Hybrid Cloud Apps with OpenShift and Kubernetes

Delivering Highly Available
Applications and Services

Michael Elder, Jake Kitchener, and Dr. Brad Topol

Beijing · Boston · Farnham · Sebastopol · Tokyo

Hybrid Cloud Apps with OpenShift and Kubernetes

by Michael Elder, Jake Kitchener, and Dr. Brad Topol

Published by O'Reilly Media, Inc., 1005 Gravenstein Highway North, Sebastopol, CA 95472.

O'Reilly books may be purchased for educational, business, or sales promotional use. Online editions are also available for most titles (*http://oreilly.com*). For more information, contact our corporate/institutional sales department: 800-998-9938 or *corporate@oreilly.com*.

Acquisitions Editor: John Devins	**Indexer:** Sue Klefstad
Development Editor: Angela Rufino	**Interior Designer:** David Futato
Production Editor: Kate Galloway	**Cover Designer:** Karen Montgomery
Copyeditor: Shannon Turlington	**Illustrator:** Kate Dullea
Proofreader: Justin Billing	

June 2021:   First Edition

Revision History for the First Edition

2021-06-07:   First Release

See *http://oreilly.com/catalog/errata.csp?isbn=9781492083818* for release details.

978-1-492-08381-8

[LSI]

To Wendy, for your love and encouragement. To Samantha, for your fearlessness and curiosity about all things in life. To David, for your inspirational smile and laughter. To my mother, Betty, for your amazing tenacity through all of life's challenges while remaining optimistic about the future.

—Michael Elder

Great thanks go to my wife, Becky, for her love and support. To Oren goes my gratitude for his laughter and caring spirit. Thank you to my parents, Nancy and Barry Kitchener; without their example I would not have the tenacity to take on the trials of life.

—Jake Kitchener

I dedicate this book to my wife, Janet; my daughter, Morgan; my son, Ryan; my sister, Marci; and my parents, Harold and Mady Topol. I could not have done this without your love and support during this process.

—Brad Topol

Table of Contents

Foreword

Software is integral to every industry today. From web and mobile apps that accelerate the digital transformation of business, to more efficient backend systems that support the growth of your business, to technology that's embedded in devices as part of everyday life, containers have established themselves as a fundamental aspect of software delivery and operation across the spectrum.

The operations and applications teams powering these transformations are seeing their application footprints grow tremendously in multiple locations, clouds, data centers, and out to the edge. The bigger the organization, the broader the footprint and the more complex the challenges. As cloud becomes an integral part of application deployment, organizations also wish to modernize their existing footprints and accelerate their development teams.

So what has powered these trends? Open source technologies enable standardization, which leads to an explosion of ecosystem benefits and approaches, which then leads to a need for new standardization. As one of the most successful open source ecosystems, Kubernetes has created a significant change in how we build and run applications.

A key question that is probably on your mind is how to balance velocity and flexibility—scaling, integrating, and simplifying—while increasing your teams' ability to deliver value. Your organization may be heavily driven by your application teams, organically adopting new services in cloud footprints. In that case, you are likely focused on how to bring consistency of operational concerns to greenfield projects while minimizing disruption to teams.

Your organization may have a broader focus—actively spanning the full spectrum of compute, including devices at the edge, gateways and local application processing in data centers, visualization, and archival in the cloud. These true "hybrid" applications have unique needs at each location, but that location-specific behavior only strengthens the need to keep operational concerns aligned.

Finally, your organization may run workloads similar to a large percentage of enterprise applications that are becoming truly cloud-agnostic. Thanks to modern application development frameworks, tools, and application infrastructure like Kubernetes, the underlying details of the infrastructure are less of a barrier to application portability and availability. For an organization aspiring to be cloud-agnostic, you are probably building a platform to consolidate and automate the life cycle of your business. The modern platforms to support hybrid cloud must address a number of serious challenges such as security, data consolidation, cost management, and increasing developer velocity to serve the applications that run your business.

As one of the founding members of the Kubernetes project and as lead OpenShift architect, I've spent the last seven years working to help large enterprises and small teams find that middle ground, as well as to ensure a consistent application environment across cloud, datacenter, and edge that enables customer platforms to succeed.

As Kubernetes has matured, so has the complexity and scale of user successes. The hockey stick of growth has taken us into broad adoption, and it's the right time to take stock of the challenges, patterns, and technologies that can help bring that growth under control.

This book dives deep on the problems and solutions that the most successful enterprise Kubernetes teams have encountered and gives you a trusted path to follow. The fusion of perspectives is key—from Brad's work in the community driving consistency across open source projects and finding common ground for users, to Jake's expertise in building and running cloud-scale Kubernetes with IBM Kubernetes Service and IBM Red Hat OpenShift Service, to Michael's deep focus on helping organizations consolidate and secure multicluster Kubernetes as architect to Red Hat's Advanced Cluster Management product.

Together they represent an immense amount of practical experience in how to leverage Kubernetes effectively at scale in a way that can help organizations support their growing application fleet, whether it be cloud-first, multicloud, or connected to the edge.

As we continue to standardize and simplify how applications are built and deployed across a wide range of environments, open source and open ecosystems help organizations collaborate towards shared goals. Kubernetes and other tools in our ecosystem are fundamental building blocks toward that end, and this book will help you navigate the trade-offs and opportunities along the way.

— Clayton Coleman
Senior Distinguished Engineer at Red Hat
Architect, Containerized Application Infrastructure
(OpenShift and Kubernetes)

Preface

OpenShift, the Red Hat distribution of Kubernetes, is rapidly becoming the platform of choice for containerized applications. As enterprises attempt to scale and operate OpenShift, there are many practices that must be understood to manage resources, expose those resources for application teams, govern those resources, and deliver changes continuously to those environments.

Based on our expertise built on managing and supporting thousands of bare metal and virtual machine clusters for some of the largest enterprise applications, we will focus on how to operationalize both basic Kubernetes and OpenShift with specific techniques and examples to make your organization effective.

Why We Wrote This Book

Although a lot of content exists on how to get started with Kubernetes and OpenShift, our goal was to focus on a book that covered more advanced concepts, such as the effective management of cluster resources and availability models that can be applied to ensure business continuity. In addition, we wanted to dig deep into topics, tools, and best practices that are critical to operating Kubernetes and OpenShift successfully in production environments. We give particular attention to topics like security, advanced resource management, continuous delivery, multicluster management, and high availability. Additionally, the book explores best practices for supporting hybrid cloud applications, which are applications that integrate the best features and functions from a combination of multiple cloud environments coupled with traditional IT environments. In this book, we offer our in-depth knowledge and experience of these production-level topics to the broader OpenShift and Kubernetes community.

Who This Book Is For

This book is for DevOps engineers, Kubernetes and OpenShift platform operations engineers, site reliability engineers, NetOps engineers, cloud native computing application developers, and IT architects. In addition, the book will be of particular interest to those who either create and manage Kubernetes or OpenShift clusters or consume and use these platforms for delivering applications and services.

How This Book Is Organized

This book is structured to enable operators and developers to gain a solid understanding of the advanced concepts required to run Kubernetes and OpenShift in production. Chapter 1 provides an overview of both basic Kubernetes and OpenShift. It then discusses fundamental concepts of Kubernetes and describes the Kubernetes architecture. In Chapter 2, we give a primer on the relationship between OpenShift and Kubernetes and describe how to get a variety of Kubernetes and OpenShift environments up and running. Chapter 3 is a deep dive into advanced resource management topics, including specialized scheduling, resource reservations, specialized node types, and capacity planning and management. Chapter 4 covers key fundamentals for supporting high availability inside a single cluster. In Chapter 5, we present an overview of production-level approaches for continuous delivery and promotion of code across multiple enterprise clusters. Chapters 6 and 7 focus on the use of multiple production clusters. In these chapters, we describe several hybrid cloud use cases, and we cover in depth such advanced topics as multicluster provisioning, upgrading, and policy support. These concepts are reinforced in Chapter 8, where we provide a working example of multicluster application delivery. Finally, in Chapter 9 we conclude with a discussion of the future of Kubernetes and OpenShift and list additional references on a variety of helpful topics for running applications in production Kubernetes and OpenShift environments.

Conventions Used in This Book

The following typographical conventions are used in this book:

Italic
> Indicates new terms, URLs, email addresses, filenames, and file extensions.

`Constant width`
> Used for program listings, as well as within paragraphs to refer to program elements such as variable or function names, databases, data types, environment variables, statements, and keywords.

`Constant width bold`
> Shows commands or other text that should be typed literally by the user.

`Constant width italic`
> Shows text that should be replaced with user-supplied values or by values determined by context.

This element signifies a tip or suggestion.

This element signifies a general note.

This element indicates a warning or caution.

Using Code Examples

Supplemental material (code examples, exercises, etc.) is available for download at *https://github.com/hybrid-cloud-apps-openshift-k8s-book*.

If you have a technical question or a problem using the code examples, please send email to *bookquestions@oreilly.com*.

This book is here to help you get your job done. In general, if example code is offered with this book, you may use it in your programs and documentation. You do not need to contact us for permission unless you're reproducing a significant portion of the code. For example, writing a program that uses several chunks of code from this book does not require permission. Selling or distributing examples from O'Reilly books does require permission. Answering a question by citing this book and quoting example code does not require permission. Incorporating a significant amount of example code from this book into your product's documentation does require permission.

We appreciate, but generally do not require, attribution. An attribution usually includes the title, author, publisher, and ISBN. For example: "*Hybrid Cloud Apps with OpenShift and Kubernetes* by Michael Elder, Jake Kitchener, and Dr. Brad Topol (O'Reilly). Copyright 2021 Michael Elder, Jake Kitchener, Brad Topol, 978-1-492-08381-8."

If you feel your use of code examples falls outside fair use or the permission given above, feel free to contact us at *permissions@oreilly.com*.

O'Reilly Online Learning

 For more than 40 years, *O'Reilly Media* has provided technology and business training, knowledge, and insight to help companies succeed.

Our unique network of experts and innovators share their knowledge and expertise through books, articles, and our online learning platform. O'Reilly's online learning platform gives you on-demand access to live training courses, in-depth learning paths, interactive coding environments, and a vast collection of text and video from O'Reilly and 200+ other publishers. For more information, visit *http://oreilly.com*.

How to Contact Us

Please address comments and questions concerning this book to the publisher:

O'Reilly Media, Inc.
1005 Gravenstein Highway North
Sebastopol, CA 95472
800-998-9938 (in the United States or Canada)
707-829-0515 (international or local)
707-829-0104 (fax)

We have a web page for this book, where we list errata, examples, and any additional information. You can access this page at *https://oreil.ly/hybrid-cloud*.

Email *bookquestions@oreilly.com* to comment or ask technical questions about this book.

For news and information about our books and courses, visit *http://oreilly.com*.

Find us on Facebook: *http://facebook.com/oreilly*

Follow us on Twitter: *http://twitter.com/oreillymedia*

Watch us on YouTube: *http://youtube.com/oreillymedia*

Acknowledgments

We would like to thank the entire Kubernetes and OpenShift communities for their passion, dedication, and tremendous commitment to these open source projects. Without the code developers, code reviewers, documentation authors, and operators contributing to these projects over the years, Kubernetes and OpenShift would not have the rich feature sets, strong adoption, and large ecosystems they enjoy today.

We would like to extend our grateful thanks to the technical reviewers who provided valuable feedback to this text: Dan "Pop" Papandrea, Daniel Berg, Joshua Packer, Scott Berens, and Burr Sutter.

We would like to thank our Kubernetes colleagues Clayton Coleman, Derek Carr, David Eads, Paul Morie, Zach Corleissen, Jim Angel, Tim Bannister, Celeste Horgan, Irvi Aini, Karen Bradshaw, Kaitlyn Barnard, Taylor Dolezal, Jorge Castro, Jason DeTiberus, Stephen Augustus, Guang Ya Liu, Sahdev Zala, Wei Huang, Michael Brown, Jonathan Berkhahn, Martin Hickey, Chris Luciano, Srinivas Brahmaroutu, Morgan Bauer, Qiming Teng, Richard Theis, Tyler Lisowski, Bill Lynch, Jennifer Rondeau, Seth McCombs, Steve Perry, and Joe Heck for the wonderful collaboration over the years.

We would also like to thank the contributors to the Open Cluster Management project and its related projects, including the OpenShift Hive project, Open Policy Agent, and ArgoCD.

We would like to thank the many open source contributors who have enabled projects and examples beyond Kubernetes, in particular the authors and originators of the example PAC-MAN application, including Ivan Font, Mario Vázquez, Jason DeTiberus, Davis Phillips, and Pep Turró Mauri. We would also like to thank the authors and contributors of the many example Open Cluster Management policies, including Yu Cao, Christian Stark, and Jaya Ramanathan.

We would also like to thank our editor, Angela Rufino, for her patience in working through the book writing process during a very dynamic year and a worldwide pandemic. In addition, we would like to thank our copyeditor, Shannon Turlington, for her meticulous review of our work and the large number of suggested improvements she provided.

A very special thanks to Willie Tejada, Todd Moore, Bob Lord, Dave Lindquist, Kevin Myers, Jeff Brent, Jason McGee, Chris Ferris, Vince Brunssen, Alex Tarpinian, Jeff Borek, Nimesh Bhatia, Briana Frank, and Jake Morlock for all of their support and encouragement during this endeavor.

—Michael, Jake, and Brad

## CHAPTER 1

Kubernetes and OpenShift Overview

Over the past few years, Kubernetes has emerged as the de facto standard platform for managing, orchestrating, and provisioning container-based cloud native computing applications. *Cloud native computing applications* are essentially applications that are built from a collection of smaller services (microservices) and take advantage of the speed of development and scalability capabilities that cloud computing environments typically provide. Over time, Kubernetes has matured to provide the controls required to manage even more advanced and stateful workloads, such as databases and AI services. The Kubernetes ecosystem continues to experience explosive growth, and the project benefits greatly from being a multiple-vendor and meritocracy-based open source project backed by a solid governance policy and a level playing field for contributing.

Although many Kubernetes distributions are available for customers to choose from, the Red Hat OpenShift Kubernetes distribution is of particular interest. OpenShift has achieved broad adoption across a variety of industries; over one thousand enterprise customers across the globe currently use it to host their business applications and drive their digital transformation efforts.

This book focuses on enabling you to become an expert at running both traditional Kubernetes and the OpenShift distribution of Kubernetes in production environments. In this first chapter, we begin with a broad overview of both Kubernetes and OpenShift and the historical origin of both platforms. We then review the key features and capabilities that have made Kubernetes and OpenShift the dominant platforms for creating and deploying cloud native applications.

Kubernetes: Cloud Infrastructure for Orchestrating Containerized Applications

The emergence of Docker in 2013 introduced numerous developers to containers and container-based application development. Containers were presented as an alternative to virtual machines (VMs) for creating self-contained deployable units. Containers rely on advanced security and resource management features of the Linux operating system to provide isolation at the process level instead of relying on VMs for creating deployable units of software. A Linux process is much more lightweight and orders of magnitude more efficient than a VM for common activities like starting up an application image or creating new image snapshots. Because of these advantages, developers favored containers as the desired approach to creating new software applications as self-contained units of deployable software. As the popularity of containers grew, so did a need for a common platform for provisioning, managing, and orchestrating containers across a cluster. For more than a decade, Google had embraced the use of Linux containers as the foundation for applications deployed in its cloud.[1] Google had extensive experience orchestrating and managing containers at scale and had developed three generations of container-management systems: Borg, Omega, and Kubernetes (*https://kubernetes.io*). The latest generation of container management developed by Google, Kubernetes was a redesign based on lessons learned from Borg and Omega and was made available as an open source project. Kubernetes delivered several key features that dramatically improved the experience of developing and deploying a scalable container-based cloud application:

Declarative deployment model
> Most cloud infrastructures that existed before Kubernetes was released took a procedural approach based on a scripting language like Ansible, Chef, Puppet, and so on for automating the deployment of applications to production environments. In contrast, Kubernetes used a declarative approach of describing what the desired state of the system should be. Kubernetes infrastructure was then responsible for starting new containers when necessary (e.g., when a container failed) to achieve the desired declared state. The declarative model was much more clear at communicating which deployment actions were desired, and this approach was a huge step forward compared with trying to read and interpret a script to determine what the desired deployment state should be.

---

[1] Brendan Burns et al., "Borg, Omega, and Kubernetes: Lessons Learned from Three Container-Management Systems over a Decade," *ACM Queue* 14 (2016): 70–93, *http://bit.ly/2vIrL4S*.

Built-in replica and autoscaling support

In some cloud infrastructures that existed before Kubernetes, support for replicas of an application and autoscaling capabilities were not part of the core infrastructure and, in some cases, never successfully materialized due to platform or architectural limitations. *Autoscaling* refers to the ability of a cloud environment to recognize that an application is becoming more heavily used, so the cloud environment automatically increases the capacity of the application, typically by creating more copies of the application on extra servers in the cloud environment. Autoscaling capabilities were provided as core features in Kubernetes and dramatically improved the robustness and consumability of its orchestration capabilities.

Built-in rolling upgrades support

Most cloud infrastructures do not provide support for upgrading applications. Instead, they assume the operator will use a scripting language, such as Chef, Puppet, or Ansible, to handle upgrades. In contrast, Kubernetes actually provides built-in support for rolling out upgrades of applications. For example, Kubernetes rollouts are configurable such that they can leverage extra resources for faster rollouts that have no downtime, or they can perform slower rollouts that do canary testing, reducing the risk and validating new software by releasing software to a small percentage of users to ensure that the new version of the application is stable. Kubernetes also supports pausing, resuming, and rolling back the version of an application.

Improved networking model

Kubernetes mapped a single IP address to a *pod*, which is Kubernetes's smallest unit of container deployment, aggregation, and management. This approach aligned the network identity with the application identity and simplified running software on Kubernetes.[2]

Built-in health-checking support

Kubernetes provided container health-checking and monitoring capabilities that reduced the complexity of identifying when failures occur.

Even with all the innovative capabilities available in Kubernetes, many enterprise companies were still hesitant to adopt this technology because it was an open source project supported by a single vendor. Enterprise companies are careful about which open source projects they are willing to adopt, and they expect open source projects like Kubernetes to have multiple vendors contributing to them; they also expect open source projects to be meritocracy based with a solid governance policy and a level

---

2 Brendan Burns et al., "Borg, Omega, and Kubernetes: Lessons Learned from Three Container-Management Systems over a Decade," *ACM Queue* 14 (2016): 70–93, *http://bit.ly/2vIrL4S*.

playing field for contributing. In 2015, the Cloud Native Computing Foundation (CNCF) was formed to address these issues facing Kubernetes.

CNCF Accelerates the Growth of the Kubernetes Ecosystem

In 2015, the Linux Foundation initiated the creation of the CNCF.[3] The CNCF's mission is to make cloud native computing ubiquitous.[4] In support of this new foundation, Google donated Kubernetes to the CNCF to serve as its seed technology. With Kubernetes as the core of its ecosystem, the CNCF has grown to more than 440 member companies, including Google Cloud, IBM Cloud, Red Hat, Amazon Web Services (AWS), Docker, Microsoft Azure, VMware, Intel, Huawei, Cisco, Alibaba Cloud, and many more.[5] In addition, the CNCF ecosystem has grown to hosting 26 open source projects, including Prometheus, Envoy, gRPC, etcd, and many others. Finally, the CNCF nurtures several early-stage projects and has had eight projects accepted into its Sandbox program for emerging technologies.

With the weight of the vendor-neutral CNCF foundation behind it, Kubernetes has grown to having more than 3,200 contributors annually from a wide range of industries.[6] In addition to hosting several cloud native projects, the CNCF provides training, a Technical Oversight Board, a Governing Board, a community infrastructure lab, and several certification programs to boost the ecosystem for Kubernetes and related projects. As a result of these efforts, there are currently over one hundred certified distributions of Kubernetes. One of the most popular distributions of Kubernetes, particularly for enterprise customers, is Red Hat's OpenShift Kubernetes. In the next section, we introduce OpenShift and give an overview of the key benefits it provides for developers and IT operations teams.

OpenShift: Red Hat's Distribution of Kubernetes

Although many companies have contributed to Kubernetes, the contributions from Red Hat are particularly noteworthy. Red Hat has been a part of the Kubernetes ecosystem from its inception as an open source project, and it continues to serve as the second-largest contributor to Kubernetes. Based on this hands-on expertise with Kubernetes, Red Hat provides its own distribution of Kubernetes that it refers to as *OpenShift*. OpenShift is the most broadly deployed distribution of Kubernetes across the enterprise. It provides a 100% conformant Kubernetes platform and supplements

---

3 Steven J. Vaughan-Nicholls, "Cloud Native Computing Foundation Seeks to Forge Cloud and Container Unity," *ZDNet* (July 21, 2015), *https://oreil.ly/WEoE0*.

4 Linux Foundation, CNCF Charter (updated December 10, 2018), *https://oreil.ly/tHHvr*.

5 The CNCF Members page (*https://oreil.ly/Tj3Vw*) provides more details on membership growth of the CNCF.

6 See the Kubernetes Companies Table Dashboard (*https://oreil.ly/mkSTm*) for a current list.

---

it with a variety of tools and capabilities focused on improving the productivity of developers and IT operations.

OpenShift was originally released in 2011.[7] At that time, it had its own platform-specific container runtime environment.[8] In early 2014, the Red Hat team met with the container orchestration team at Google and learned about a new container orchestration project that eventually became Kubernetes. The Red Hat team was incredibly impressed with Kubernetes, and OpenShift was rewritten to use Kubernetes as its container orchestration engine. As a result of these efforts, OpenShift was able to deliver a 100% conformant Kubernetes platform as part of its version 3 release in June 2015.[9]

The Red Hat OpenShift Container Platform is Kubernetes with additional supporting capabilities to make it operational for enterprise needs. The Kubernetes community provides fixes for releases for a period of up to 12 months. OpenShift differentiates itself from other distributions by providing long-term support (three or more years) for major Kubernetes releases, security patches, and enterprise support contracts that cover both the operating system and the OpenShift Kubernetes platform. Red Hat Enterprise Linux (RHEL) has long been a de facto distribution of Linux for organizations large and small. Red Hat OpenShift Container Platform builds on RHEL to ensure consistent Linux distributions from the host operating system through all containerized functions on the cluster. In addition to all these benefits, OpenShift enhances Kubernetes by supplementing it with a variety of tools and capabilities focused on improving the productivity of both developers and IT operations. The following sections describe these benefits.

Benefits of OpenShift for Developers

While Kubernetes has a lot of functionality for provisioning and managing container images, it does not provide much support for creating new images from base images, pushing images to registries, or identifying when new versions become available. In addition, the networking support provided by Kubernetes can be quite complicated to use. To fill these gaps, OpenShift offers several benefits to developers beyond those provided by the core Kubernetes platform:

---

7 Joe Fernandes, "Why Red Hat Chose Kubernetes for OpenShift," Red Hat OpenShift Blog (November 7, 2016), *https://oreil.ly/r66GM*.

8 Anton McConville and Olaph Wagoner, "A Brief History of Kubernetes, OpenShift, and IBM," IBM Developer Blog (August 1, 2019), *https://oreil.ly/IugtP*.

9 "Red Hat Delivers OpenShift Enterprise 3 to Power a New Web-Scale Distributed Application Platform" [press release], Red Hat (June 24, 2015), *https://oreil.ly/jlane*.

Source-to-Image

When using basic Kubernetes, the cloud native application developer is responsible for creating their own container images. Typically, this involves finding the proper base image and creating a `Dockerfile` with all the necessary commands for taking a base image and adding in the developer's code to create an assembled image that Kubernetes can deploy. This requires the developer to learn a variety of Docker commands that are used for image assembly. With its Source-to-Image (S2I) capability, OpenShift is able to handle merging the cloud native developer's code into the base image. In many cases, S2I can be configured such that all the developer needs to do is commit their changes to a Git repository, and S2I will see the updated changes and merge them with a base image to create a new assembled image for deployment.

Push images to registries

Another key step that must be performed by the cloud native developer when using basic Kubernetes is storing newly assembled container images in an image registry such as Docker Hub. In this case, the developer needs to create and manage the repository. In contrast, OpenShift provides its own private registry and developers can use that option, or S2I can be configured to push assembled images to third-party registries.

Image streams

When developers create cloud native applications, the development effort results in a large number of configuration changes, as well as changes to the container image of the application. To address this complexity, OpenShift provides the image stream functionality, which monitors for configuration or image changes and performs automated builds and deployments based on the change events. This feature takes the burden off the developer of having to perform these steps manually whenever changes occur.

Base image catalog

OpenShift provides a base image catalog with a large number of useful base images for a variety of tools and platforms, such as WebSphere Liberty, JBoss, PHP, Redis, Jenkins, Python, .NET, MariaDB, and many others. The catalog provides trusted content that is packaged from known source code.

Routes

Networking in base Kubernetes can be quite complicated to configure. OpenShift has a route construct that interfaces with Kubernetes services and is responsible for adding Kubernetes services to an external load balancer. Routes also provide readable URLs for applications and a variety of load-balancing strategies to support several deployment options, such as blue-green, canary, and A/B testing deployments.[10]

While OpenShift has a large number of benefits for developers, its greatest differentiators are the benefits it gives IT operations. In the next section, we describe several of the core capabilities for automating the day-to day-operations of running OpenShift in production.

Benefits of OpenShift for IT Operations

In May 2019, Red Hat announced the release of OpenShift 4.[11] Red Hat acquired CoreOS, which had a very automated approach to managing Kubernetes's life-cycle behavior and was an early advocate of the "operator" concept. This new version of OpenShift was completely rewritten to build on capabilities from CoreOS's innovative management practices and OpenShift 3's reputation for reliability, which dramatically improved how the OpenShift platform is installed, upgraded, and managed.[11] To deliver these significant life-cycle improvements, OpenShift heavily used the latest Kubernetes innovations and best practices for automating the management of resources in its architecture. As a result of these efforts, OpenShift 4 is able to deliver the following benefits for IT operations:

Automated installation
OpenShift 4 supports an innovative installation approach that is automated, reliable, and repeatable.[12] Additionally, the OpenShift 4 installation process supports full stack automated deployments and can handle installing the complete infrastructure, including components like DNS and the VM.

Automated operating system and OpenShift platform updates
OpenShift is tightly integrated with the lightweight RHEL CoreOS operating system, which itself is optimized for running OpenShift and cloud native applications. Thanks to the tight coupling of OpenShift with a specific version of RHEL CoreOS, the OpenShift platform is able to manage updating the operating system as part of its cluster management operations. The key value of this approach for IT operations is that it supports automated, self-managing, over-the-air updates. This enables OpenShift to support cloud native and hands-free operations.

---

10 For more details on OpenShift routes, please see Using Route-Based Deployment Strategies (*https://oreil.ly/ hmpJz*) in the OpenShift documentation.

11 Joe Fernandes, "Introducing Red Hat OpenShift 4: Kubernetes for the Enterprise," Red Hat OpenShift Blog (May 8, 2019), *https://oreil.ly/yNb8s*.

12 Christian Hernandez, "OpenShift 4.1 Bare Metal Install Quickstart," Red Hat OpenShift Blog (July 31, 2019), *https://oreil.ly/yz4pR*.

Automated cluster size management

OpenShift supports the ability to automatically increase or decrease the size of the cluster it is managing. Like all Kubernetes clusters, an OpenShift cluster has a certain number of worker nodes on which the container applications are deployed. In a typical Kubernetes cluster, adding worker nodes is an out-of-band operation that IT operations must handle manually. In contrast, OpenShift provides a component called the *machine operator* that is capable of automatically adding worker nodes to a cluster. An IT operator can use a MachineSet object to declare the number of machines needed by the cluster, and OpenShift will automatically perform the provisioning and installation of new worker nodes to achieve the desired state.

Automated cluster version management

OpenShift, like all Kubernetes distributions, is composed of a large number of components. Each of these components has its own version number. To manage updating each of these components, OpenShift relies on a Kubernetes innovation called the *operator construct*. OpenShift uses a cluster version number to identify which version of OpenShift is running, and this cluster version number denotes which versions of the individual OpenShift platform components need to be installed. With its automated cluster version management, OpenShift is able to install the proper versions of all these components automatically to ensure that it is properly updated when the cluster is updated to a new version.

Multicloud management support

Many enterprise customers that use OpenShift have multiple clusters, and these clusters are deployed across multiple clouds or in multiple data centers. To simplify the management of multiple clusters, OpenShift 4 has introduced a new unified cloud console that allows customers to view and manage multiple OpenShift clusters.[13]

As we will see later in this book, OpenShift and the capabilities it provides become extremely prominent when it's time to run in production and IT operators need to address operational and security-related concerns.

Summary

In this chapter, we gave an overview of Kubernetes and OpenShift, including the historical origins of both platforms. We then presented the key benefits provided by both Kubernetes and OpenShift that have driven the huge growth in popularity of these platforms. This has helped us have a greater appreciation for the value that Kubernetes and OpenShift provide to cloud native application developers and IT

---

13 Fernandes, "Introducing Red Hat OpenShift 4: Kubernetes for the Enterprise."

operations teams. Thus, it is no surprise that these platforms are experiencing explosive growth across a variety of industries. In Chapter 2, we will build a solid foundational overview of Kubernetes and OpenShift that presents the Kubernetes architecture, discusses how to get Kubernetes and OpenShift production environments up and running, and introduces several key Kubernetes and OpenShift concepts that are critical to running successfully in production.

Getting Started with OpenShift and Kubernetes

In this chapter, we cover a variety of topics that present a foundational understanding of Kubernetes and OpenShift. We begin with an overview of the Kubernetes architecture and then describe several deployment options that will enable you to get both a basic Kubernetes environment and an OpenShift environment up and running. Next, we give an introduction to the command-line tools `kubectl` and `oc`, which are used for interacting with Kubernetes and OpenShift respectively. We then introduce a short review of the fundamental Kubernetes concepts of pods, deployments, and service accounts. In the second half of this chapter, we present several enhancement concepts that OpenShift provides over traditional Kubernetes. We then conclude this chapter with a discussion of more advanced topics that are often used when running Kubernetes or OpenShift in production.

Kubernetes Architecture

The Kubernetes architecture (*https://oreil.ly/QEYUe*) at a high level is relatively straightforward. It is composed of a *master node* and a set of *worker nodes*. The nodes can be either physical servers or VMs. Users of the Kubernetes environment interact with the master node using either a CLI (`kubectl`), an API, or a GUI. The master node is responsible for scheduling work across the worker nodes. In Kubernetes, the unit of work that is scheduled is called a *pod*, and a pod can hold one or more containers. The primary components that exist on the master node are the *kube-apiserver, kube-scheduler, kube-controller-manager,* and *etcd*:

kube-apiserver
    The kube-apiserver makes available the Kubernetes API that is used to operate the Kubernetes environment.

kube-scheduler

The kube-scheduler component is responsible for selecting the nodes on which pods should be created.

kube-controller-manager

Kubernetes provides several high-level abstractions for supporting replicas of pods, managing nodes, and so on. Each of these is implemented with a controller component, which we describe later in this chapter. The kube-controller-manager is responsible for managing and running controller components.

etcd

The etcd component is a distributed key-value store and is the primary datastore of the Kubernetes control plane. This component stores and replicates all the critical information states of your Kubernetes environment. The key feature of etcd is its ability to support a watch. A *watch* is a remote procedure call (RPC) mechanism that allows for callbacks to functions on key-value create, update, or delete operations. Kubernetes's outstanding performance and scalability characteristics depend on etcd being a highly efficient data storage mechanism.

The worker nodes are responsible for running the pods that are scheduled on them. The primary Kubernetes components that exist on worker nodes are the kubelet, *kube-proxy*, and *container runtime*:

kubelet

The kubelet is responsible for making sure that the containers in each pod are created and stay up and running. The kubelet will restart containers upon recognizing that they have terminated unexpectedly or failed other health checks defined by the user.

kube-proxy

One of Kubernetes's key strengths is the networking support it implements for containers. The kube-proxy component provides networking support in the form of connection forwarding, load balancing, and mapping of a single IP address to a pod. Kube-proxy is unique in that it gives a distributed load-balancing capability that is critical to the high availability architecture of Kubernetes.

container runtime

The container runtime component is responsible for running the containers that exist in each pod. Kubernetes supports several container runtime environment options, including Docker, rkt, CRI-O, and containerd.[1]

---

1 Lantao Liu and Mike Brown, "Kubernetes Containerd Integration Goes GA," Kubernetes Blog (May 24, 2018), *https://oreil.ly/SlHmh*.

Figure 2-1 shows a graphical representation of the Kubernetes architecture encompassing a master node and two worker nodes.

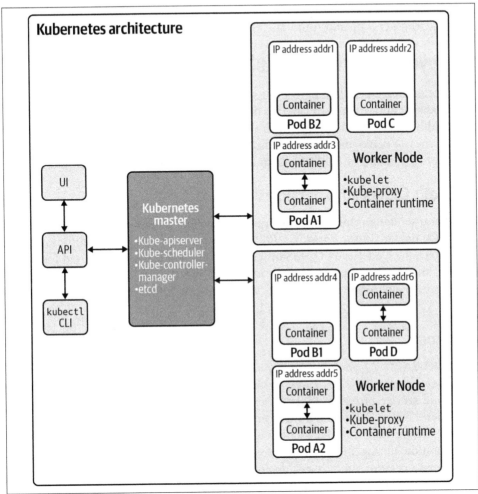

Figure 2-1. Graphical representation of the Kubernetes architecture

As shown in Figure 2-1, users interact with the Kubernetes API server using either a GUI or by kubectl CLI. Both of these use the Kubernetes API to interact with the kube-apiserver on the Kubernetes master node. The Kubernetes master node's kube-scheduler component schedules pods to run on different worker nodes. Each pod contains one or more containers and is assigned its own IP address.In many real-world applications, Kubernetes deploys multiple replicas (running copies) of the same pod to improve scalability and ensure high availability. Pods A1 and A2 are pod replicas that differ only in the IP address they are allocated. Similarly, Pods B1 and B2 are also replica copies of the same pod. The containers located in the same pod are permitted to communicate with one another using standard interprocess communication (IPC) mechanisms.

In the next section, we present several approaches to getting OpenShift and Kubernetes environments up and running.

Deployment Options for Kubernetes and OpenShift

Kubernetes and OpenShift have both reached incredible levels of popularity. As a result, several options are available for deploying either basic Kubernetes or Red Hat's OpenShift Kubernetes distribution. In the following sections, we summarize the different types of deployment options that are currently available, including Red Hat's CodeReady Containers, IBM Cloud, and several OpenShift deployment options.

Red Hat's CodeReady Containers

Red Hat provides a minimal preconfigured OpenShift version 4 cluster called Code-Ready Containers (*https://oreil.ly/1rI07*) that you can run on your laptop or desktop computer. The CodeReady OpenShift environment is intended to be used for development and testing purposes. CodeReady Containers provide a fully functional cloud development environment on your local machine and contain all the tooling necessary for you to develop container-based applications.

IBM Cloud

IBM Cloud (*https://cloud.ibm.com*) gives users their choice of either a traditional Kubernetes cluster or a Red Hat OpenShift cluster. IBM Cloud's Kubernetes offering is a cloud service providing Kubernetes as a Service that brings all of the standard Kubernetes features, including intelligent scheduling, self-healing, horizontal scaling, service discovery and load balancing, automated rollout and rollbacks, and secret and configuration management. In addition, IBM Cloud's Kubernetes Service includes automated operations for cluster deployment, updates, and scaling, expert security, optimized configuration, and seamless integration with the IBM Cloud Infrastructure platform. It produces highly available multizone clusters across 6 regions and 35 datacenters. IBM Cloud offers both a free Kubernetes cluster with over 40 free services and pay-as-you-go options.

IBM Cloud also provides users with highly available, fully managed OpenShift clusters (*https://oreil.ly/qsOdD*). IBM's OpenShift offering implements unique security and productivity capabilities designed to eliminate substantial time spent on updating, scaling, and provisioning. Additionally, IBM Cloud's OpenShift delivers the resiliency to handle unexpected surges and protects against attacks that can lead to financial and productivity losses. In addition to pay-as-you-go and subscription options, IBM Cloud offers a free preconfigured OpenShift version 4.3 environment that is available for four hours at no charge.

OpenShift Deployment Options

Several deployment options for OpenShift are defined at the Getting Started with OpenShift (*https://www.openshift.com/try*) website. The options described include installing OpenShift version 4 on your laptop, deploying it in your datacenter or public cloud, or having Red Hat manage OpenShift for you. In addition, Red Hat offers hands-on OpenShift tutorials and playground OpenShift environments for unstructured learning and experimentation. Figure 2-2 shows the myriad of OpenShift deployment options available.

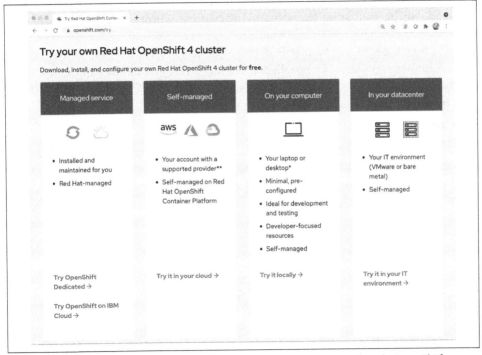

Figure 2-2. OpenShift deployment options available at Get Started with OpenShift (https://www.openshift.com/try)

In the next section, we describe the command-line tools used for interacting with these platforms.

Kubernetes and OpenShift Command-Line Tools

As discussed in Chapter 1, OpenShift provides a 100% conformant Kubernetes platform and supplements it with a variety of tools and capabilities focused on improving the productivity of developers and IT operations. In this section, we begin with an introduction to kubectl and oc, which are the standard command-line tools used for interacting with Kubernetes and OpenShift respectively. We present several concepts that OpenShift uses to represent the enhancements it serves over traditional Kubernetes. OpenShift concepts that we describe include authentication, projects, applications, security contexts, and image streams.

After covering some core concepts in Kubernetes, the next sections give several examples in the form of YAML files. For all Kubernetes environments, the samples included can be run using the standard Kubernetes command-line tool kubectl. Many Kubernetes environments, including the ones mentioned earlier in this chapter, describe how kubectl can be installed. Once you have your Kubernetes environment up and running and kubectl installed, all of the YAML file samples in the following sections can be run by first saving the YAML to a file (e.g., *kubesample1.yaml*) and then by running the following kubectl command:

```
$ kubectl apply -f kubesample1.yaml
```

As previously discussed, the OpenShift distribution of Kubernetes adds several new enhancements and capabilities beyond those used by traditional Kubernetes. OpenShift provides access to these features by extending the capabilities of kubectl. To make it explicit that the OpenShift version of kubectl has extended functionality, OpenShift renamed its version of kubectl to be a new command-line tool called oc. Thus, the following is equivalent to the previous kubectl command:

```
$ oc apply -f kubesample1.yaml
```

In addition to one-for-one matching support for all kubectl commands, oc adds commands for administrative functions like managing roles and role bindings for users and groups.

For more information on the breadth of commands available from the OpenShift oc CLI, please see the OpenShift command line documentation (*https://oreil.ly/7NQW3*).

Kubernetes Fundamentals

Kubernetes has several concepts that are specific to its model for managing containers. In this section we briefly review key Kubernetes concepts, including pods, deployments, and service accounts.

What's a Pod?

Because Kubernetes supports the management and orchestration of containers, you would assume that the smallest deployable unit supported by Kubernetes would be a container. However, the designers of Kubernetes learned from experience[2] that it was more optimal to have the smallest deployable unit be something that could hold multiple containers. In Kubernetes, this smallest deployable unit is called a *pod*. A pod can hold one or more application containers. The application containers that are in the same pod have the following benefits:

- They share an IP address and port space
- They share the same hostname
- They can communicate with one another using native IPC

In contrast, application containers that run in separate pods are guaranteed to have different IP addresses and different hostnames. Essentially, containers in different pods should be viewed as running on different servers even if they ended up on the same node.

Kubernetes contributes a robust set of features that make pods easy to use:

Easy-to-use pod management API
> Kubernetes provides the kubectl CLI, which supports a variety of operations on pods, including creating, viewing, deleting, updating, interacting, and scaling pods.

File copy support
> Kubernetes makes it very easy to copy files back and forth between your local host machine and your pods running in the cluster.

Connectivity from your local machine to your pod
> In many cases, you will want to have network connectivity from your local host machine to your pods running in the cluster. Kubernetes supports port forwarding whereby a network port on your local host machine is connected via a secure tunnel to a port on your pod that is running in the cluster. This is an excellent feature to assist in debugging applications and services without having to expose them publicly.

---

2 Brendan Burns et al., "Borg, Omega, and Kubernetes: Lessons Learned from Three Container-Management Systems over a Decade," *ACM Queue* 14 (2016): 70–93, *http://bit.ly/2vIrL4S*.

Volume storage support

Kubernetes pods support the attachment of remote network storage volumes to enable the containers in pods to access persistent storage that remains long after the lifetime of the pods and the containers that initially utilized the storage.

Probe-based health-check support

Kubernetes provides health checks in the form of probes to ensure that the main processes of your containers are still running. In addition, Kubernetes administers liveness checks that ensure the containers are actually functioning and capable of doing real work. With this health-check support, Kubernetes can recognize if your containers have crashed or become nonfunctional and restart them on your behalf.

How Do I Describe What's in My Pod?

Pods and all other resources managed by Kubernetes are described using a YAML file. The following is a simple YAML file that describes a rudimentary pod resource:

```
apiVersion: v1
kind: Pod
metadata:
 name: nginx
spec:
 containers:
 - name: nginx
   image: nginx:1.7.9
   ports:
   - containerPort: 80
```

This YAML file contains the following fields and sections:

`apiVersion`

This field is used to declare which version of the Kubernetes API schema is being used. Kubernetes continues to experience rapid growth in features and functionality. It manages the complexity that results from its growth in capabilities by supporting multiple versions of its API. By setting the `apiVersion` field, you can control the API version that your resource uses.

`kind`

Use the `kind` field to identify the type of resource the YAML file is describing. In the preceding example, the YAML file declares that it is describing a `Pod` object.

`metadata`

The `metadata` section contains information about the resource that the YAML is defining. In the preceding example, the `metadata` contains a name field that declares the name of this pod. The `metadata` section can contain other types of identifying information, such as labels and annotations. We describe these in more detail in "Deployments" on page 20.

spec

The spec section provides a specification for what the desired state for this resource should be. As shown in the example, the desired state for this pod is to have a container with the name nginx that is built from the Docker image identified as nginx:1.7.9. The container shares the IP address of the pod it is contained in, and the containerPort field is used to allocate this container a network port (in this case, 80) that it can use to send and receive network traffic.

 The apply command will either create a resource or update any existing matching resources. There is also a supported create command that will assume the resources described by the YAML document do not yet exist. You can typically use apply wherever you use create. In some cases, such as the special generateName attribute, only create is supported.

To run the previous example, save the file as *pod.yaml*. You can now run it by doing the following:

```
$ kubectl apply -f pod.yaml
```

After running this command, you should see the following output:

```
pod/nginx created
```

To confirm that your pod is actually running, use the kubectl get pods command to verify:

```
$ kubectl get pods
```

After running this command, you should see output similar to the following:

```
NAME   READY STATUS  RESTARTS AGE
nginx 1/1    Running 0        21s
```

When the pod is running, you can also view the logs of the process running within the pod with the logs command (if there are multiple containers, select the specific container you want to view with the -c option):

```
$ kubectl logs nginx
```

If you need to debug your running container, you can create an interactive shell that runs within the container by using the following command:

```
$ kubectl exec -it nginx - bash
```

This command instructs Kubernetes to run an interactive shell for the container that runs in the pod named nginx. Because this pod has only one container, Kubernetes knows which container you want to connect to even if you have not specified the container name. Accessing the container interactively to modify it at runtime is typically considered a bad practice. However, interactive shells can be useful as you are learning or debugging apps before deploying to production. After you run the preceding command, you can interact with the container's runtime environment, as shown here:

```
root@nginx:/# ls
bin boot dev etc home lib lib64 media mnt opt proc root run sbin selinux
srv sys tmp usr var
root@nginx:/# exit
```

If your pod has multiple containers within it, you will need to include the container name as well in your kubectl exec command. To do this, use the -c option and include the container name in addition to the pod name. Here is an example:

```
$ kubectl exec -it nginx -c nginx -- bash
root@nginx:/# exit
exit
```

To delete the pod that you just created, run the following command:

```
$ kubectl delete pod nginx
```

You should see the following confirmation that the pod has been deleted:

```
pod "nginx" deleted
```

When using Kubernetes, you can expect to have large numbers of pods running in a cluster. In the next section, we describe how labels and annotations are used to help you keep track of and identify your pods.

Deployments

Deployments are a high-level Kubernetes abstraction that not only allow you to control the number of pod replicas that are instantiated, but also provide support for rolling out new versions of the pods. Deployments are configurable such that they can leverage extra resources for faster rollouts that have no downtime, or they can perform slower rollouts that do canary testing. The advantage of a slower rollout is that it can reduce the risk and validate new software by releasing the software to a small percentage of users, thus ensuring that the new version of the application is stable. Deployments rely on the ReplicaSet resource to manage pod replicas and then add pod version management support on top of this capability. Deployments also enable newly rolled-out versions of pods to be rolled back to previous versions if there is something wrong with the new versions of the pods. Furthermore, deployments support two options for upgrading pods, Recreate and RollingUpdate:

Recreate

The `Recreate` pod upgrade option is very straightforward. In this approach, the deployment resource modifies its associated `ReplicaSet` to point to the new version of the pod. It then proceeds to terminate all the pods. The `ReplicaSet` then notices that all the pods have been terminated and thus spawns new pods to ensure that the number of desired replicas are up and running. The `Recreate` approach will typically result in your pod application not being accessible for a period of time, and thus it is not recommended for applications that need to always be available.

RollingUpdate

Kubernetes's deployment resource also provides a `RollingUpdate` option. With the `RollingUpdate` option, your pods are replaced with the newer versions incrementally over time. This approach results in there being a mixture of both the old version and the new version of the pod running simultaneously and thus avoids having your pod application unavailable during this maintenance period. The readiness of each pod is measured and used to inform kube-proxy and ingress controllers which pod replicas are available to handle network requests to ensure that no requests are dropped during the update process.

The following is an example YAML specification for a deployment that uses the `RollingUpdate` option:

```
apiVersion: apps/v1
kind: Deployment
metadata:
 name: nginx
 labels:
  app: webserver
 annotations:
  deployment.kubernetes.io/revision: "1"
spec:
 replicas: 3
 selector:
  matchLabels:
   app: webserver
 strategy:
  rollingUpdate:
   maxSurge: 1
   maxUnavailable: 1
  type: RollingUpdate
 template:
  metadata:
   labels:
    app: webserver
  spec:
   containers:
   - name: nginx
     image: nginx:1.7.9
```

```
    ports:
    - containerPort: 80
```

The previous deployment example encompasses many of the characteristics that we have seen in ReplicaSets and pods. In its metadata it contains labels and annotations. For the deployment, an annotation with deployment.kubernetes.io/revision as the key and 1 as its value provides information that this is the first revision of the contents in this deployment. Similar to ReplicaSets, the deployment declares the number of replicas it provides and uses a matchLabels field to declare what labels it uses to identify the pods it manages.

 Label matching is a very common aspect of Kubernetes API. If you need to organize or categorize resources, add descriptive labels that serve as lightweight metadata. You can also query or find resources using the -l option in kubectl like kubectl get or kubectl patch.

Similar to ReplicaSets, the deployment has both a spec section for the deployment and a nested spec section inside a template that is used to describe the containers that comprise the pod replicas managed by this deployment.

The fields that are new and specific to a deployment resource are the strategy field and its subfields of type and RollingUpdate. The type field is used to declare the deployment strategy being used and can currently be set to Recreate or RollingUpdate.

If the RollingUpdate option is selected, the subfields of maxUnavailable and maxSurge need to be set as well. The options are used as follows:

maxSurge

The maxSurge RollingUpdate option enables extra resources to be allocated during a rollout. The value of this option can be set to a number or a percentage. As a simple example, assume a deployment is supporting three replicas and max Surge is set to 2. In this scenario, there will be a total of five replicas available during the RollingUpdate.

At the peak of the deployment, there will be three replicas with the old version of the pods running and two with the new version of the pods running. At this point, one of the old version pod replicas will need to be terminated, and then another replica of the new pod version can be created. At this stage, there would be a total of five replicas, three that have the new revision and two that have the old version of the pods. Finally, having reached a point of the correct number of pod replicas being available with the new version, the two pods with the old version can be terminated.

maxUnavailable

This `RollingUpdate` option is used to declare the number of the deployment replica pods that may be unavailable during the update. It can be set to either a number or a percentage.

The following YAML example shows a deployment that has been updated to initiate a rollout:

```
apiVersion: apps/v1
kind: Deployment
metadata:
 name: nginx
 labels:
  app: webserver
 annotations:
  kubernetes.io/change-cause: "Update nginx to 1.13.10"
spec:
 replicas: 3
 selector:
  matchLabels:
   app: webserver
 strategy:
  rollingUpdate:
   maxSurge: 1
   maxUnavailable: 1
  type: RollingUpdate
 template:
  metadata:
   labels:
    app: webserver
  spec:
   containers:
   - name: nginx
     image: nginx:1.13.10
     ports:
     - containerPort: 80
```

Note that a new annotation label with a key of `kubernetes.op/change-cause` has been added with a value that denotes an update to the version of nginx running in the container. Also notice that the name of the image used by the container in the `spec` section has changed to `nginx:1.13.10`. This declaration is what actually drives the pod replicas managed by the deployment to now have a new version of the container images when the upgrade occurs.

To demonstrate the capabilities of deployments, let's run the two previous examples. Save the first deployment example as *deploymentset.yaml* and the second example as *deploymentset2.yaml*. You can now run the first deployment example by doing the following:

```
$ kubectl apply -f deploymentset.yaml
```

After running this command, you should see the following output:

```
deployment.apps/nginx created
```

To confirm that your pod replicas managed by the deployment are actually running, use the kubectl get pods command to verify:

```
$ kubectl get pods
```

After running this command, you should see output similar to the following:

```
NAME                     READY STATUS  RESTARTS AGE
nginx-758fbc45d-2znb7 1/1   Running 0        68s
nginx-758fbc45d-gxf2d 1/1   Running 0        68s
nginx-758fbc45d-s9f9t 1/1   Running 0        68s
```

With deployments, we have a new command called kubectl get deployments that provides status on the deployments as they update their images. Run this command as follows:

```
$ kubectl get deployments
```

After running this command, you should see output similar to the following:

```
NAME   READY UP-TO-DATE AVAILABLE AGE
nginx 3/3    3          3         2m6s
```

Now to make things interesting, let's update the image in our deployment by applying the second deployment example that we saved in *deploymentset2.yaml*. Note that we could have just updated the original YAML that we saved in *deploymentset.yaml* instead of using two separate files. We begin the update by doing the following:

```
$ kubectl apply -f deploymentset2.yaml
```

After running this command, you should see the following output:

```
deployment.apps/nginx configured
```

Now, when we rerun the kubectl get deployments command, which provides status on the deployments as they update their images, we see a much more interesting result:

```
$ kubectl get deployments
NAME   READY UP-TO-DATE AVAILABLE AGE
nginx 2/3    3          2         34s
```

As shown in this output, the deployment currently has three pod replicas running. Three of the pod replicas are up to date, which means they are now running the updated nginx image. In addition, there are three pod replicas in total, and of these three replicas, two are available to handle requests. After some amount of time, when the rolling image update is complete, we reach the desired state of having three updated pod replicas available. We can confirm this by rerunning the kubectl get deployments command and viewing that the output now matches our desired state:

```
$ kubectl get deployments
NAME   READY UP-TO-DATE AVAILABLE AGE
nginx 3/3    3            3        46s
```

To delete the deployment that was just created, run the following command:

```
$ kubectl delete deployment nginx
```

You should get the following confirmation that the deployment has been deleted:

```
deployment.apps "nginx" deleted
```

Deployments also include commands for pausing rollouts, resuming rollouts, and rolling back the update of an image. The commands are quite helpful if you have some concerns about the new image being rolled out that merits investigation or if you determine that the updated image being rolled out is problematic and needs to be rolled back to a previous version. See the Kubernetes Deployment documentation (*https://oreil.ly/BJ115*) for more information on how to use these deployment capabilities.

In the next section, we examine the extra steps that are needed to run the previous examples in a secure Kubernetes production-level environment such as OpenShift.

Running the Pod and Deployment Examples in Production on OpenShift

The pod and deployment examples presented in the previous sections are perfect for instructional purposes and for running in a local development environment. When running in production on a highly secure Kubernetes platform such as OpenShift, there are other factors that need to be addressed. First, the nginx container image we used in the previous examples is configured to run as a privileged root user. By default, secure production Kubernetes platforms such as OpenShift are configured to not allow a container image to run as root. This is because running a container image as root increases the risk that malicious code could find a way to cause harm to the host system.[3] To address this issue, we will replace the nginx container used earlier in this chapter with a version of the image that does not need to run as a privileged root user. The nginx container image from Bitnami runs as a nonroot container and can be used in a production OpenShift environment. The following example is an updated version of our previously created *pod.yaml,* which uses the Bitnami nonroot nginx container image:

```
apiVersion: v1
kind: Pod
metadata:
  name: nginx
```

---

3 Tomas Pizarro Moreno, "Running Non-root Containers on OpenShift," Bitnami Engineering (October 27, 2017), *https://oreil.ly/pxSGf.*

```
spec:
 containers:
 - name: nginx
 image: bitnami/nginx:1.18
 ports:
 - containerPort: 80
```

Remember that all resources are either *cluster scoped,* meaning that only one resource of that kind can exist within the cluster, or *namespace scoped,* meaning that the resources are isolated from other similar resources on the cluster. Within OpenShift, you may also see the term *project,* which predated the concept that Red Hat worked with the community to generalize as namespace. *Project* and *namespace* are synonymous, and OpenShift will respond to either `get projects` or `get namespaces`. You can think of namespaces as like folders within a filesystem that you use to assign to a group of users who are collaborating on a collection of files. We will talk more about namespaces or projects in "OpenShift Enhancements" on page 28.

Another issue with our earlier pod and deployment examples that needs to be addressed is that when they were created, we did not isolate our resources from others by creating a Kubernetes namespace that was specific to our resources. Instead, the earlier examples placed our resources in the Kubernetes default namespace. To encourage proper isolation of applications, secure production Kubernetes platforms such as OpenShift will enforce that your Kubernetes resources are not created in the default namespace but instead are created in a user-defined namespace that provides the required isolation. To create a properly configured namespace, OpenShift provides the `oc new-project` command. OpenShift's project capability is described more thoroughly in "OpenShift Enhancements" on page 28. For now, however, we will use the `oc new-project` command to create a new project called book, which will provide the required isolation to be able to run our pod example. We create our new project by running the following command:

```
$ oc new-project book
```

We can then use the `oc apply -f` command, pass in our updated *pod.yaml,* and use the `-n` option to declare that we want our resources created in the book namespace:

```
$ oc apply -f pod.yaml -n book
pod/nginx configured
```

Now that we have used a nonroot container image and are no longer using the default namespace, our pod example will be permitted by OpenShift to run in production. We can confirm this is the case by using the `oc get pods` command:

```
$ oc get pods
NAME   READY STATUS   RESTARTS AGE
nginx 1/1   Running 0          63s
```

We can clean up and remove the pod example by using the oc delete pod command:

```
$ oc delete pod nginx
pod "nginx" deleted
```

The same techniques we used for the pod example can be applied to the deployment examples as well. Simply update the nginx image that is used in *deploymentset.yaml*, and make sure to use the book namespace when doing the oc apply command. In the next section, we'll introduce another fundamental Kubernetes concept called *service accounts*, which are used to provide authentication for key parts of the Kubernetes platform.

Service Accounts

When you interact with your cluster, you often represent yourself as a user identity. In the world of Kubernetes, we build intelligence into the system to help it interact with its world. Many times, pods may use the Kubernetes API to interact with other parts of the system or to spawn jobs. When we deploy a pod, it may interact with volume storage, interact with the host filesystem, interact with the host networking, or be sensitive to which operating system user it is given access to use for filesystem access. In most cases, you want to restrict the default permissions for a given pod from doing anything more than the absolute basics. Basically, the less surface area that a pod is given access to in the cluster, the host operating system, the networking layer, and your storage layer, the fewer attack vectors that can be exploited.

For a pod to interact with the system, it is assigned a service account. Think of this as a functional identity. The service accounts are subjects that can authenticate with kube-apiserver via tokens and are authorized for certain behaviors.

In some Kubernetes systems, the service account projected into the pod can have identity outside of Kubernetes. A powerful use case is when using the open source Istio (*https://istio.io*) service mesh project with Kubernetes. In this scenario, the Istio identity is projected via the service account, and this allows one pod to authenticate with another when making service requests. Some cloud providers and other security tools also allow for projection of a service account identity into the pod, and this allows for authentication with these external platforms.

In OpenShift, service accounts are also used to associate a grouping of security privileges with each pod. The object that OpenShift uses for creating specialized groupings of security privileges is called a *security context constraint*. In the next section, we provide a more detailed discussion of security context constraints, as well as several other important enhancements that OpenShift delivers to supplement basic Kubernetes.

OpenShift Enhancements

OpenShift introduces several new concepts that it uses to simplify development and operations. Approaches that are specific to OpenShift include authentication, projects, applications, security contexts, and image streams.

Authentication

Security is paramount to the OpenShift Kubernetes platform. As a result, all users must authenticate with the cluster to be able to access it. OpenShift supports a variety of common authentication methods, including basic authentication with username and password, OAuth access tokens, and X.509 client certificates.[4] OpenShift provides the oc login command for performing authentication, which is run by doing the following:

```
$ oc login
```

In a basic authentication use case, when this command is run, the user will be asked to enter the OpenShift Container Platform server URL and whether or not secure connections are needed, and then the user will be asked to input their username and password. In addition, OpenShift's configurable OAuth server allows for users to integrate OpenShift identity with external providers, such as LDAP servers.

Projects

Standard Kubernetes provides the concept of a *namespace* (*https://oreil.ly/IAiIw*), which allows you to define isolation for your Kubernetes resources. Namespaces enable cluster resources to be divided among a large number of users, and the isolation that results from the scoping that they administer keeps users from accidentally using someone else's resource due to a naming collision. Namespaces are incredibly useful, and OpenShift has adapted namespaces for grouping applications. OpenShift accomplishes this by taking a Kubernetes namespace and adding a special standard list of annotations to the namespace. OpenShift refers to this specific type of namespace as a *project*. OpenShift uses projects as its mechanism for grouping applications. Projects support the notion of access permissions. This enables you to add one or more users who have access to the project, and role-based access control is used to set the permissions and capabilities that various users have when accessing a project.

Projects are created using the oc new-project command and by providing a project name, description, and display name as shown:

---

4 The OpenShift authentication documentation (*https://oreil.ly/23ON5*) provides more detail on supported authentication methods.

```
$ oc new-project firstproject --description="My first project"
--display-name="First Project"
```

OpenShift makes it easy to switch between projects by using the `oc project` command. Here we switch to a different project called `secondproject`:

```
$ oc project secondproject
```

To view the list of projects that you are authorized to access, you can use the `oc get projects` command:

```
$ oc get projects
```

For more information on the use of projects, please see the OpenShift project documentation (*https://oreil.ly/xXs4d*).

Applications

When using a basic Kubernetes environment, one of the more tedious steps that needs to be performed by a cloud native application developer is creating their own container images. Typically, this involves finding the proper base image and creating a `Dockerfile` with all the necessary commands for taking a base image and adding in the developer's code to create an assembled image that can be deployed by Kubernetes. OpenShift introduced the application construct (*https://oreil.ly/3RpbY*) to greatly simplify the process of creating, deploying, and running container images in Kubernetes environments.

Applications are created using the `oc new-app` command. This command supports a variety of options that enable container images to be built many ways. For example, with the `new-app` command, application images can be built from local or remote Git repositories, or the application image can be pulled from a Docker Hub or private image registry. In addition, the `new-app` command supports the creation of application images by inspecting the root directory of the repository to determine the proper way to create the application image. For example, the OpenShift `new-app` command will look for a `JenkinsFile` in the root directory of your repository, and if it finds this file, it will use it to create the application image. Furthermore, if the `new-app` command does not find a `JenkinsFile`, it will attempt to detect the programming language that your application is built in by looking at the files in your repository. If it is able to determine the programming language that was used, the `new-app` command will locate an acceptable base image for the programming language you are using and will use this to build your application image.

The following example illustrates using the the `oc new-app` command to create a new application image from an OpenShift example ruby hello world application:

```
$ oc new-app https://github.com/openshift/ruby-hello-world.git
```

This command will create the application as part of whichever OpenShift project was most recently selected to be the current context for the user. For more information on the application image creation options supported by the new-app command, see the OpenShift application creation documentation (*https://oreil.ly/3RpbY*).

Security Context Constraints

Security is always at the forefront in OpenShift. But with added security can come extra complexity and aggravation. If enhanced security is used and a container is not given the proper security options, it will fail. If security is relaxed to avoid issues, then vulnerabilities can result. In an effort to enable users to leverage enhanced security with less aggravation, OpenShift includes a security construct called *security context constraints.*

The security context constraints identify a set of security privileges that a pod's container is guaranteed to execute with. Thus, before the pod's container begins execution, it knows what security privileges it will get. The following is a list of the common security privilege options that are provided by security context constraints:

Allow pods to run privileged containers
> Security context constraints can declare if a pod is permitted to run privileged containers or if it can run only nonprivileged containers.

Require Security-Enhanced Linux (SELinux)
> SELinux (*https://oreil.ly/SlHNy*) is a security architecture for Linux that defines access controls for applications, processes, and files on a system. SELinux presents extra protections beyond what standard Linux uses. Security context constraints provide the MustRunAs attribute value for declaring if SELinux must be run by a pod's container and a RunAsAny attribute value for declaring if the pod's container can run either standard Linux or SELinux.

Run the pod's container as a specific user or as nonroot
> Containers running as root have a bigger vulnerability footprint than containers running as a nonroot. Security context constraints provide a MustRunAsNonRoot attribute value to denote that a Pod's container is not permitted to run as root. Additionally, the security context constraints use a RunAsAny attribute value that permits a pod's container to run as either a root or nonroot user. Finally, the security context constraint administers a MustRunAsRange attribute value that allows a pod's container to run if the user ID is within a specific range of user IDs.

Allow the pod's container access to File System Group block storage
> Security context constraints can be used to limit the block storage that a pod's container has access to. Block storage portions are identified through the use of a File System Group identifier. Security context constraints provide a RunAsAny

attribute value that permits a pod's container to access any File System Group of block storage, as well as a MustRunAs attribute value, which is used to denote that the pod's block storage must be in the range of File System Group IDs listed in the security context constraint.

OpenShift includes several built-in security context constraint profiles that can be reused. To view the list of projects that you are authorized to access, you can use the oc get scc command:

```
$ oc get scc

NAME                  AGE
anyuid                182d
hostaccess            182d
hostmount-anyuid      182d
hostnetwork           182d
node-exporter         182d
nonroot               182d
privileged            182d
restricted            182d
```

As shown, OpenShift contributes security context constraint profiles for common scenarios, such as privileged, restricted, or running as nonroot. To see all the individual capability settings for the security constraint profile, use the oc describe scc command and pass in the name of the profile that you want more details on. For example, if you wanted more details on how powerful the privileged constraint profile is, you would invoke the oc describe scc command as follows:

```
$ oc describe scc privileged
```

Running this command will list a large number of constraint attributes associated with this profile. Here are a few of the more interesting ones:

```
Settings:
  Allow Privileged: true
  Allow Privilege Escalation: true
  Default Add Capabilities: <none>
  Required Drop Capabilities: <none>
  Allowed Capabilities: *
  Allowed Seccomp Profiles: *
  Allowed Volume Types: *
  Allowed Flexvolumes: <all>
  Allowed Unsafe Sysctls: *
  Forbidden Sysctls: <none>
  Allow Host Network: true
  Allow Host Ports: true
  Allow Host PID: true
  Allow Host IPC: true
  Read Only Root Filesystem: false
  Run As User Strategy: RunAsAny
  SELinux Context Strategy: RunAsAny
  FSGroup Strategy: RunAsAny
  Supplemental Groups Strategy: RunAsAny
```

For comparison purposes, we can run the same command for the restricted profile. As shown in the following output, the constraint attribute values are much more restrictive than those in the privileged profile:

```
$ oc describe scc restricted

Settings:
 Allow Privileged: false
 Allow Privilege Escalation: true
 Default Add Capabilities: <none>
 Required Drop Capabilities: KILL,MKNOD,SETUID,SETGID
 Allowed Capabilities: <none>
 Allowed Seccomp Profiles: <none>
 Allowed Volume Types: configMap,downwardAPI,emptyDir,persistentVolumeClaim,
projected,secret
 Allowed Flexvolumes: <all>
 Allowed Unsafe Sysctls: <none>
 Forbidden Sysctls: <none>
 Allow Host Network: false
 Allow Host Ports: false
 Allow Host PID: false
 Allow Host IPC: false
 Read Only Root Filesystem: false
 Run As User Strategy: MustRunAsRange
 SELinux Context Strategy: MustRunAs
 FSGroup Strategy: MustRunAs
 Supplemental Groups Strategy: RunAsAny
```

The key point here is that security context constraint profiles are able to group and encapsulate large groups of capability attributes and ensure that all the attributes are met before a pod is permitted to execute. This reduces the chance of improperly setting the capability attributes and reduces the chance of an unexpected pod failure due to an incorrect security setting.

Security context constraint profiles are associated with pods by using the Kubernetes service account object. For more information on the use of security context constraints, see the OpenShift security context constraints documentation (*https://oreil.ly/W41Sq*).

Image Streams

One of the key steps in deploying a cloud native application is retrieving the correct container application image from a repository. When running in production, there are several possible pitfalls with this retrieval process. First, container images are retrieved by a tag identifier, but it is possible that container images can be overwritten, and thus the image that is referenced by the tag can change. If this change goes unnoticed, it could result in introducing unexpected errors into the cloud native application that is deployed. Second, when running in production, the image retrieval process also needs to be supplemented with support for automating builds and deployments, and many image repositories are limited in their ability to support this automation. Third, in some cases a container image needs to have multiple tags associated with it because the container image is used for different purposes in different environments. Unfortunately, many image repositories do not support the ability to associate multiple tags with a container application image.

To address all of these issues, OpenShift introduced the concept of *image streams*.[5] Image streams are intended to provide a more stable pointer for tagged images. The image stream maintains an SHA-256 secure hash function to the image it points to in order to ensure that the image is not mistakenly changed. Image streams also support multiple tags for images to better support using them in multiple environments. In addition, image streams include triggers that enable builds and deployments to be started automatically when the image stream is updated. Furthermore, image streams can not only reference container images from external repositories, but can also be scheduled to periodically reimport the external container image to ensure that they always have the most recently updated copy of the container image they are referencing in the external repository.

Creating and updating image streams is relatively straightforward. The oc import-image command is used to create an image stream. In the following example, the oc import-image command is used to create an initial image stream called nginx with an initial image stream tag for the imported image that has the value 1.12:

```
$ oc import-image nginx:1.12 --from=centos/nginx-112-centos7 --confirm
```

As shown in this example, the initial container image that is being imported into the nginx image stream is the image that is located at centos/nginx-112-centos7. The confirm option states that the image stream should be created if it doesn't already exist.

Once the image stream is created, we can examine it using the oc describe command. In the following example, the is value is the short name for an input stream resource. The specific input stream that we want described is the one with the name nginx:

```
$ oc describe is/nginx
```

The output from this command looks like this:

```
Name: nginx
Namespace: default
Created: 52 seconds ago
Labels: <none>
Annotations: openshift.io/image.dockerRepositoryCheck=2020-06-12T20:16:15Z
Image Repository: default-route-openshift-image-registry.apps-
crc.testing/default/nginx
```

---

5 The documentation on image streams (*https://oreil.ly/T7vSF*) provides more information.

```
Image Lookup: local=false
Unique Images: 1
Tags: 1

1.12
  tagged from centos/nginx-112-centos7

*centos/nginx-112-
  centos7@sha256:af171c38298e64664a9f999194480ce7e392858e773904df22f7585a1731ad0d
```

We can add an extra tag for this image by using the `oc tag` command. We add an `nginx:latest` tag to the existing `nginx:1.12` tag by doing the following:

```
$ oc tag nginx:1.12 nginx:latest
```

Finally, we can tag an image from an external repository and schedule this image to be periodically reimported by calling the `oc tag` command. As shown in the following example, we reference the image from the external repository, associate it with an image stream tag, and then add the scheduled option to denote that the tag should be periodically updated:[6]

```
$ oc tag docker.io/nginx:1.14 nginx:1.14 --scheduled
```

For more information on the use of image streams, please see the documentation on managing image streams (*https://oreil.ly/YMfdZ*).

Kubernetes and OpenShift Advanced Topics

Several advanced concepts are frequently used when running Kubernetes or OpenShift in production. In this section, we discuss these advanced topics, including webhooks, admission controllers, role-based access control, and operators.

Webhooks

A *webhook* is an HTTP callback.[7] Essentially, a webhook enables information to be pushed to an external entity when an interesting event is occurring. Typically, an HTTP Post operation is used to push the event information, and the event information is most commonly represented as a JSON payload. In Kubernetes, webhooks are used for a variety of security-related operations. For example, Kubernetes can use a webhook to query an external service to determine if a user has the correct privileges to perform a specific operation.

---

6 Maciej Szulik, "How to Simplify Container Image Management in Kubernetes with OpenShift Image Streams," Red Hat OpenShift Blog (March 23, 2017), *https://oreil.ly/JEV4u*.

7 Wikipedia provides an overview of webhooks (*https://oreil.ly/PLH43*).

Webhooks are also used by OpenShift as a mechanism for triggering builds (*https://oreil.ly/bmfyW*). With webhooks, you can configure your GitHub repository to send an alert whenever there is a change in the repository. This alert can be used to kick off a new build and, if the build succeeds, perform a deployment as well.

Webhooks are also used heavily by Kubernetes admission controllers, which are described in the next section. For more information on the use of webhooks in Kubernetes, see Webhook Mode in the Kubernetes documentation (*https://oreil.ly/Aiw7t*).

Admission Controllers

The key to keeping your Kubernetes platform secure is to protect it from requests that can cause harm. *Admission controllers* are one of the mechanisms that Kubernetes uses to protect the platform from harmful requests. In some cases, an admission controller will prevent a request from creating the Kubernetes object at all. In other cases, the admission controller will allow the request to be processed, but it will modify the request to make it safer. As an example, if a request comes in to start a pod and the request does not specify whether the pod should be started in privileged or nonprivileged mode, the admission controller could change the request such that in this situation the pod is requested to be started in nonprivileged mode.

A number of admission controllers are embedded in the kube-controller-manager, and many are enabled in Kubernetes by default to keep the Kubernetes platform secure. In some cases, the admin needs enforcement beyond the scope of the included admission controllers. Kubernetes allows the admin to add additional admission controllers via registration of webhooks to process requests on Kubernetes objects. We will go into more detail regarding admission controllers in Chapter 3.

Role-Based Access Control

Authorization in Kubernetes is integrated into the platform. Kubernetes authorization uses a role-based access control (RBAC) model and provides a fully featured authorization platform that allows operators to define various roles via the Kubernetes objects ClusterRole and Role and to bind them to users and groups using Cluster RoleBinding and RoleBinding. Think of RBAC as a way of setting permissions on a file system, but in the case of Kubernetes, it's setting permissions on the Kubernetes object model. We'll cover the details of how to use RBAC and how best to build a multitenancy model around it in Chapter 4.

Operators

Kubernetes has built-in abstractions like deployments that are extremely well-suited stateless applications. In addition, Kubernetes has a very elegant design based on control loops that enables it to support a declarative programming model and allows the platform to execute robustly at large scale even when failures are common.

To support complex stateful applications, Kubernetes needed an extensibility model that would enable users to add custom resources and perform life-cycle management for those resources. Additionally, it would be ideal if the extensibility model could also support the control loop architecture that is used extensively inside the Kubernetes platform. Kubernetes includes the operator pattern (*https://oreil.ly/OujZb*), which provides an extensibility model for custom resources that meet all of these requirements.

Operators support the creation of custom resources. What this means is that you can define a new resource type in Kubernetes by creating a custom resource definition, and this new resource can be stored in the Kubernetes etcd database just like any standard Kubernetes resource. Additionally, you can create a custom controller for your resource that performs the same type of control loop behavior that the standard Kubernetes controllers perform. The custom controller can then monitor the actual state of your stateful application, compare it to the desired state, and then take actions to attempt to achieve the desired state for the application. For example, let's say you create an operator for a special type of database, which is a stateful application. The operator and its controller can make sure that the actual number of replicas of the database that are running matches the desired number of copies. Furthermore, since the operator has a custom controller, any custom life-cycle management code that is needed for starting up new copies of the database or updating existing copies of the database can be added to the controller.

The operator pattern is well-designed, and a key advantage is that it is seamless. The custom resources associated with an operator are managed using the kubectl command-line tool and look just like a standard Kubernetes resource from a management perspective. To ease the creation of operators, an operator software development kit exists to generate the custom resource definitions and a large portion of the controller code required to run the operator's control loop. As a result of the clean architectural design of the operator framework and also due to extensive tooling available, creating new operators as the means of adding stateful applications continues to grow in popularity. There is now an Operator Hub (*https://operatorhub.io*) that hosts a large number of existing and reusable operators for managing a variety of applications for the Kubernetes platform. We will go into more detail about operators and their consumption within Kubernetes in Chapter 7.

Summary

In this chapter, we covered a wide range of topics to give you a broad foundation and solid introduction to Kubernetes and OpenShift. We touched upon several topics that are critical for running in production, and we will explore many of these topics in greater detail in subsequent chapters of this book. In addition, this chapter helps to illustrate how the Kubernetes and OpenShift ecosystems have matured into platforms that provide a lot of enterprise-level functionality and flexibility. In Chapter 3, we cover a crucial production topic: advanced management of Kubernetes resources while running in production.

Advanced Resource Management

Managing available resources is a critical aspect of effectively running Kubernetes workloads in production. Without the proper sizing of workloads and management of CPU, memory, disk, graphics processing units (GPUs), pods, containers, and other resources, it is impossible for engineers and operations teams to control the service-level agreement (SLA) of applications and services between a client and provider. This SLA is the defining contract that determines the level of availability and performance that the client can expect from the system and is often backed by financial penalties.

We'll discuss a variety of tools and techniques available to the Kubernetes engineer for controlling the allocation of these resources. In this chapter, we begin with a discussion of proper scheduling of pod resources, where we cover topics like priority scheduling, quality of service, and the impact resource limits can have on scheduling pods. Next, we provide an overview of capacity planning and management approaches for ensuring the scalability of your Kubernetes platform. We then conclude this chapter with a discussion of admission controllers and how they can be used to enforce additional constraints on resources.

Pod Resources and Scheduling

Proper scheduling of workload is critical to maintaining the availability and performance of your applications. Without effective scheduling, you can end up with an overloaded worker node with insufficient memory and CPU resources. The most desired outcome in these situations is a graceful shutdown of workload instances that have additional replicas running in the system, resulting in little or no service disruption. In contrast, the worst-case scenario is that the Linux Out of Memory (OOM)

Killer[1] comes through and starts randomly destroying processes. In extreme cases, an improperly configured `kubelet` component on a Kubernetes node could actually destroy the worker node itself.

Driving Scheduler Decisions via Resource Requests

One of the key mechanisms that Kubernetes uses for making scheduling decisions is the resource request construct. A *resource request* for a container is the mechanism that the developer uses to inform Kubernetes how much CPU, memory, and disk resources will be needed to run the associated container. The Kubernetes official documentation on pod resources (*https://oreil.ly/Sxnzu*) provides an excellent overview of resource requests. Let's take a look at a basic Pod that uses resource requests:

```
apiVersion: v1
kind: Pod
metadata:
  name: frontend
spec:
  containers:
  - name: web
    image: icr.io/sample/web:v1
    env:
    resources:
      requests:
        memory: "50Mi"
        cpu: "150m"
        ephemeral-storage: "50Mi"
  - name: logging
    image: icr.io/sample/logging:v2
    resources:
      requests:
        memory: "40Mi"
        cpu: "100m"
        ephemeral-storage: "200Mi"
```

All of this information provided in the pod and container definition are the hints used by the Kubernetes scheduler for placement in the cluster. When we look more closely at scheduling, we'll gain a better understanding of how the scheduler processes this information.

Node Available Resources

During the scheduling process, Kubernetes is looking for nodes that fit the requested resources of the pod to be scheduled. To determine this, the scheduler is looking at allocatable resources minus allocated resources to find available resources. *Allocatable*

---

1 The Out of Memory Killer is a Linux process with the job of weighing all running processes on the system and selecting one or more for termination when the system is critically low on available memory.

resources are the resources that can be consumed by user-controlled pods on a worker node. In Kubernetes, the allocatable resource quantity for a worker node is defined by the total resource available in the node minus the capacity that is reserved for system daemons and Kubernetes runtime components.[2]

 The `--kube-reserved` and `--system-reserved` kubelet flags are critical to maintaining the stability of your worker nodes. Without proper configuration, the user pods can easily overwhelm the resources available on the node and start to compete with system processes and kubelet, kube-proxy, and other container runtime components for resources. We recommend a healthy reservation for kube and system components to ensure the health of the node when faced with hungry user container components.

For administrators managing Kubernetes in production, it's critical to properly configure these resource reservations for both the Kubernetes platform and the system. What's the best way to determine how to set these flags? Experience and real-world testing are invaluable. Trial and error aren't fun, but given how varied every Kubernetes worker may be, it's worth spending some time testing out various settings. A good starting place may lie with your friendly cloud provider. IBM Cloud has done extensive scale testing and evaluation of production systems to come up with a set of safe resource reservations (*https://oreil.ly/7g71U*). As mentioned in the upstream documentation, these reservations are largely based on pod limits per node, kube resource reservations, and kernel memory for system resource reservations. If your configuration has any significant system-level runtime components, you may need to adjust.

These reservations play two key roles. Here we are looking at how they impact allocatable resources for each worker. Later in this chapter, we'll talk about the postscheduling life cycle where these reservations play a role in the life cycle of a pod with pod quality of service.

Scheduling

We're now armed with critical knowledge for the scheduling process with resource reservations and node-allocatable resources. Finding a node that fits our resource requirements is not the only metric at play in scheduling.

---

2 See the Kubernetes documentation, "Reserve Compute Resources for System Daemons" (*https://oreil.ly/YQjrt*).

Kubernetes uses several different factors to determine the placement of pods on worker nodes. Let's cover some of the basic concepts of scheduling and how you can leverage this knowledge to build applications and services with higher availability and performance.

The kube-scheduler (*https://oreil.ly/jca9A*) uses a two-phase process that first filters for nodes that can run the pod and then scores the filtered nodes to determine which is a best fit. A number of predicates (*https://oreil.ly/oVThs*) are used to determine if a node is fit for running a given pod. The priorities (*https://oreil.ly/NA3Z9*) then rank the remaining nodes to determine final placement. There are numerous predicates and policies. We'll cover a few that have the greatest impact on the day-to-day operation of a Kubernetes or OpenShift cluster:

PodFitsResources

The most commonly considered predicate, PodFitsResources evaluates the resource requests of the pods and filters out any nodes that do not have sufficient available resources. There may be instances where there are sufficient total available resources in the cluster but not one node has enough resources available to fit the pod. We'll discuss pod priority and preemption, which can assist with this, in the next section.

PodMatchNodeSelector

While seemingly not that complex, this predicate is responsible for handling all of the pod and node affinity and anti-affinity rules that can be specified. These rules are critical for handling blast radius control and the availability of applications across zones.

PodToleratesNodeTaints

Taints are often used to isolate groups of nodes that may be dedicated to specific workloads in a cluster. In some cases, administrators may use this to reserve a set of nodes for a specific namespace or tenant.[3]

When you think about availability, you should consider the "blast radius" of any specific failure. If a node fails, all pods on that node will become unavailable. If an availability zone fails, all nodes supporting the control plane and the application pods will become unavailable. When you think about the "blast radius," it really is just a way of reasoning about the impact (and the cascading effects) of that failure.

---

3 See the Kubernetes documentation on Taints and Tolerations Example Use Cases (*https://oreil.ly/gSnJ9*).

Pod Priority and Preemption

There are occasions where a pod with resource needs that cannot be met needs to be scheduled. If pod priority and preemption (*https://oreil.ly/nrgbg*) are used, the scheduler can evict lower-priority pods to make room for the higher-priority pod. Priority classes will also factor into which pods will be scheduled first. If a high-priority pod and a low-priority pod are both pending, the low-priority pod will not be scheduled until the high-priority pod is running.

One interesting use case for priority classes is to have pods with larger resource requests be assigned to the higher priority class. In some situations, this can help by moving smaller pods onto other nodes and making room for a larger pod to fit. While this can result in smaller, lower-priority pods being unscheduled and stuck in Pending, it does help to better use the capacity of your cluster by compressing smaller pods into the gaps available on nodes. Let's consider an example.

Initial state:

- Pod P has resource requests of CPU: 1,000, priority 100
- Pod Q has resource requests of CPU: 100, priority 10
- Node N has 900 available CPU out of 1,000 total
- Node O has 300 available CPU out of 300 total
- Pod P is Pending
- Pod Q is Running on Node N

In this example, Pod P will not fit on either Node N or Node O. However, because Pod P has higher priority than Pod Q, Q will be evicted from Node N; thus, Pod P can fit onto Node N and be scheduled. Pod Q will then enter the scheduler again and can fit on Node O. The result is that both pods are now scheduled.

End state:

- Pod P is running on Node N
- Pod Q is running on Node O
- Node N has 0 available CPU
- Node O has 200 available CPU

This may not be a common use case for users, but it is an interesting process that can be used to maximize the utilization of the available node resources.

Post-Scheduling Pod Life Cycle

Now that our pod has been scheduled to a node, we're done, right? Not so. Once the pod is running on a node, a number of factors will determine the ongoing life cycle of the pod. Kubernetes controls the resource consumption of pods, may evict pods to protect the health of the node, and may even preempt a running pod to make way for a higher-priority pod, as discussed in "Scheduling" on page 41.

We've already reviewed resource requests, which are used for making scheduling decisions in Kubernetes. Once pods are in the Running state, resource limits are the attributes most critical to the pod's life cycle. It's worth noting that resource requests continue to serve a valuable purpose as they help to determine the quality of service of the pod and are factored into eviction decisions.

Pod Quality of Service

The intersection of requests and limits is *quality of service* (QoS) (*https://oreil.ly/QukmD*). QoS does not have any impact on scheduling; only requests are factored here. However, QoS does determine the pod eviction selection process and what we would have called overcommit in the world of virtualized infrastructure. There are yet other factors in eviction that we'll discuss in detail in "Node Eviction" on page 50.

Before containers, there were VMs. A VM was a huge leap forward in efficiency for developers and operations teams alike. The VM allowed users to take a single physical computer system and subdivide it into multiple logical operating system instances. If you ever worked with a VM infrastructure management platform, especially Open-Stack, then you have likely run across the concept of overcommit. Overcommit is a number or multiplier that determines how much more CPU, memory, and disk would be allocated than is actually available for a given node. Kubernetes does not have the notion of overcommit, but rather QoS. However, you will notice some similarities between the two.

In the world of VMs, the VM creator picks a CPU and memory size for a given VM, and that is how much memory is carved out of the physical host system for that VM: no more, no less. In Kubernetes, the creator of a pod or container can choose how much CPU and memory they would like to have for their pod or container (resource request) and chooses limits separately. This allows for more efficient utilization of resources in the Kubernetes cluster where there are pods that are less sensitive to their available CPU and memory. The delta between the resource requests and resource limits is how Kubernetes provides the ability to overcommit node resources.

It's important to note that some resources are compressible and some are incompressible. What does this mean? Well, unless it's 1990 and you are running RAM Doubler and Disk Doubler, then these resources are finite and cannot be shared. These non-shareable resources (RAM and disk) are known as *incompressible*. When there is competition for disk or memory, then processes will lose out and be evicted to make room for other processes. However, CPU can be split, or compressed, to allow multiple processes to compete for CPU cycles. Let's say that there are two processes that each wants to do one thousand pieces of work per time unit. If the CPU can do one thousand cycles per unit of time, then both processes continue to run, but they will take double the time to complete their task.

Pod QoS Levels

Now that we have completed our detailed investigation of resource types, we can discuss QoS a bit further. There are three QoS levels. *Guaranteed* is the highest level of QoS. These are pods that have their resource requests and limits set to the same value for all resources. *Burstable* pods have requests set, but their limit values are higher, which permits them to consume more resources if needed. *BestEffort* pods have no requests or limits set. Following are some examples of resource settings for container specs within a pod:

Here is a Guaranteed example:

```
resources:
   limits:
      memory: "200Mi"
   requests:
      memory: "200Mi"
```

Here is a Burstable example:

```
resources:
   limits:
      memory: "200Mi"
   requests:
      memory: "100Mi"
```

And here is a BestEffort example:

```
resources: {}
```

> When requests and limits are equal, you do not need to explicitly set both. If only the limit is set, then the requests are automatically assumed to be the same as the limit by the Kubernetes scheduler.

Remember, we mentioned that if there is competition for memory or disk, then one or more processes will be killed. How does Kubernetes decide which processes to kill? It uses QoS to make this decision. If a Kubernetes worker node comes under resource pressure, then it will first kill off BestEffort pods, then Burstable, and then Guaranteed. For a Guaranteed pod to be evicted from a node, it would require some system-level resource pressures.

Because this QoS is defined on a container-by-container basis and is under the container creator's control, we have the opportunity for much higher resource utilization without putting our critical containers at risk of being starved for resources or potentially having their performance diminished. We get the best of both worlds in Kubernetes.

What about pod priority? It sounds a lot like QoS. However, as we saw in "Scheduling" on page 41, pod priority affects preemption during scheduling but does not affect the eviction algorithms.

The takeaway from all this QoS discussion is that your developers' configuration of resource requests and limits will have a significant impact on how your cluster behaves and handles pods. It's also worth noting that using anything other than Guaranteed QoS can make debugging your workloads and managing capacity very difficult. Your developers keep asking why their pods are constantly dying, only to find out that they are being evicted to make room for higher QoS pods from other teams. As an admin, you are trying to figure out how to manage the capacity of your cluster, but you can't tell how much room is really available because half of your pods are Burstable. Yes, there are monitoring tools that will calculate the cluster's true available capacity based on allocatable resources versus requested resources on all your nodes, but your users are in for a rude awakening when their Burstable capacity starts getting reclaimed to make way for Guaranteed pods. Sure, you may end up leaving a bit of CPU or memory on the table, but your cluster admin and your development teams will have a much more predictable result in production.

 Avoid the use of BestEffort QoS at all costs in production. It can result in very unpredictable scheduling. The result is an environment that may be very unstable as pods compete for resources.

Testing Resource Limits

Limits control how many resources a container is given access to after it is running. Various container runtimes may have different methods for implementing this. For our purposes, we'll focus on traditional Linux container runtimes. The following rules apply for the CRI-O (*https://cri-o.io*) and containerd (*https://containerd.io*) container runtimes. The basic implementation of limits for CPU and memory are implemented using Linux control groups (cgroups). Specifically, in these examples, we are using an OpenShift 4.7 cluster and the CRI-O 1.17.4-19 container runtime.

CPU limits

Let's see what this means for actual running pods. We will start by looking at compressible CPU resources in a Burstable configuration, as it is the most interesting. We have created a test deployment we can use to scale and view the impact on our CPU resources:

```
apiVersion: apps/v1
kind: Deployment
metadata:
 labels:
   run: cpu-use
 name: cpu-use
spec:
 replicas: 1
 selector:
   matchLabels:
     run: cpu-use
 template:
   metadata:
     labels:
       run: cpu-use
   spec:
     containers:
     - command:
       - stress
       - --cpu
       - "5"
       image: kitch/stress
       imagePullPolicy: Always
       name: cpu-use
       resources:
         limits:
           cpu: 1000m
         requests:
           cpu: 200m
     nodeSelector:
       kubernetes.io/hostname: "<worker node>"
```

This sample will let us scale our workload up and down on a four-vCPU worker node and see what the impact is on CPU.

At three replicas, all pods are hitting their CPU limit:

```
$ kubectl top pods
NAME                        CPU(cores)   MEMORY(bytes)
cpu-use-ffd7fd8f8-b2wds     998m         0Mi
cpu-use-ffd7fd8f8-cw6lz     999m         0Mi
cpu-use-ffd7fd8f8-wcn2x     999m         0Mi
```

But when we scale up to higher numbers of pods, we can see there is competition for resources and the cgroups start slicing the CPU thinner. And if we max out the schedulable pods based on our CPU request of 200m, we still end up with even distribution of CPU:

```
$ kubectl top pods
NAME                         CPU(cores)   MEMORY(bytes)
cpu-use-575444f9c6-2fctp     264m         0Mi
cpu-use-575444f9c6-4x2w6     264m         0Mi
cpu-use-575444f9c6-89q8z     263m         0Mi
cpu-use-575444f9c6-bw6fl     265m         0Mi
cpu-use-575444f9c6-dq4pn     265m         0Mi
cpu-use-575444f9c6-g968p     265m         0Mi
cpu-use-575444f9c6-jmpwl     265m         0Mi
cpu-use-575444f9c6-ktmbp     264m         0Mi
cpu-use-575444f9c6-lmjlz     265m         0Mi
cpu-use-575444f9c6-rfvx6     264m         0Mi
cpu-use-575444f9c6-rg77n     264m         0Mi
cpu-use-575444f9c6-skt25     263m         0Mi
cpu-use-575444f9c6-srhhf     264m         0Mi
cpu-use-575444f9c6-svz9z     264m         0Mi
```

Now let's take a look at what happens when we add BestEffort load. Let's start with cpu-noise, which has no requests or limits (BestEffort) and has enough load to consume five vCPU if available. We start with the following load:

```
$ kubectl top pods
NAME                          CPU(cores)   MEMORY(bytes)
cpu-noise-6575cc6657-2qhl8    3724m        0Mi
```

Once we add a cpu-use pod to the mix with requests and limits, this new pod is given not only its requested CPU, but also its limit:

```
$ kubectl top pods
NAME                          CPU(cores)   MEMORY(bytes)
cpu-noise-6575cc6657-2qhl8    2491m        0Mi
cpu-use-679cbc8b6d-95bpk      999m         0Mi
```

Finally, we scale up cpu-use and get to see the real difference between Burstable and BestEffort QoS:

```
$ kubectl top pods
NAME                          CPU(cores)   MEMORY(bytes)
cpu-noise-6575cc6657-2qhl8    7m           0Mi
cpu-use-679cbc8b6d-6nnkp      850m         0Mi
cpu-use-679cbc8b6d-n6gwp      844m         0Mi
cpu-use-679cbc8b6d-rl7vv      863m         0Mi
cpu-use-679cbc8b6d-z7hhb      865m         0Mi
```

In these results, we see that the Burstable pods are well past their requested CPU resources, but the cpu-noise BestEffort pod is just getting scraps.

This is the part where you take note and remember that CPU requests are your friend. You'll be ensuring that your pod won't be at the bottom of the CPU barrel.

Memory limits

We've taken a closer look at the rather interesting control of compressible CPU resources. It's worth looking at memory, but it is not quite as interesting. Let's get started with our memory-use workload first:

```
apiVersion: apps/v1
kind: Deployment
metadata:
  labels:
    app: memory-use
  name: memory-use
spec:
  replicas: 1
  selector:
    matchLabels:
      app: memory-use
  template:
    metadata:
      labels:
        app: memory-use
    spec:
      containers:
      - command:
        - stress
        - --cpu
        - "1"
        - --vm
        - "5"
        - --vm-keep
        image: kitch/stress
        imagePullPolicy: Always
        name: memory-use
        resources:
          limits:
            cpu: 10m
            memory: 1290Mi
          requests:
            cpu: 10m
            memory: 1290Mi
      nodeSelector:
        kubernetes.io/hostname: "10.65.59.69"
```

The result is that we can fit right around six pods per 16 GB host after accounting for node reservations and other critical pods:

```
$ kubectl top pods
NAME                             CPU(cores)   MEMORY(bytes)
memory-use-66b45dbd56-j4jj7      3m           943Mi
memory-use-774b6549db-bqpj5      9m           1280Mi
memory-use-774b6549db-k9f78      9m           1280Mi
memory-use-774b6549db-qmq62      9m           1280Mi
memory-use-774b6549db-vtm96      9m           1280Mi
memory-use-774b6549db-wwj2r      9m           1280Mi
```

If we start to apply memory pressure with our `memory-noise` deployment (same as above, just no resource requests or limits), then we'll start to see eviction and OOM Killer take over; our Guaranteed pods are spared in the mayhem:

```
$ kubectl top pods
NAME                            READY   STATUS      RESTARTS   AGE
memory-noise-85df694f5d-2szg2   0/1     Evicted     0          12m
memory-noise-85df694f5d-598mz   1/1     Running     1          3m49s
memory-noise-85df694f5d-7njvb   1/1     Running     1          7m23s
memory-noise-85df694f5d-7pjjc   0/1     Evicted     0          12m
memory-noise-85df694f5d-8vl8h   0/1     Evicted     0          12m
memory-noise-85df694f5d-7njvb   0/1     OOMKilled   1          8m23s
memory-use-774b6549db-bqpj5     1/1     Running     0          59m
memory-use-774b6549db-k9f78     1/1     Running     0          62m
memory-use-774b6549db-qmq62     1/1     Running     0          62m
memory-use-774b6549db-vtm96     1/1     Running     0          62m
memory-use-774b6549db-wwj2r     1/1     Running     0          62m
```

 "OOMKilled" is a status condition indicating that the process running within the pod was killed because it reached an OOM error. The supporting node could have had all memory exhausted because of unrestricted pods running on the same compute host, or the container process could have reached its specified memory limit (and was thus terminated). The oom_killer is a process in the Linux kernel that takes over whenever a process is identified for termination due to memory constraints.

Hopefully, these examples help to clarify what you can expect from the `kubelet` and Linux memory allocation and management techniques. Ensure that your developers have a clear understanding as well. Once developers realize they will be first in line for OOM Killer's wrath when they don't provide strong requests and limits for their containers, they typically give much better container definitions.

Node Eviction

Eventually, we'll exhaust the noncompressible resources of our worker node, and it is at that point that eviction starts to take over. We won't go into the details of things like eviction thresholds here; the official Kubernetes documentation (*https://oreil.ly/imjls*) provides plenty of information about these settings.

It is, however, worth reviewing the process for evicting end-user pods (*https://oreil.ly/G9chi*). In short, when the `kubelet` is unable to free sufficient resources on the node to alleviate any resource pressure, it will first evict BestEffort or Burstable pods that are exceeding their resource requests. The last pods it will evict are those Guaranteed pods that are underutilizing their resource requests or limits. If only Guaranteed pods are used on a node, then resource pressure may be coming from system-reserved or kube-reserved processes on the node. It will start evicting user Guaranteed pods in self-preservation. It's worth investigating the kubelet configuration for reserved resources to ensure a more stable and predictable node in the future.

The last resort in the situation where a system out of memory situation is encountered before pods can be gracefully evicted is the OOM Killer process itself. More details can be found in the Kubernetes documentation (*https://oreil.ly/hO0h2*). Typically, this comes from a process that is consuming resources at a very rapid pace, such that the kubelet cannot address the memory-pressure situation as fast as the process is consuming memory. Debugging can be quite a chore. If your pods all have limits in place, then this becomes less of an issue since the cgroup limits placed on individual pods will OOM Kill the process before the node reaches memory pressure. Containers and pods with no memory limits are your most likely culprits and should be avoided.

Capacity Planning and Management

As with many modern platforms and service frameworks, our focus is more about capacity management than it is about predicting the future. You can plan for how you will scale your Kubernetes platform for your enterprise. Part of this planning should include how and when to scale master and/or worker nodes, as well as when it is the right time to add additional clusters to your fleet.

Single cluster or multiple clusters? It is unrealistic to expect to run a single cluster for all your workloads. There are some factors to consider. Geographic distribution, tenancy, single-cluster scalability, and blast radius are other factors to consider.

Kubernetes Worker Node Capacity

The starting point for effective and consistent worker node capacity management comes from using Guaranteed QoS for your pods. While it's possible to manage capacity with Burstable or BestEffort pods, it can be extremely challenging to decide when a cluster needs to be scaled.

What is it like to manage capacity without Guaranteed QoS? Administrators are left trying to formulate a guess on when scale is needed based on a combination of monitoring tools for the worker node resources and application metrics coming from the services and applications running on the cluster. Do your monitoring tools show that you have 25% unused memory and CPU and your application metrics are all hitting their *service-level objectives* (SLOs)? Fantastic, you've gotten lucky. It's only a matter of time before those resources start getting pinched and your SLOs start to suffer. It's at this point where you can just start throwing more and/or bigger worker nodes at the cluster in hopes that your SLOs come back in line. However, it may be that there are ill-behaving pods elsewhere in the cluster that are forcing you into this position and you are just throwing money away. With Guaranteed QoS, your CPU will never be compressed, and your memory utilization will never result in randomly evicted pods.

A number of tools are at our disposal to help monitor and manage the capacity of our cluster. Let's consider some of the options available to us.

Monitoring

Monitoring is critical to having a strong understanding of how your capacity is being used. Even with all Guaranteed QoS pods, you'll want to have monitoring data to see if you have significantly underutilized resources or rogue system or kube processes that are consuming resources. Monitoring systems gather metrics from the entire system and aggregate this data into a centralized tool. These metrics can include CPU consumption, available memory, disk performance, network throughput, and application-specific data. With this centralized tool, we typically have the ability to view historical data, as well as to define alarms and thresholds to notify engineers of impending issues. Together, this historical data and alerting provide powerful insight into the performance and scale of the system. Two first-rate monitoring options to consider are Prometheus (*https://prometheus.io*) and Sysdig Monitor (*https://oreil.ly/3p9YR*).

Limit ranges and quotas

We've now talked extensively about resource requests and limits. Fortunately, Kubernetes has even more tools at your disposal to assist with controlling resource usage.

Limit ranges (*https://oreil.ly/BvBNH*) enable an administrator to enforce the use of requests and limits. This includes setting defaults for all containers and pods to inject them at runtime, as well as setting minimum and maximum values for a namespace.

> Limit ranges are really a safeguard against poorly configured pods. Administrators should strongly encourage application owners to set their own proper requests and limits based on performance testing data.

Quotas allow an administrator to set maximum requests and limits per namespace. While potentially aggravating for the developer who expects unlimited access to resources, this gives the cluster administrator ultimate control over preventing resource contention. Administrators should consider setting alerts in combination with total cluster capacity as well as on individual namespace quotas to help plan for future capacity needs. Quotas provide the control needed to ensure that additional compute resources can be onboarded before user demand for resources exceeds the cluster supply.

Autoscaling

Kubernetes autoscaling comes in two flavors. The first of these is the cluster autoscaler, which modifies the number of worker nodes in the cluster. The other is workload autoscaling, which takes many forms, such as horizontal pod autoscaler, vertical pod autoscaler, addon-resizer, and cluster proportional autoscaler. Typically, a cluster administrator is more concerned with the cluster autoscaler, and the workload autoscaling options are more the domain of those responsible for the applications and services running on the cluster.

Cluster autoscaler. The cluster autoscaler (*https://oreil.ly/ccMvo*) works by evaluating pods that remain in Pending state due to insufficient resources and responds by adding additional worker nodes or removing underutilized worker nodes. In clusters where most pods are using Guaranteed QoS, the cluster autoscaler can be a very efficient solution to the management of worker node capacity.

Horizontal pod autoscaler. The most common form of autoscaling used is horizontal pod autoscaling (HPA) (*https://oreil.ly/Y6vOg*). Autoscaling factors in the actual CPU utilization of a pod based on metrics provided via the metrics API `metrics.k8s.io` (or directly from heapster, pre-Kubernetes 1.11 only). With this approach, the resource requests and limits just need to be reasonable for the given workload, and the autoscaler will look at real-world CPU utilization to determine when to scale. Let's look at an example via our application:

```
apiVersion: apps/v1
kind: Deployment
metadata:
  labels:
    app: hello
  name: hello
spec:
  selector:
    matchLabels:
      app: hello
  template:
    metadata:
      labels:
        app: hello
    spec:
      containers:
      - image: kitch/hello-app:1.0
        name: hello
        resources:
          requests:
            cpu: 20m
            memory: 50Mi
---
apiVersion: v1
kind: Service
metadata:
```

```
      labels:
        run: hello
      name: hello
    spec:
      ports:
      - port: 80
        protocol: TCP
        targetPort: 8080
      selector:
        run: hello
```

We now have a simple web app to begin exploring autoscaling. Let's see what we can do from a scaling perspective. Step one—create an autoscaling policy for this deployment:

```
$ kubectl autoscale deploy hello --min=1 --max=5 --cpu-percent=80
deployment.apps "hello" autoscaled

$ kubectl get hpa hello
NAME     REFERENCE           TARGETS    MINPODS   MAXPODS   REPLICAS
hello    Deployment/hello    0%/80%     1         5         1
```

Excellent! We are ready to scale! Let's throw some load, using Locust (*http://locust.io*) or similar, at our fancy new web application and see what happens next. Now when we check to see the CPU utilization of our pod, we can see it is using 43m cores:

```
$ kubectl top pods -l run=hello
NAME                        CPU(cores)   MEMORY(bytes)
hello-7b68c766c6-mgtdk      43m          6Mi
```

This is more than double the resource request we specified:

```
$ kubectl get hpa hello
NAME     REFERENCE           TARGETS    MINPODS   MAXPODS   REPLICAS
hello    Deployment/hello    215%/80%   1         5         1
```

Note that the HPA has increased the number of replicas:

```
$ kubectl get hpa hello
NAME     REFERENCE           TARGETS    MINPODS   MAXPODS   REPLICAS   AGE
hello    Deployment/hello    86%/80%    1         5         3          10m
```

Utilization is still above our policy limit, and thus in time the HPA will continue to scale up and reduce the load below the threshold of the policy:

```
$ kubectl get hpa hello
NAME     REFERENCE           TARGETS    MINPODS   MAXPODS   REPLICAS   AGE
hello    Deployment/hello    62%/80%    1         5         4          15m
```

It's important to note that the metrics collection and HPA are not real-time systems. The Kubernetes documentation (*https://oreil.ly/9R9cE*) provides a bit more detail about the controller-manager settings and other intricacies of the HPA.

Finally, we reduce the load on the deployment by killing the load-generating pod, and it is automatically scaled down again:

```
$ kubectl get hpa hello
NAME      REFERENCE          TARGETS   MINPODS   MAXPODS   REPLICAS   AGE
hello     Deployment/hello   0%/80%    1         5         1          45m
```

How does this help us in hybrid scenarios? It guarantees that regardless of the inherent performance of any one cluster or worker node, the autoscaler will ensure that we have the appropriate resources allocated to support our workload.

HPA can be configured to use all kinds of metrics, including request response times or request rates, in order to meet application service-level requirements.

Vertical pod autoscaler. The vertical pod autoscaler (VPA) (*https://oreil.ly/ostge*) is an excellent solution for a situation in which you have a deployment that needs to scale up rather than out. Whereas the HPA adds more replicas as memory and CPU utilization increase, the VPA increases the memory and CPU requests of your deployment. For this example, let's reuse our hello example. We begin by installing the VPA according to the steps provided. If you recall, we started with requests of 20m. First, let's apply our VPA:

```
apiVersion: poc.autoscaling.k8s.io/v1alpha1
kind: VerticalPodAutoscaler
metadata:
  name: hello-vpa
spec:
  selector:
    matchLabels:
      run: hello
  updatePolicy:
    updateMode: Auto
```

Now, let's apply load using a load generation tool such as Locust (*http://locust.io*) to the application and observe the appropriate response:

```
$ kubectl top pods -l run=hello
NAME                      CPU(cores)   MEMORY(bytes)
hello-7b68c766c6-mgtdk    74m          6Mi
```

We can then view the resource requests for our `hello` deployment and see that they have been automatically adjusted to match real-world utilization of our application:

```
resources:
      requests:
        cpu: 80m
        memory: 50Mi
```

The VPA is a powerful tool that can enable us to scale our applications and services in a manner that is best suited to their performance characteristics. Scaling out an application doesn't always provide the most efficient use of available resources. Leveraging the VPA in these situations can lead to improved performance and lower costs if applied appropriately.

Cluster proportional autoscaler. A couple of other common autoscaler implementations are used in addition to the HPA. The first of these is the cluster proportional autoscaler (*https://oreil.ly/pvIDT*), which looks at the size of the cluster in terms of workers and resource capacity to decide how many replicas of a given service are needed. Famously, this is used by CoreDNS; for example:

```
spec:
  containers:
  - command:
    - /cluster-proportional-autoscaler
    - --namespace=kube-system
    - --configmap=coredns-autoscaler
    - --target=Deployment/coredns
    - --default-params={"linear":{"coresPerReplica":256,"nodesPerReplica":16,
"preventSinglePointFailure":true}}
    - --logtostderr=true
    - --v=2
```

The number of cores and nodes are used to determine how many replicas of CoreDNS are needed.

Addon-resizer. Another great example is the addon-resizer (*https://oreil.ly/3sF7E*) (aka pod_nanny), which performs vertical scaling of resource requests based on cluster size. It scales the resource's requests of a singleton based on the number of workers in the cluster. This autoscaler has been used by the Kubernetes metrics-server (*https://oreil.ly/GIyey*), which is a core component responsible for providing a simple API frontend to basic worker node and pod metrics. Here we can see the use of the pod_nanny to scale the metrics-server as the cluster grows in size, with extra-cpu and extra-memory defining how much additional CPU and memory resources should be allocated to the metrics-server for each additional worker node in the cluster:

```
- /pod_nanny
    - --config-dir=/etc/config
    - --cpu=100m
    - --extra-cpu=1m
    - --memory=40Mi
    - --extra-memory=6Mi
    - --threshold=5
    - --deployment=metrics-server
    - --container=metrics-server
    - --poll-period=300000
    - --estimator=exponential
    - --use-metrics=true
```

This autoscaling technique is very helpful as it can resize applications based on known scaling measurements as cluster size grows. This can help to avoid issues with OOM or CPU starvation for an application before a traditional horizontal or vertical autoscaler would even be able to collect enough metrics to make a judgment on the need to scale up.

Kubernetes Master Capacity

The Kubernetes scalability special interest group (sig-scalability) (*https://oreil.ly/IjmVi*) is a group of Kubernetes community members focused on measuring and improving the scalability of Kubernetes itself. The sig-scalability team has done fantastic work to quantify and improve the limits of a Kubernetes cluster, yet it still has its boundaries.[4] The limits specified by the sig-scalability team are based primarily on the impact of adding nodes and pods. The limiting factor in kube scalability is the performance of etcd/kube-apiserver to handle the load of the controllers and objects they are managing. In the standard tests, there are a limited number of objects and controllers at work. In these tests, the kubelet, controller-manager, and scheduler are the primary consumers of etcd/apiserver resources.

Table 3-1 lists the recommended master node systems based on the number of worker nodes based on the data from sig-scalability (*https://oreil.ly/lXkTu*).

Table 3-1. Recommended resources needed for Kubernetes control plane based on cluster worker node counts

Worker nodes	Master vCPU	Master memory
1–10	2	8
11–100	4	16
101–250	8	32
251–500	16	64
500+	32	128

The maximum cluster size documented officially (*https://oreil.ly/DxmGf*) is as follows:

- No more than 5,000 nodes
- No more than 150,000 total pods
- No more than 300,000 total containers
- No more than 100 pods per node

---

[4] See the Kubernetes documentation, "Considerations for Large Clusters" (*https://oreil.ly/qaWKY*).

However, as we'll discuss in this chapter, there are far more factors to consider.

In addition to pods and worker nodes, it's important to consider the number of Kubernetes services, secrets, ConfigMaps, persistent volumes, and other standard Kubernetes objects and controllers. There have been considerable improvements in kube-proxy to mitigate the performance impact of a large number of services, but it's still a factor. Remember that kube-proxy needs to track changes to the endpoints of all services in order to keep iptables or IP Virtual Server (IPVS) configurations up to date. There is no hard limit on the number of services that we know of, but more endpoints and more ports will have a huge impact on the scalability of each kube-proxy and increase the load on etcd/apiserver. Consider also the load of secrets and ConfigMaps on etcd/apiserver. Every mounted secret means another watch on that secret for the kubelet. In aggregate, these secret watches can have a significant impact on etcd/apiserver performance and scale.

 One option to consider to help Kubernetes scale more efficiently is to skip mounting the service account secret into your pods. This means the kubelet will not need to watch this service account secret for changes.

Here is an example of how to skip mounting the service account token into the pod:

```
apiVersion: v1
kind: ServiceAccount
metadata:
  name: build-robot
automountServiceAccountToken: false
```

This will help with scalability of the kube-apiserver as well as the node itself. Workload for kube-apiserver is reduced because the kubelet will not need to call the kube-apiserver to get the token. The node performance is improved because there are fewer volume mounts for tokens.

Not convinced that many factors contribute to the scalability of the cluster? Consider that the modern Kubernetes workload often includes a significant number of other objects and controllers. Kubernetes 1.7 introduced the ability for users to define their own objects via *custom resource definitions* (CRDs). These CRDs, along with the Kubernetes controller model for reconciling declared states, enabled users to extend the capabilities of Kubernetes to manage almost any resource imaginable. Although they are very powerful tools, CRDs and controllers can sometimes lead to an explosion of objects in the Kubernetes data model. Along with all those new objects may come many active actors writing and reading to and from that model. Left unchecked, these controllers and new objects can have a massive impact on scale and performance.

With so many moving parts contributing to the scale limitations of your kube cluster, the one thing you can count on is this: in production, you will need to shard. In Chapters 5, 6, and 8, we go into more detail on how to manage multiple clusters and distribute workload across them. We provide a formula for sharding that allows for further expansion of our scaling capabilities. For the purposes of this discussion, we simply need to establish what the scalability limits are of a single Kubernetes cluster running *your* unique workload. There is simply no substitute for automated scale testing that you can repeat regularly. One of your teams wants to introduce a new set of CRDs and a controller for them? Time to run scale testing! Before they can ship that new code to production, you need to understand the impacts of those changes. It may be that you find that it is a significant enough impact that you can break the scale capabilities of your clusters in production. In such cases, you may need to roll out a new set of clusters for these services. What if this service is already in production? You may need to migrate this service off of an existing set of multitenant clusters.

Admission Controller Best Practices

Admission controllers are powerful tools available to the administrator of Kubernetes clusters to enforce additional constraints and behaviors on objects in the cluster. Most commonly, these controllers are used to enforce security, performance, and other best practices. These add-ons to the cluster can either modify or constrain objects that are being created, updated, or deleted in the kube-apiserver.

It's important to note that as with many features of Kubernetes, enabling admission controllers can have an impact on the performance and scale of your cluster. This is especially true when using webhook-based admission controllers.

Standard Admission Controllers

Upstream Kubernetes includes a number of admission controllers as part of all control planes. As of Kubernetes 1.18, the set of admission controllers enabled by default (*https://oreil.ly/DzrON*) are as follows:

- NamespaceLifecycle
- LimitRanger
- ServiceAccount
- TaintNodesByCondition
- Priority
- DefaultTolerationSeconds

- DefaultStorageClass

- StorageObjectInUseProtection

- PersistentVolumeClaimResize

- RuntimeClass

- CertificateApproval

- CertificateSigning

- CertificateSubjectRestriction

- DefaultIngressClass

- MutatingAdmissionWebhook

- ValidatingAdmissionWebhook

- ResourceQuota

Not all of these are particularly interesting, and the official documentation (*https://oreil.ly/4EHzv*) has plenty of information about what they all do. There are two on this list that we'll spend more time on: `MutatingAdmissionWebhook` and `ValidatingAdmissionWebhook`.

Before we move on to those dynamic admission controllers, we'll cover a few of the standard controllers in more detail:

LimitRanger

Earlier in this chapter, we talked about the importance of resource limits to ensure that pod resource consumption is kept in check. `LimitRanger` ensures that the `LimitRange` settings configured on a namespace are adhered to. This provides one more tool for cluster administrators to keep workloads in check.[5]

Priority

As we discussed earlier, `PriorityClasses` play a key role in the scheduling and post-scheduling behavior of pods. The `Priority` admission controller helps to map useful names to an integer that represents the relative value of one class versus another.

ResourceQuota

Critical to the function of a production-ready cluster, this controller is responsible for enforcing the quotas we discussed in "Limit ranges and quotas" on page 52.

---

5 See the Kubernetes documentation on Limit Ranges (*https://oreil.ly/gPLXG*).

`PodSecurityPolicy`
> This controller is not enabled by default but should be in any production-ready Kubernetes or OpenShift cluster. Pod security policies (*https://oreil.ly/fLhIC*) are essential for enforcing security and compliance.

Collectively, these additional admission controllers provide a great deal of the core behaviors we have come to take as standard for Kubernetes. These admission controllers help to build the rules that govern how administrators and users deploy their workloads within set boundaries of performance, scale, and security.

Admission Webhooks

It's helpful to talk a bit about what admission webhooks are and how they work. The upstream documentation (*https://oreil.ly/pSA4X*) also refers to them as *dynamic admission controllers* and provides excellent information about these tools. An *admission webhook* is a Kubernetes configuration that references a web service that can run either on the cluster or external to the cluster and provides modification (mutating) or validation of objects as they are modified in the kube-apiserver. A simple example of a webhook configuration is provided for reference:

```
apiVersion: admissionregistration.k8s.io/v1
kind: ValidatingWebhookConfiguration
metadata:
  name: "pod-policy.example.com"
webhooks:
- name: "pod-policy.example.com"
  rules:
  - apiGroups:   [""]
    apiVersions: ["v1"]
    operations:  ["CREATE"]
    resources:   ["pods"]
    scope:       "Namespaced"
  clientConfig:
    service:
      namespace: "example-namespace"
      name: "example-service"
    caBundle: "xxxxxxxxxx"
  admissionReviewVersions: ["v1", "v1beta1"]
  sideEffects: None
  timeoutSeconds: 5
```

Notable features of this config are the rules that determine which objects the kube-apiserver should call the webhook for and the `clientConfig`, which determines the target endpoint and authentication mechanism to be used for the calls.

In our example, we have a `clientConfig` that references an in-cluster service to contact for webhook calls. Alternatively, the `service:` stanza can be replaced with a `url:` "https://myexample webhook:9443/path" to refer via a specific address rather than a service.

ValidatingAdmissionWebhook

Validating webhooks are powerful tools that can be used to enforce security constraints, resource constraints, or best practices for a cluster. A great example is Portieris (*https://oreil.ly/xpu1F*), which is used to validate that only images from approved registries are used for containers. The kube-apiserver calls the validating webhook and expects a Boolean response to determine if the request should be admitted.

An important operational note is that a dependency chain could inadvertently be built that prevents the validating application from starting in the cluster. As noted, it is not uncommon for admission controllers to be run in the cluster; if we were to run Portieris in our cluster in the `portieris` namespace and then created a webhook rule that required validation before starting any pods in the `portieris` namespace, we would have to remove the webhook configuration before we could even restart the pods that were serving the webhook. Be sure to avoid such circular dependencies by excluding namespaces from the webhook configuration where appropriate.

MutatingAdmissionWebhook

Mutating webhooks are commonly used to inject sidecars into pods, modify resource constraints, apply default settings, and other useful enforcement. There may often be a validating and a mutating option for similar purposes. There may be a validating webhook that ensures that pods are not started without having a specific service account in use, and a mutating alternative might modify the service account of the pod dynamically. Both have similar results: one requires the user to make the modifications required on their own before running their applications, while the other modifies on the fly. There are pros and cons to both approaches. Mutating is typically best reserved for adding function to a pod, such as a sidecar. Validating is better suited for enforcing best practices and forcing users to make the modifications on their own, thus raising awareness of those practices for the team.

Summary

In this chapter, we explored the tools that govern how user applications consume resources in the cluster and how administrators can put rules in place with admission controllers to guide their users to success. We also covered how the Kubernetes scheduler uses these user-provided details to efficiently schedule workload in the cluster. Finally, we covered some of the tools of the trade that can be used to help ensure strong performance of our applications with monitoring and autoscaling.

When combined, these resource definitions, autoscaling techniques, and admission controls provide the groundwork for more advanced management of resources in any Kubernetes or OpenShift cluster. Proper application of all of these tools can lead to a higher level of application performance, more stability for the system, and lower costs through efficient resource utilization. Now that we have a foundation for understanding how resources are managed in Kubernetes and OpenShift, we will move on to how to use these tools to increase the availability of applications and services.

## CHAPTER 4

Single Cluster Availability

A solid foundation for each individual cluster is critical to the availability of your applications and services. Even with these advanced distributed application capabilities, there are some systems for which multicluster isn't an option. Most stateful applications and databases are not capable of geographic distribution and are very complicated to properly operate across multiple clusters. Many modern data storage solutions require low latency multizone solutions, making it less than optimal to break up the data clusters into higher latency environments. It is also important to consider that many data platforms have StatefulSet solutions to help operate them, requiring a single-cluster architecture. We think that having a strong foundation of what it means for a system to be *available* and *highly available* is critical to understanding the value and architecture of OpenShift and Kubernetes. Note that we'll discuss how to take advantage of multicluster architectures for the ultimate in availability and flexibility in Chapter 5. This chapter should help prepare you with the knowledge required to make intelligent decisions about what your availability goals are and how to leverage Kubernetes and OpenShift to achieve them.

System Availability

In modern service and application delivery, we typically talk about system availability in terms of what percentage of time an application or service is available and responding normally. A common standard in the technology service industry is to describe SLOs in terms of nines. We hear the terms *four nines* or *five nines* to indicate the percentage of time that the service is available. Four nines is 99.99%, and five nines is 99.999%. We'll use these standards throughout this chapter. This SLO is the agreement within the SLA that the service provider has with its stakeholder or customer. These SLOs are often measured on a monthly basis, or sometimes annually.

Measuring System Availability

In his day job, one of the authors, Jake, is responsible for the delivery of IBM Cloud Kubernetes Service (*https://oreil.ly/7SAB7*) and Red Hat OpenShift on IBM Cloud (*https://oreil.ly/FMJGW*). These are global services that provide managed Kubernetes and OpenShift solutions with the simplicity of an API-driven, user-friendly cloud experience. For these services, the site reliability engineering (SRE) team measures SLOs on a monthly basis as that coincides with the client billing cycle. It's helpful to think about how much downtime is associated with these nines. We can see in Table 4-1 that our disruption budget or allowable downtime can be very low once we get into higher levels of availability. When performing this analysis, your team needs to carefully consider what it is willing to commit to.

Table 4-1. Availability table; calculations based on an average 730-hour month

Availability percentage	Downtime per month
99% (two nines)	7 hours 18 minutes
99.5% (two and a half nines)	3 hours 39 minutes
99.9% (three nines)	43 minutes 48 seconds
99.95% (three and a half nines)	21 minutes 54 seconds
99.99% (four nines)	4 minutes 22.8 seconds
99.999% (five nines)	26.28 seconds

There are two key performance indicators (KPIs) that a team will strive to improve in order to achieve an agreed-upon SLO. They are *mean time to recovery* (MTTR) and *mean time between failures* (MTBF). Together, these KPIs directly impact availability:

$$Availability = \frac{MTBF}{MTBF + MTTR}$$

It's helpful to think about how we can arrive at our desired availability percentage. Let's say we want to get to a 99.99% availability. In Table 4-2, we compare some different MTTR and MTBF numbers that can get us to this availability.

Table 4-2. Four nines (99.99%) availability calculations

MTBF	MTTR
1 day	8.64 seconds
1 week	60.48 seconds
1 month	4 minutes 22.8 seconds
1 year	52 minutes 33.6 seconds

For those following along at home, this means that to get to four-nines availability in a system that will experience a failure once a day, you have to identify and repair that failure in under nine seconds. The engineering investment required to achieve platform stability and software quality to dramatically extend the MTBF is simply massive. For many customers, four nines is prohibitively expensive. Getting to that level of availability takes hardware, engineering, and a support staff. For contrast, let's take a look at a two nines comparison in Table 4-3.

Table 4-3. Two nines 99% availability calculations

MTBF	MTTR
30 minutes	18.18 seconds
1 hour	36.36 seconds
1 day	14 minutes 32.4 seconds
1 week	1 hour 41 minutes 48 seconds

What are we to make of these numbers? Well, there are a few things to take away from this. First, if you have a target of four nines, then you will need an unbelievably reliable system with failures occurring on the order of once a year if you are going to have any hope of hitting the target. Even at two nines, if you have a single failure a day, then you are going to need to identify and repair that failure in under 15 minutes. Second, we need to consider the likelihood of these failures. A failure once a day, you say? Who has a failure once a day? Well, consider this: the SLA for a single VM instance is typically around 90%, which means 73.05 hours of downtime per month. A single VM is going to be down on average three days per month. If your application depends on just 10 systems, then the odds are that at least one of those is going to be down every day.

Does this picture look grim and insurmountable? If not, then you are quite the optimist. If it is looking challenging, then you have recognized that hitting these failure rate numbers and recovery times with standard monitoring and recovery runbooks is unlikely. Enter the world of highly available systems.

What Is a Highly Available System?

In the simplest terms, *high availability (HA)* refers to a system that has the characteristic of not having any single point of failure. Any one "component" can sustain a failure and the system as a whole experiences no loss of availability. This attribute is sometimes referred to as having the ability to treat individual components as cattle rather than pets. This concept was first introduced by Bill Baker of Microsoft in his talk "Scaling SQL Server 2012."[1] It was later popularized by Gavin McCance when

---

1 Unfortunately, PASS has ceased operations, and the talk given in early 2012 is not available.

talking about OpenStack at CERN.[2] As long as the overall herd is healthy, we don't need to be concerned with the health of the individuals. We like to keep *all* of our pets healthy and in top shape, but it is rather time-consuming and expensive. If you have only a handful of pets, this can be sustainable. However, in modern cloud computing, we typically see a herd of hundreds or thousands. There simply are not enough SRE engineers on the planet to keep the entire herd healthy.

In a system that has a single point of failure, even the most cared-for components occasionally have a failure that we cannot prevent. Once discovered via monitoring, some time is always required to bring them back to health. Hopefully, our introduction to system availability convinces you of the challenges of MTBF and MTTR.

It is helpful for us to have a diagram of the simplest of highly available systems. A simple stateless web application with a load balancer is a great example, as shown in Figure 4-1.

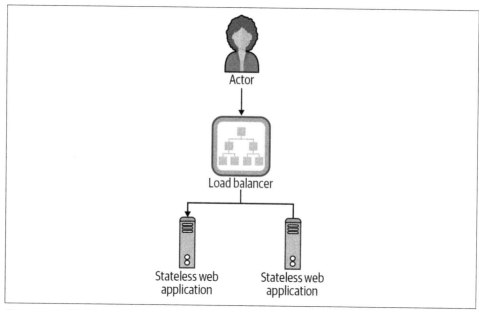

Figure 4-1. Highly available stateless web application with load balancer

In this simplest of HA systems, if either one of these two web application instances fails, the load balancer can detect that failure and stop routing traffic to the failed instance. The actor doesn't know about the individual instances; all of the actor's

---

2 Gavin McCance, "CERN Data Centre Evolution," talk presented at SCDC12: Supporting Science with Cloud Computing (November 19, 2012), *https://oreil.ly/F1Iw9*.

interactions are with the load balancer. The load balancer is even capable of doing retries if a request to one of the instances fails or does not respond fast enough.

Now, obviously the load balancer itself could also fail, but load balancers generally have much higher availability numbers than your typical web application. A typical cloud load balancer has an SLA of 99.99%, which would be the ceiling for the availability of any application running behind that load balancer. Where a cloud load balancer is not available, you can deploy them in pairs with virtual IPs and *Virtual Router Redundancy Protocol* (VRRP), which can move a single IP address between two load balancer instances. The public cloud providers can simplify all of this with their application and network load balancer services, which are capable of handling all of the HA aspects of the load balancer itself.

All done, right? Well, not quite; there are so many components and services to run in a modern application and service platform. In our experience, many large cloud services could consist of multiple groups of five to six microservices. Then add in the fact that your application or service might be globally distributed and/or replicated. Consider our own Red Hat OpenShift on IBM Cloud service availability in Figure 4-2.

Figure 4-2. Red Hat OpenShift on IBM Cloud locations

That's six global multizone regions along with 14 other datacenters worldwide. Our team runs over 40 microservices in each of those multizone regions, and about half that in the single-zone datacenters. The numbers add up quickly. Imagine if we had to manually deploy each microservice and configure a load balancer for each one of them in each of these locations. We'd need an army of engineers just writing custom configuration data. Enter OpenShift and Kubernetes.

OpenShift and Kubernetes Application and Service Availability

Many components in Kubernetes and OpenShift contribute to the availability of the overall system. We'll discuss how we keep the application healthy, how we deal with networking, and how we are able to address potential issues with compute nodes.

The application

For our stateless application, the simple load balancer is the key to high availability. However, as we discussed, if we rely on manually deploying and configuring load balancers and applications, then keeping them up to date won't be a whole lot of fun. In Chapter 2, we discussed Kubernetes deployments. This elegant construct makes it simple to deploy multiple replicas of an application. Let's look at the livenessProbe, which is an advanced capability and one of the more critical features of the deployment-pod-container spec. The livenessProbe defines a probe that will be executed by the kubelet against the container to determine if the target container is healthy. If the livenessProbe fails to return success after the configured failure Threshold, the kubelet will stop the container and attempt to restart it.

 To handle transient issues in a container's ability to serve requests, you may use a readinessProbe, which will determine the routing rules for Kubernetes services but won't restart the container if it fails. If the readinessProbe fails, the state of the pod is marked NotReady and the pod is removed from the service endpoint list. The probe continues to run and will set the state back to Ready upon success. This can be useful if a pod has an external dependency that may be temporarily unreachable. A restart of this pod won't help, and thus using a livenessProbe to restart the pod has no benefit. See the community docs (*https://oreil.ly/GqNnW*) for more details on the available probes in Kubernetes and OpenShift.

The following example shows a simple deployment that includes a livenessProbe with common parameters:

```
apiVersion: apps/v1
kind: Deployment
metadata:
  name: nginx
  labels:
    app: webserver
spec:
  replicas: 3
  selector:
    matchLabels:
      app: webserver
  template:
    metadata:
```

```
      labels:
        app: webserver
    spec:
      containers:
      - name: nginx
        image: nginx:1.7.9
        ports:
          - containerPort: 80
        livenessProbe:
          httpGet:
            path: /
            port: 80
          initialDelaySeconds: 3
          periodSeconds: 3
          timeoutSeconds: 2
          failureThreshold: 2
```

Let's take a closer look at the options we have chosen in our example for `liveness Probe` and how they translate into real-world behaviors:

`httpGet`
> The type of check that will be performed. You can also use `tcp` or `exec` commands that will execute to test if the container is healthy.

`initialDelaySeconds`
> How long the `kubelet` will wait before attempting the first probe.

`periodSeconds`
> How often the `kubelet` will test the probe.

`timeoutSeconds`
> How long the `kubelet` client will wait for a response.

`failureThreshold`
> The number of consecutive failures that the `kubelet` must run through before marking the probe as failed. In the case of our `livenessProbe`, the result is restarting this container.

> Be sure to thoroughly test your `livenessProbe` and the timing settings. We have heard of numerous cases where a slow application startup results in a `CrashLoopBackOff` scenario where a pod never starts up successfully due to never having sufficient `initialDelay Seconds` to start completely. The `livenessProbe` never succeeds because the `kubelet` starts to check for liveness before the application is ready to start receiving requests. It can be painful for rolling updates to set very long initial delay settings, but it can improve stability of the system where there is a lot of variability in initial liveness times.

Together, we have all the makings of a traditional load balancer health check. HAProxy is a popular traditional software load balancing solution. If we look at a standard HAProxy configuration, we'll see many of the same critical health-checking components:

```
frontend nginxfront
  bind 10.10.10.2:80
  mode tcp
  default_backend nginxback

backend nginxback
  mode tcp
  balance roundrobin
  option httpchk GET /
  timeout check 2s
  default-server inter 3s fall 2
  server 10.10.10.10:80 check
  server 10.10.10.11:80 check
  server 10.10.10.12:80 check
```

The interesting thing to note here is that we're looking at the same configuration settings for a load balancer configuration in legacy infrastructure as we are for a deployment in Kubernetes. In fact, the actual check performed is identical. Both initiate an HTTP connection via port 80 and check for a 200 response code. However, the net resulting behavior is quite different. In the case of HAProxy, it just determines if network traffic should be sent to the backend server. HAProxy has no idea what that backend server is and has no ability to change its runtime state. In contrast, Kubernetes isn't changing the network routing directly here. Kubernetes is only updating the state of each of the pods in the deployment (Ready versus NotReady), and it will restart that container if it fails its livenessProbe. Restarting the pod won't fix all issues that are causing unresponsiveness, but it often can solve minor issues.

 livenessProbe isn't just great for ensuring that your containers are healthy and ready to receive traffic. It's a fantastic programmable solution for the pragmatic operator who is tired of cleaning up Java Virtual Machine (JVM) leaking threads and memory to the point of becoming unresponsive. It's a nice backup to the resource limits that we set in place in Chapter 3 in an attempt to limit these resource leaks.

It's worth noting that associating these health-checking configurations with the runtime components rather than a networking feature of the system is a deliberate choice. In Kubernetes and OpenShift, the livenessProbe is performed by the kubelet rather than by a load balancer. As we can see in Figure 4-3, this probe is executed on every node where we find a pod from the deployment.

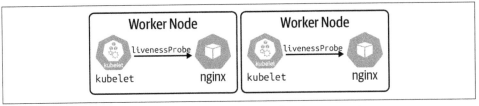

Figure 4-3. kubelet performing livenessProbe to local nginx pod

Every kubelet (one per worker node) is responsible for performing all of the probes for all containers running on the kubelet's node. This ensures a highly scalable solution that distributes the probe workload and maintains the state and availability of pods and containers across the entire fleet.

The infrastructure

Where does the networking come from in Kubernetes? That's the job of the Kubernetes service. Here is where things get interesting. Let's look at how traffic travels to our nginx pod. First, our service definition:

```
apiVersion: v1
kind: Service
metadata:
 labels:
 app: webserver
 name: nginx-svc
spec:
 ports:
 - port: 80
 protocol: TCP
 targetPort: 8080
 selector:
 app: webserver
 type: ClusterIP
 clusterIP: 172.21.102.110
```

This service definition tells Kubernetes that it should route any traffic in the cluster that is sent to 172.21.102.110 on port 80 to any pods that match the selector app=webserver on port 8080. The advantage here is that as we scale our webserver application up and down or update it and the pods are replaced, the service keeps the endpoints up to date. A great example of endpoint recovery can be seen if we delete all the pods and let our deployment replace them automatically for us:

```
$ kubectl get endpoints nginx-svc
NAME        ENDPOINTS                                                    AGE
nginx-svc 172.30.157.70:80,172.30.168.134:80,172.30.86.21:80 3m21s

$ kubectl delete pods --all
pod "nginx-65d4d9c4d4-cvmjm" deleted
pod "nginx-65d4d9c4d4-vgftl" deleted
pod "nginx-65d4d9c4d4-xgh49" deleted
```

```
$ kubectl get endpoints nginx-svc
NAME        ENDPOINTS                                               AGE
nginx-svc 172.30.157.71:80,172.30.168.136:80,172.30.86.22:80 4m15s
```

This automatic management of the endpoints for a service begins to show some of the power of Kubernetes versus traditional infrastructure. There's no need to update server configurations in HAProxy. The Kubernetes service does all the work to keep our "load balancer" up to date. To assemble that list of endpoints, the Kubernetes service looks at all pods that are in the Ready state and matches the label selector from the service definition. If a container fails a probe or the node that the pod is hosted on is no longer healthy, then the pod is marked NotReady and the service will stop routing traffic to that pod. Here we again see the role of the livenessProbe (as well as the readinessProbe), which is not to directly affect routing of traffic, but rather to inform the state of the pod and thus the list of endpoints used for routing service traffic.

In a situation where we have multiple replicas of our application spread across multiple worker nodes, we have a solution with the service where even if a worker node dies, we won't lose any availability. Kubernetes is smart enough to recognize that the pods from that worker node may no longer be available and will update the service endpoint list across the full cluster to stop sending traffic to the pods on the failed node.

We've just discussed what happens when a compute node dies: the service itself is smart enough to route traffic around any pods on that node. In fact, the deployment will then also replace those pods from the failed node with new pods on another node after rescheduling them, which is very handy for dealing with compute failures. What about the need to provide a "load balancer" for the service? Kubernetes takes a very different approach in this matter. It uses the kube-proxy component to provide the load-balancing capabilities. The interesting thing about kube-proxy is that it is a fully distributed component providing a load-balancing solution that blends the distributed nature of client-side load balancers and the frontend of a traditional load balancer. There is not a separate client-side load balancer for every client instance, but there is one per compute node.

Note that kube-proxy is responsible for translating service definitions and their endpoints into iptables[3] or IPVS[4] rules on each worker node to route the traffic appropriately. For simplicity, we do not include the iptables/IPVS rules themselves in our diagram; we represent them with kube-proxy, as shown in Figure 4-4.

---

3 The Wikipedia entry on iptables (*https://oreil.ly/6Pmwf*) provides more information.

4 The Wikipedia entry on IP Virtual Server (*https://oreil.ly/LSYXT*) provides more information.

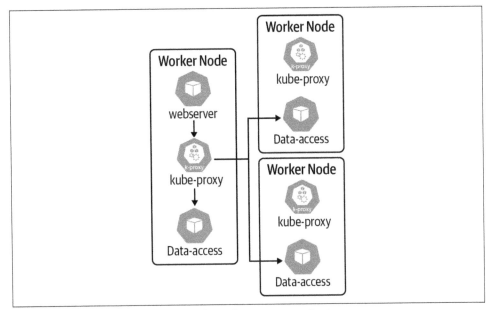

Figure 4-4. kube-proxy routing traffic to data-access endpoints

In the example in Figure 4-4, note that the webserver (client) will route traffic to the local kube-proxy instance, and then kube-proxy sends traffic along to the data-access service pods running on the local and/or remote nodes. Thus, if any one of these nodes fails, then the client application and the kube-proxy that does the load balancing for that node die together. As a result, the kube-proxy is a key component that provides a simplified and distributed solution for high availability in the Kubernetes system.

We have now reviewed how Kubernetes has engineered a solution to maintain system uptime despite a failure of any single compute node, service instance, or "load balancer" (kube-proxy), thus allowing us to maintain the availability of our entire system automatically. No SRE intervention is required to identify or resolve the failure. Time and again, we see issues where a Kubernetes-hosted system does suffer some failure despite this. This is often the result of poorly written probes that are unable to account for some edge-case application failure. Kubernetes does an excellent job of providing the platform and guidelines for ultimate availability, but it is not magic. Users will need to bring well-engineered and properly configured applications and services to see this potential.

There are other networking solutions for load balancing as well. The kube-proxy is great, but as we have noted, it really works only when routing traffic from a client that lives in the cluster. For routing client requests from outside the cluster, we'll need a slightly different approach. Solutions such as an ingress controller, OpenShift Router, and Istio Ingress Gateway enable the same integration with the Kubernetes service concept but provide a way to route traffic from outside the cluster to the service and applications running inside the cluster. It is important to note that you will need to combine these Layer 7 routing solutions with an external Layer 4 load balancer in order to maintain proper availability. Figure 4-5 shows how an external load balancer is combined with an OpenShift Router to get a request from the actor outside the cluster to the web server that is running in the cluster. Note that when these network solutions are used, they do not route their traffic through kube-proxy; they do their own load balancing directly to the endpoints of the service.

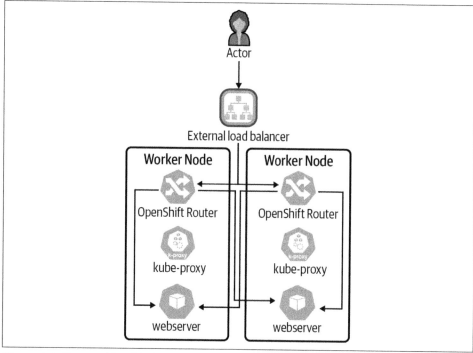

Figure 4-5. External load balancer and OpenShift Router

All of the same rules and logic for redundancy and availability apply here as we have discussed thus far. The external load balancer is just like the HAProxy example we provided earlier in this chapter. There simply is no escaping the laws of networking. You still need a highly available solution to get traffic from the outside world into the cluster. The advantage here is that we don't need to set up a separate load balancer for every application in our cluster. The OpenShift Router, ingress controller, and Istio Ingress Gateway can all serve many different applications in the cluster because they support Layer 7 routing, not just Layer 4. Layer 7 routers can inspect HTTP(S) headers to understand the target URL and use that information to send traffic to the correct service. It's important to note that the OpenShift Router and ingress controller still rely on the Kubernetes service to do the liveness and readiness probe work to determine which pods the Router or ingress controller should send traffic to.

While these are more complex solutions, we simply need to have something that allows for routing external traffic to services hosted in our cluster. We have left discussion of the NodePort concept upon which the external load balancer solution is based to the reader to investigate from the Kubernetes documentation (*https://oreil.ly/ NxmdG*).

The result

Looking back to our initial availability discussion, Kubernetes has supplied a mechanism to identify and repair an issue. Based on our application livenessProbe settings, it would take a maximum of six seconds to identify the problem and then some amount of time to reroute traffic (mitigating any failed requests), and then it would automatically repair the failed container by restarting it. That container-restart process in an efficient application can be quite speedy indeed, subsecond. Even conservatively at 10 seconds, that looks pretty good for our MTTR. We could be more aggressive with our settings and do a livenessProbe every two seconds, kick a restart on just a single failure, and get to a sub-five-second MTTR.

A quick note on livenessProbe and readinessProbe settings: remember that the kubelet is going to be making requests to every instance of these containers across the entire cluster. If you have hundreds of replicas running and they are all being hit every two seconds by the probes, then things could get very chatty in your logging or metrics solution. It may be a nonissue if your probes are hitting fairly light endpoints that are comparable to those that may be hit hundreds or thousands of times a second to handle user requests, but it's worth noting all the same.

Now that we have some idea of the kind of MTTR we could achieve with Kubernetes for our application, let's take a look at what this does for some of our availability calculations to determine MTBF for our system in Table 4-4.

Table 4-4. MTBF calculations for MTTR

MTTR	MTBF for 99% availability	MTBF for 99.99% availability
5 seconds	8.26 minutes	13 hours 53 minutes
10 seconds	16.5 seconds	27 hours 46 minutes
1 minute	99 seconds	6 days 22.65 hours
10 minutes	16 minutes 30 seconds	69 days 10.5 hours

Looking at this data, we can start to see how with the power of just the simple Kubernetes deployment concept, we can get to some reasonable availability calculations that we could sustain.

Done and dusted, right? Not so fast. Different failure modes can have a variety of different results for Kubernetes and OpenShift. We'll take a look at these failures next.

Failure Modes

You can experience a variety of different types of failures in your Kubernetes and OpenShift systems. We'll cover many of these failures, how to identify them, what the application or service impact is, and how to prevent them.

Application Pod Failure

A single application pod failure (Figure 4-6) has the potential to result in almost no downtime, as based on our earlier discussion around probes and the kubelet ability to automatically restart failed pods.

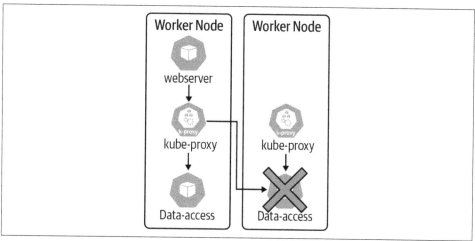

Figure 4-6. Application pod failure

It is worth noting that longer probe intervals can result in longer MTTR as that increases the time to detect the failure. It's also interesting to note that if you are using readinessProbes, it can take some time for a readiness failure to propagate through the Kubernetes or OpenShift system. The total time for recovery can be:

```
(readinessProbe Internal * failureThreshold) + iptables-min-sync-period
```

The iptables-min-sync-period is a new configuration setting we have not discussed yet. This setting (or ipvs-min-sync-period in the case of IPVS mode) of kube-proxy determines the shortest period of time that can elapse between any two updates of the iptables rules for kube-proxy.[5] If one endpoint in the cluster is updated at t0 and then another endpoint update occurs five seconds later but the `min-sync` is set to 30 seconds, then kube-proxy (iptables/IPVS) will still continue to route traffic to potentially invalid endpoints. The default for this setting is one second and thus minimal impact. However, in very large clusters with huge numbers of services (or huge numbers of endpoints), this interval may need to be increased to ensure reasonable performance of the iptables/IPVS control plane. The reason for this is that as there are more and more services to manage, the size of the iptables or IPVS rule set can become massive, easily tens of thousands of rules. If the `iptables-min-sync-period` is not adjusted, then kube-proxy can become overwhelmed with constantly trying to update the rules. It's important to remember this relationship. Cluster size can impact performance and responsiveness of the entire system.

Worker Node Failure

One of the most common failures seen in any OpenShift or Kubernetes cluster is the single worker node failure (Figure 4-7). Single node faults can occur for a variety of reasons. These issues include disk failure, network failure, operating system failure, disk space exhaustion, memory exhaustion, and more. Let's take a closer look at what takes place in the Kubernetes system when there is a node failure. The process to recover a single node will directly impact our availability calculations of the system.

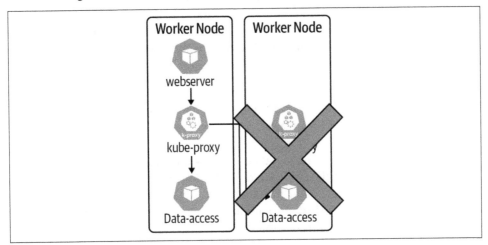

Figure 4-7. Worker node failure

---

5 See the Kubernetes documentation on kube-proxy (*https://oreil.ly/HReuF*) for more information.

The following are the time intervals that occur when responding to a worker node failure:

T0

Failure occurs on node.

T1 = T0 + `nodeLeaseDurationSeconds`

Kubernetes and OpenShift now use a lease system to track the health of worker nodes. Each `kubelet` registers a lease object for itself with the control plane. If that lease expires, then the node is immediately marked as `NotReady`. As soon as the node is marked `NotReady`, then the service controller will denote that any pods on that node may have failed and any service endpoints associated with the pods on that node should be removed. This is how Kubernetes decides to stop routing traffic to pods on a failed node. The result is the same as the `liveness Probe` failing for the pod but affects all pods on the failed node. `nodeLease DurationSeconds` is configured on the `kubelet` and determines how long the lease will last. The default time is 40 seconds.

T2 = T1 + `iptables-min-sync-period`

This is the additional time that may be required to update the fleet of kube-proxy configurations across the cluster. This behavior is identical to the behavior that was discussed earlier in our application pod failure scenario where any changes in the endpoint list for a service need to be synced to all of the kube-proxy instances across the cluster. Once the sync completes, then all traffic is routed properly, and any issues from the failed node will be resolved minus the capacity lost. The default minimum sync period is 30 seconds.

T3 = T2 + `pod-eviction-timeout`

This setting is configured on the kube-controller-manager and determines how long the controller will wait after a node is marked `NotReady` before it will attempt to terminate pods on the `NotReady` node. If there are controllers managing the pods that are terminating, then typically they will start a new replacement pod, as is the case with the deployment controller logic. This does not affect routing of traffic to the pods on the bad node; that was addressed at T2. However, this will recover any diminished capacity associated with the pods from the failed node. The default timeout is five minutes.

As we can see, the impact of a node failure is on a similar order of magnitude as an application pod failure. Note that here we are calculating the worst-case scenario to get to T2 where service is recovered. Some node failures may be detected and reported faster, and as a result, the T1 time can be quicker as we don't have to wait for the lease to expire for the node to be marked `NotReady`. Also remember that the iptables may sync faster; this is just the worst-case scenario.

Worker Zone Failure

A zone failure is handled much the same as a worker node failure. In a total zone failure (Figure 4-8), such as a network failure, we would typically expect all nodes to be marked as NotReady within a reasonably small window of time.

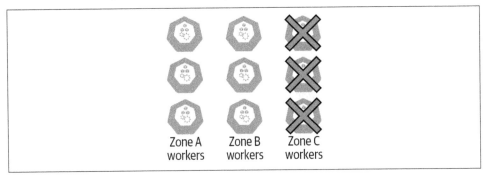

Figure 4-8. Worker zone failure

A zone failure can be "detected" by Kubernetes and OpenShift if the number of nodes in a single zone that is failing exceeds the unhealthy-zone-threshold percentage.[6] If a zone failure is detected, there is no change to the service endpoint evaluation process. All pods on the failed nodes will be removed as endpoints for any associated services. The unhealthy-zone-threshold will change what happens to the pod eviction process. If the cluster is below the large-cluster-size-threshold (defined as a count of nodes), then all pod eviction in the zone will stop. If unhealthy-zone-threshold is above the large cluster size, then pod eviction starts, but nodes are processed at a much slower rate as defined by the secondary-node-eviction-rate. This is in an effort to prevent a storm of pod scheduling and allows the system some additional time to recover without "overreacting" to a temporary failure.

Control Plane Failure

There are a variety of different control plane failure scenarios. There are network-related failures between worker nodes and the control plane, and there are control plane component failures. We'll get into the details of the high availability features of the various control plane components later in this section. Before we get started with those details, it's worth talking about what happens when there is any kind of total control plane failure. How does the cluster overall respond to a failure like the one shown in Figure 4-9?

---

6 See the Kubernetes documentation on Nodes Reliability (*https://oreil.ly/uzHtJ*) for more information.

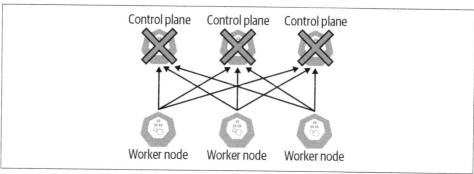

Figure 4-9. Complete control plane failure

The good news is that all of the workloads running on the worker nodes are unaffected in this scenario. All of the kube-proxy configurations, ingress controllers, pods, DaemonSets, network policies, and so on continue to function exactly as they were at the time of the control plane failure. The bad news is that no changes or updates can be made to the system in this state. In addition, if a worker node fails during this scenario, then there is no detection or updating of the cluster to compensate for the failure. Fortunately, the likelihood of such a failure is low if the control plane is implemented properly. We'll cover some of the HA features of the control plane now.

Rather than keep everyone waiting, we'll start with the most complex, potentially most challenging, and easily most critical component within the control plane. The component worthy of the title of "most critical" is etcd. Kubernetes and OpenShift use the open source key value store etcd as their persistent storage solution. The etcd datastore is where all objects in the system are persisted. All of the data and information related to the nodes, deployments, pods, services, and so on are stored in etcd.

etcd failures

You can encounter many different issues with etcd. Some are easier to mitigate than others. Connectivity failures from the kube-apiserver to etcd may be the most common. The modern etcd client has load balancing and resiliency built in. Note that if you have a traditional load balancer that sits in front of your etcd instance, then much of this does not apply, as you likely have a single endpoint registered for etcd. Regardless, the kube-apiserver will use the --etcd-servers setting to determine what IP(s) and/or hostname(s) the etcd go client is configured with. There is excellent documentation about the load balancing behavior (*https://oreil.ly/TUc0U*) in the community. It's worth noting that most modern Kubernetes and OpenShift versions are now using the clientv3-grpc1.23 variant in their client. This version of the client maintains active gRPC subconnections at all times to determine connectivity to the etcd server endpoints.

The failure recovery behavior of the etcd client enables the system to deal with communication failures between the kube-apiserver and etcd. Unfortunately, the etcd client cannot handle issues like performance degradation of a peer or network partitioning. This can be mitigated to some extent with excellent readiness checking of the etcd peers. If your system allows for readiness checking (for example, etcd hosted on Kubernetes), you can configure readiness checks that can look for network partitioning or severe performance degradation using something like:

```
etcdctl get --consistency=s testKey --endpoints=https://localhost:port
```

Using this code will ensure that the local peer is able to properly perform a serialized read and is a stronger check to make sure that not only is this peer listening but also it can handle get requests. A put test can be used (which also ensures peer connectivity), but this can be a very expensive health check that introduces tons of key revisions and may adversely impact the etcd cluster. We are conducting an ongoing investigation to determine whether etcd performance metrics are a reliable indicator that a peer is suffering performance degradation and should be removed from the cluster. At this point, we can only recommend standard monitoring and SRE alerting to observe performance issues. There is not yet strong evidence that you can safely kill a peer because of performance issues and not potentially adversely impact overall availability of the cluster.

> It would be poor form to have all of this discussion about improving availability of etcd without also mentioning how critical it is to have a proper disaster-recovery process in place for etcd. Regular intervals of automated backups are a must-have. Ensure that you regularly test your disaster-recovery process for etcd. Here's a bonus tip for etcd disaster recovery: even if quorum is broken for the etcd cluster, if etcd processes are still running, you can take a new backup from that peer even without quorum to ensure that you minimize data loss for any time delta from the last regularly scheduled backup of etcd. Always try to take a backup from a remaining member of etcd before restoring. The Kubernetes documentation (*https://oreil.ly/jCvAb*) has some excellent info on etcd backup and restore options.

The most significant concern with etcd is maintaining quorum of the etcd cluster. etcd will break quorum any time less than a majority of the peers are healthy. If quorum breaks, then the entire Kubernetes/OpenShift control plane will fail and all control plane actions will begin to fail. Increasing the number of peers will increase the number of peer failures that can be sustained. Note that having an even number of peers doesn't increase fault tolerance and can harm the cluster's ability to detect split brain-network partitions.[7]

kube-apiserver failures

The kube-apiserver is responsible for handling all requests for *create, read, update, and delete* (CRUD) operations on objects in the Kubernetes or OpenShift cluster. This applies to end-user client applications as well as internal components of the cluster, such as worker nodes, kube-controller-manager, and kube-scheduler. All interactions with the etcd persistent store are handled through the kube-apiserver.

The kube-apiserver is an active/active scale-out application. It requires no leader election or other mechanism to manage the fleet of kube-apiserver instances. They are all running in an active mode. This attribute makes it straightforward to run the kube-apiserver in a highly available configuration. The cluster administrator may run as many instances of kube-apiserver as they wish, within reason, and place a load balancer in front of the apiserver. If properly configured, a single kube-apiserver failure will have no impact on cluster function. See Figure 4-10 for an example.

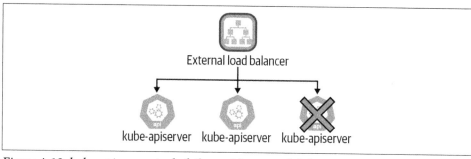

Figure 4-10. kube-apiserver single failure with no availability impact

kube-scheduler and kube-controller-manager failures

These two components have very similar availability features. They both run with a single active instance at all times and use the same leader election features. They leverage the lease object to manage the leader of the cluster. If a follower instance of either component fails, there is no impact to the overall cluster functionality. If the leader fails, then for the `--leader-elect-lease-duration` there will be no leader. However, no component interacts with the scheduler or controller manager directly. These two components interact asynchronously on object state changes in the cluster.

Loss of leader for the kube-controller-manager can result in a delay of recovery from a node failure, as an example. If a pod fails for some reason, then the controller

---

7 For more information, see the etcd FAQ (*https://oreil.ly/XrFaC*).

manager will not respond to update the endpoints of the associated service. So while a concurrent leader failure with other system failures can result in a prolonged MTTR for the system, it will not result in an extended failure or outage.

A failed kube-scheduler leader should have almost no impact on availability. While the leader is down awaiting a new election, no new pods will be scheduled to nodes. So while you may experience diminished capacity due to lack of scheduling of pods from a concurrent failed node, you'll still have service and routing updates to the cluster at this time.

Network Failure

Networking failures come in many different varieties. We could see failures of routing-table updates that cause packets to be misrouted. In other scenarios, we might see load-balancer failures. There could be a network-switch failure. The list of potential issues is endless. To simplify our discussion of this topic, we will bundle net-work failures into two common flavors: *North-South network failures* occur when traffic from outside our Kubernetes or OpenShift cluster can no longer enter or exit, and *East-West network failures* describe a situation where network traffic cannot travel between the nodes in our cluster.

North-South network failure

This failure scenario refers to the situation where the cluster itself may be healthy, control plane and data plane, but there may be issues routing traffic into the cluster from external sources. In Figure 4-11, we have a situation where connectivity from the external load balancer to the worker node has failed.

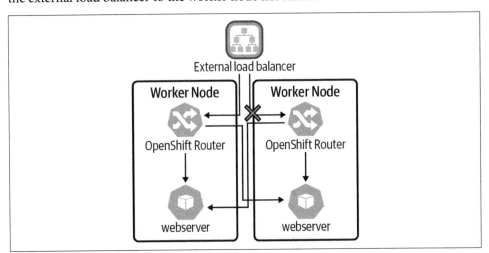

Figure 4-11. North-South networking failure

The result is that the load balancer health checks to any NodePorts exposed from the connection to the failed worker node will fail, the load balancer will stop routing traffic to that worker node, and life goes on. In fact, the MTTR here will be quite good, as it will take only the time required for the external load balancer to fail the health check to stop routing traffic down the failed link, or potentially it would have zero downtime if connection time limits and retries are integrated into this load-balancer solution. Load balancers were born for this stuff.

If *all* connectivity between the load balancer and the worker nodes fails, then all access from outside the cluster will have failed. The result is real downtime for any service whose purpose is to be accessed from outside the cluster. The good news is that we can implement multizone clusters to mitigate the chances of such catastrophic failures. In Chapter 8, we will discuss using multiple clusters with global DNS-based load balancing for further improvements to mitigating geographic network outages. In addition, these North-South failures only affect access to services from outside the cluster. Everything operating within the cluster may still function without any service interruption.

East-West network failure

We may also encounter scenarios where nodes may lose cross-zone connectivity or network partitioning. This is most frequently experienced in multizone clusters when there is a network failure between zones. In Figure 4-12 we look at a full zone failure.

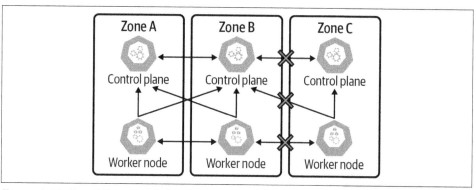

Figure 4-12. East-West total failure

In this scenario, we are faced with a "clean" zone failure where Zone C is fully partitioned. The worker node in the zone will continue to try and renew its lease to the control plane node in Zone C. If this were successful, it would lead to issues. However, the Zone C control plane will drop out of the cluster and stop responding to requests. Two things happen for this to occur. First, etcd in Zone C will begin to fail as it will not be able to contact etcd in other zones to participate in the quorum on the etcd cluster. As a result, the kube-apiserver in Zone C will also start to report back as unhealthy. The worker in Zone C won't be able to renew its lease with the control plane. As a result, it will just sit tight and do nothing. The kubelet will restart any containers that fail. However, as we can see, there is no connectivity between the Zone C worker and other zones. Any application communication will begin to fail.

The good news is that all will be well in Zones A and B. The control plane etcd will retain quorum (electing a new leader in A or B if the leader was previously in C), and all control plane components will be healthy. In addition, the lease for the worker in Zone C will expire, and thus this node will be marked as NotReady. All Zone C service endpoints will be removed, and kube-proxy will be updated to stop routing traffic to pods in Zone C.

There are probably a number of scenarios that can leave the Kubernetes or OpenShift platform slightly out of sorts. We're going to focus on one such scenario that does expose a weakness in the Kubernetes design. This is a failure where East-West traffic only fails between worker nodes. It is not uncommon to provide some network isolation between the worker nodes and control plane, which can result in this inconsistency between control plane connectivity and worker node connectivity. We've got an example depicting this in Figure 4-13.

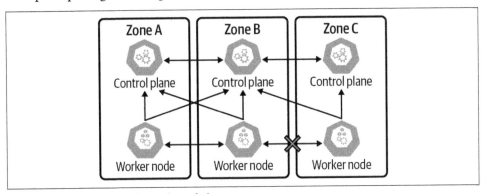

Figure 4-13. East-West data plane failure

The result here is quite interesting. All worker nodes are able to report back as healthy to the control plane. The worker nodes have no validation of communication between one another. This also includes kube-proxy, as it is not a traditional load balancer. Kube-proxy does not perform any health checking that can validate connectivity between workers. The result is that all pods, services, and endpoints remain fully intact. That sounds great, but the issue is that if any pod tries to route requests across the failed zone boundary, that request will fail and kube-proxy does not perform retries. This can be a hassle to detect and/or debug.

One approach to take is to include the addition of some cross-zone network validation components at the worker level. We also recommend monitoring and alerting for your application pods so that you can detect and alert.

There is another secret weapon in this battle. If you do not rely on kube-proxy, but rather a solution that includes things like circuit breakers and automatic retries for timeouts, then you can overcome these situations, and many others, with no modification to your applications or Kubernetes or OpenShift. Service mesh solutions like Istio (*https://istio.io*) and Red Hat Service Mesh (*https://oreil.ly/3drTt*) introduce a full mesh of sidecar containers to every pod. These sidecar containers run Envoy, a small, lightweight, efficient load balancer that includes advanced circuit breaking, load balancing, and retry capabilities. In this type of service mesh configuration, each sidecar is smart enough to stop routing traffic to any endpoint IPs with which it fails to communicate.

Summary

We now have a solid basis for understanding how we can measure and calculate availability of a system. In addition, we have a clear understanding of how Kubernetes provides the tools and architecture to implement a highly available application and service platform. It's critical to understand how the system functions and what its failure modes are in order for development teams to properly architect their applications and define their Kubernetes and OpenShift resources. SRE and operations teams should familiarize themselves with these failure modes and plan monitoring and alerting accordingly.

With these Kubernetes tools in hand, we should be ready to build a properly architected Kubernetes or OpenShift cluster with highly available services. We also have the equations necessary to derive an SLO for our services based on the choices we have made. How far can we push our availability? Armed with the analysis and tools outlined in this chapter, you have the ability to make an informed decision about your SLOs and create an implementation that meets your goals.

## CHAPTER 5

Continuous Delivery Across Clusters

Cloud native applications have the potential to disrupt entire industries. A key reason for this is their ability to support continuous delivery. When the market environment changes and applications need to be updated to address real-world constraints that pop up quickly, continuous delivery enables applications to quickly adapt to meet these newly encountered issues. Here is a brief overview of how container images, Kubernetes, and OpenShift support DevOps principles to facilitate continuous delivery:

Small batch changes
> All changes should be incremental and finite. When failures occur, small batch changes are typically easier to recover than large, disruptive changes.

Source control all the things
> A history of all changes is helpful to understand the changes that have been made and to identify the causes of regressions in the code base or configuration.

Production-like environments
> Developers should have access to environments and tools that are representative of production. Production environments typically operate at larger scales than development or quality assurance (QA) and with more complex configuration. The variance can mean that features that work fine in the early stages do not work correctly in production, which is the only place they matter.

Shift-left of operational practices
> We should expose behaviors for health management, log collection, change management, and so on earlier in the development process.

Continuous integration of changes
> All changes should be built and deployed together on an ongoing basis to iden-tify when the intermingling of various changes lead to an unforeseen issue or API incompatibility.

Highly automated testing with continuous feedback
> To manage velocity, we have to automate our testing and validation work so that we can always be testing (ABT).

In this chapter, we provide an overview of a variety of tools and methodologies for supporting continuous delivery in production across clusters. We begin with a dis-cussion of Helm, which is a popular packaging tool for Kubernetes applications. Next we introduce Kustomize, which provides the ability to repurpose your existing Kubernetes YAML files for multiple purposes and configurations while avoiding the use of templates. We then describe several popular approaches for supporting contin-uous delivery pipelines, including GitOps, Razee, and Tekton. Finally, we conclude this chapter with an extensive discussion of OpenShift pipelines and the Open Clus-ter Management project for deploying applications across multiple clusters.

Helm

Helm is the Kubernetes package manager. It enables you to create a package contain-ing multiple templates for all of the resources that make up your application. Com-mon Kubernetes resources you would expect to find included in a Helm package are `ConfigMaps`, deployments, `PersistentVolumeClaims`, services, and many others.

Helm provides its own CLI (*https://oreil.ly/9S6Ne*) that will generate a collection of template files, and it also supports passing variable values into these template files. The collection of template files that Helm generates is called a *Helm chart*. The CLI will then create complete YAML files from the template files, package up all the related files, and deploy the chart.

The `helm create` command is used to create a new package by passing in the name of the chart. So to create a new chart called `firstchart` we do the following:

```
$ helm create firstchart
```

This command creates the following files and subfolders:

- *Chart.yaml*
- *charts/*
- *templates/*
- *values.yaml*

The *templates* folder contains some generated templates for representing key Kubernetes abstractions like deployments and service accounts. These template files are:

- *NOTES.txt*
- *_helpers.tpl*
- *deployment.yaml*
- *hpa.yaml*
- *ingress.yaml*
- *Service.yaml*
- *serviceaccount.yaml*
- *tests/*

The *_helpers.tpl* file contains partial templates that are used to generate values such as Kubernetes selector labels and the name to use for the service account. Template files such as *deployment.yaml* and *serviceaccount.yaml* then use the partial templates to obtain these values. The template files also pull values from the *values.yaml* file. This file contains values such as `replicaCount` that are variables the user can change. These variables are also passed into template files such as *deployment.yaml* and *serviceaccount.yaml* and used to set desired values.

Once you have the proper set of template files and proper variables set for your application, it's time to package up all the contents associated with this Helm chart. This is accomplished by using the `helm package` command. In our example, we would call the `helm package` as follows:

```
$ helm package firstchart

Successfully packaged chart and saved it to:
/Users/bradtopol/go/k8s.io/helmexample/firstchart-0.1.0.tgz
```

As shown in the example, running the `helm package` command generates an archive file containing all the content associated with the Helm chart. Now, if we want to install the Helm chart, we just need to run the `helm install` command as follows:

```
$ helm install firstchart_release1 firstchart-0.1.0.tgz
```

The `helm install` command in its most basic form takes two arguments, the name of the release and the archive file. The `helm install` command is quite flexible and can install a Helm chart and its content in a variety of different ways. In addition, the Helm release that has been installed can be easily updated using the `helm update` command. For more information on the use of Helm and its capabilities, please see the Helm documentation (*https://helm.sh/docs*).

Kustomize

When running Kubernetes in production, you will invariably have lots of YAML files used for deploying and configuring applications. Moreover, you would typically store these configuration files in some form of source control to enable continuous delivery. Experience with running in production has shown that in many cases the configuration YAML files will need customizations for a variety of reasons. For example, there may be configuration changes for differences between development and production environments. Or custom prefix names may be needed to distinguish similar applications. To address these needs, the Kubernetes `kubectl` CLI has incorporated a recently developed tool called Kustomize (*https://kustomize.io*). The Kustomize tool provides a template-free approach to customizing Kubernetes configurations.[1] The Kustomize tool has several key features that both reduce the complexity of managing a large number of Kubernetes configurations for production deployments and facilitate the use of continuous deployment methodologies. The primary capabilities provided by Kustomize include generators, composition, patches, and overlays.

Generators

Best practices for Kubernetes deployment recommend that configuration and secret data should not be hardcoded into an application. Instead, this information should be stored in Kubernetes resources like `ConfigMaps` and secrets. Kustomize provides the notion of *generators* that can create `ConfigMaps` and secrets to simplify this aspect of deployment. Kustomize uses YAML files to describe what should be generated. The following Kustomize YAML is used to generate a Kubernetes secret:

```
secretGenerator:
- name: sample-secret
  literals:
  - username=admin
  - password=letbradin
```

To run the previous example, save the file as *kustomization.yaml* in a new folder called *generateSecret*. You can now run it by doing the following:

```
$ kubectl kustomize ./generateSecret
```

After you run the above command, Kustomize will generate a Kubernetes secret resource as shown:

```
apiVersion: v1
data:
  password: bGV0YnJhZGlu
  username: YWRtaW4=
```

---

[1] Jeff Regan and Phil Wittrock, "Introducing Kustomize; Template-free Configuration Customization for Kubernetes," Kubernetes Blog (May 29, 2018), *https://oreil.ly/fli5E*.

```
kind: Secret
metadata:
 name: sample-secret-dh2bm897df
type: Opaque
```

As an alternative, Kustomize can generate a secret where the username and password are stored in a separate file. For example, create a file called *password.txt* and store the following key value pairs in the file:

```
username=admin
password=letbradin
```

With these values now in *password.txt*, you can create a Kustomization file that generates a secret and pulls the username and password from *password.txt* as shown:

```
secretGenerator:
- name: sample-secret2
  files:
  - password.txt
```

To run the previous example, save the file as *kustomization.yaml* in a new folder called *generateSecret2*. You can now run Kustomize using this file by doing the following:

```
$ kubectl kustomize ./generateSecret2
```

After you run this command, Kustomize will generate a Kubernetes secret resource similar to the one shown:

```
apiVersion: v1
data:
 password.txt: CnVzZXJuYW1lPWFkbWluCnBhc3N3b3JkPWxldGJyYWRpbgo=
kind: Secret
metadata:
 name: sample-secret2-77bf8kf96f
type: Opaque
```

In the next section, we discuss another key feature of Kustomize: the ability to aggregate individual Kubernetes resource files into a single deployment YAML file.

Composition

Kubernetes deployments are typically created from a large set of YAML files. The YAML files themselves may be shared for multiple purposes. Kustomize supports the notion of *composition*, which enables individual YAML files to be selected and aggregated into a single deployment YAML file. The composition functionality also reduces the need to copy YAML files and then make slight modifications to those duplicate files for different purposes.

To demonstrate the capabilities of Kustomize composition, let's create some Kubernetes YAML resource files that we want to aggregate. First, create a new folder called *composition* and store the following content in a file called *deploymentset.yaml* in the *composition* folder:

```
kind: Deployment
metadata:
 name: nginx
 labels:
  app: webserver
 annotations:
  deployment.kubernetes.io/revision: "1"
spec:
 replicas: 3
 selector:
  matchLabels:
   app: webserver
 strategy:
  rollingUpdate:
   maxSurge: 1
   maxUnavailable: 1
  type: RollingUpdate
 template:
  metadata:
   labels:
    app: webserver
  spec:
   containers:
   - name: nginx
     image: nginx:1.7.9
     ports:
     - containerPort: 80
```

Next, store the following service resource YAML in a file called *service.yaml* in the *composition* folder:

```
apiVersion: v1
kind: Service
metadata:
 name: nginx
 labels:
  app: webserver
spec:
 ports:
 - port: 80
   protocol: TCP
 selector:
   app: webserver
```

You can now create a customization file that is capable of composing *deploymentset.yaml* and *service.yaml* by doing the following:

```
resources:
- deploymentset.yaml
- service.yaml
```

To run this example, save the file as *kustomization.yaml* in the *composition* folder you previously created. You can now run Kustomize using this file by doing the following:

```
$ kubectl kustomize ./composition
```

After you run this command, Kustomize will generate the aggregated deployment YAML as shown:

```
apiVersion: v1
kind: Service
metadata:
 labels:
  app: webserver
 name: nginx
spec:
 ports:
 - port: 80
   protocol: TCP
 selector:
   app: webserver
---
apiVersion: apps/v1
kind: Deployment
metadata:
 annotations:
  deployment.kubernetes.io/revision: "1"
 labels:
  app: webserver
 name: nginx
spec:
 replicas: 3
 selector:
  matchLabels:
   app: webserver
 strategy:
  rollingUpdate:
   maxSurge: 1
   maxUnavailable: 1
  type: RollingUpdate
 template:
  metadata:
   labels:
    app: webserver
  spec:
   containers:
   - image: nginx:1.7.9
     name: nginx
     ports:
     - containerPort: 80
```

In the next section, we cover Kustomize's patch capability, which enables us to avoid duplicating a full Kubernetes YAML file when all we need is a small change to an existing YAML file.

Patches

In many cases, the YAML file needed for a deployment may be very similar to an existing YAML file and only needs a small change to one of the resources. As an example, perhaps the only thing in a YAML file that needs to be changed is the number of replicas to create. For this type of situation, Kustomize provides the notion of *patches*, which are capable of making small modifications to resources described in YAML files. This is a much better approach than having to make a copy of the complete YAML file and then making the small modification to the duplicate file.

To demonstrate the capabilities of patches, let's create a Kubernetes YAML resource file that is close to what we want but needs small changes. First, create a new folder called *patch* and store the following content in a file called *deploymentset.yaml* in the *patch* folder:

```
apiVersion: apps/v1
kind: Deployment
metadata:
 name: nginx
 labels:
  app: webserver
 annotations:
  deployment.kubernetes.io/revision: "1"
spec:
 replicas: 3
 selector:
  matchLabels:
   app: webserver
 strategy:
  rollingUpdate:
   maxSurge: 1
   maxUnavailable: 1
  type: RollingUpdate
 template:
  metadata:
   labels:
    app: webserver
  spec:
   containers:
   - name: nginx
     image: nginx:1.7.9
     ports:
     - containerPort: 80
```

The deployment YAML file shown above is close to what we desire, but we now need a new version of this file that needs to provide six replicas instead of three. Rather than duplicating the whole *deploymentset.yaml* resource file and then changing the value of the `replicas` field, we can create a patch file that is much smaller and easier to maintain.

Here is a simple patch file that can be used to create a duplicate *deploymentset.yaml* with a modified `replicas` field value:

```
apiVersion: apps/v1
kind: Deployment
metadata:
 name: nginx
spec:
 replicas: 6
```

Note that this small file identifies the kind of resource, the name of the resource, and the attribute field we wish to modify. This small file gives Kustomize enough information to identify the field that needs to be patched. To use this patch file, save it in a new file called *update_replicas.yaml* in the *patch* folder you just created.

With the patch file created, we can now create a *kustomization.yaml* file that identifies the *deploymentset.yaml* file we wish to modify and also identifies the *update_replicas.yaml* file as the file that contains information on which fields to modify:

```
resources:
- deploymentset.yaml
patchesStrategicMerge:
- update_replicas.yaml
```

To run the previous example, save the file as *kustomization.yaml* in the *patch* folder you previously created. You can now run Kustomize using this file by doing the following:

```
$ kubectl kustomize ./patch
```

After you run this command, Kustomize will generate the patched deployment YAML as shown:

```
apiVersion: apps/v1
kind: Deployment
metadata:
 annotations:
  deployment.kubernetes.io/revision: "1"
 labels:
  app: webserver
 name: nginx
spec:
 replicas: 6
 selector:
  matchLabels:
   app: webserver
 strategy:
  rollingUpdate:
   maxSurge: 1
   maxUnavailable: 1
  type: RollingUpdate
 template:
  metadata:
   labels:
```

```
   app: webserver
 spec:
  containers:
  - image: nginx:1.7.9
    name: nginx
    ports:
    - containerPort: 80
```

In the next section, we describe the overlays capability, which is one of the most powerful features available in Kustomize.

Overlays

Building on the features described in the previous sections, the *overlays* functionality is where users see the most significant capabilities available from Kustomize. Overlays provide an approach where the user starts with a base folder that contains a set of Kubernetes deployment YAML files and builds on the base folder using overlay folders that enhance and customize the deployment YAML files contained in the base folder. In this section, we demonstrate how Kustomize overlays can be used to manage the differences that occur in deployment YAML files that exist when using the deployment YAML files across development, staging, and production Kubernetes environments.

To demonstrate how Kustomize can be used in this fashion, let's first create a new folder called *base* and copy into this folder the *deploymentset.yaml* and *service.yaml* files that we created in "Composition" on page 93. With these files in the *base* folder, we can now create a *kustomization.yaml* in the *base* folder that references the deployment YAML files as shown:

```
resources:
- deploymentset.yaml
- service.yaml
```

Next, we are going to create an overlay folder that tailors the base deployment files for a development environment. We begin by creating a new folder called *development*. Inside this folder, we create a new *kustomization.yaml* as shown:

```
commonLabels:
 env: development
bases:
- ../base
namePrefix: dev-
patchesStrategicMerge:
- update_replicas.yaml
```

As shown in *kustomization.yaml*, the Kustomization file starts by defining a new label called env that contains the value development. Since this label is defined as part of the commonLabels field, the effect is that this label will be set on all resources that are included in *kustomization.yaml*. The Kustomization then declares that its base will be the deployment YAML files that are located in the *base* folder. Next, the

Kustomization defines a `namePrefix` with the value `dev-`. The effect of this declaration is to add a prefix to all resource names and references. In the final portion of *kustomization.yaml*, a patch is declared that will contain modifications to the deployment YAML files found in the *base* directory. The patch is contained in the file *update_replicas.yaml*. The contents of *update_replicas.yaml* are shown here:

```
apiVersion: apps/v1
kind: Deployment
metadata:
 name: nginx
spec:
 replicas: 2
```

The *update_replicas.yaml* file contains a patch that modifies the number of replicas to now be 2 for a development environment. To run this example, make sure to save the patch in the *development* folder with the name *update_replicas.yaml*. You can now run Kustomize using the *kustomization.yaml* and *update_replicas.yaml* files by doing the following:

```
$ kubectl kustomize ./development
```

After you run this command, Kustomize will generate the patched deployment YAML as shown:

```
apiVersion: v1
kind: Service
metadata:
 labels:
  app: webserver
  env: development
 name: dev-nginx
spec:
 ports:
 - port: 80
   protocol: TCP
 selector:
  app: webserver
  env: development
---
apiVersion: apps/v1
kind: Deployment
metadata:
 annotations:
  deployment.kubernetes.io/revision: "1"
 labels:
  app: webserver
  env: development
 name: dev-nginx
spec:
 replicas: 2
 selector:
  matchLabels:
   app: webserver
   env: development
```

```
    strategy:
     rollingUpdate:
      maxSurge: 1
      maxUnavailable: 1
     type: RollingUpdate
    template:
     metadata:
      labels:
       app: webserver
       env: development
     spec:
      containers:
      - image: nginx:1.7.9
        name: nginx
        ports:
        - containerPort: 80
```

Upon reviewing the deployment file that was generated, we see several changes that resulted from the use of *kustomization.yaml* and *update_replicas.yaml* files. First, notice that a new env label with the value of development now exists in both the service and deployment resources, as well as in the template section used to create the container replicas. Also note that all names listed in the deployment YAML have a prefix of dev-. Finally, the number of replicas for the development deployment YAML has been modified to denote that only two replicas should be created.

Next, we are going to create *kustomize.yaml* and *update_replicas.yaml* files that are used to tailor the base deployment YAMLs for a staging environment. In our situation, the staging environment should have a label of env with the value of staging on all resources, the names of all resources should have a prefix of staging-, and the number of replicas that should be used for the staging environment is five. Similar to the previous example for the development environment customizations, we begin by creating a new folder called *staging*. Inside this folder, we create a new *kustomization.yaml* as shown:

```
    commonLabels:
     env: staging
    bases:
    - ../base
    namePrefix: staging-
    patchesStrategicMerge:
    - update_replicas.yaml
```

In this example, we defined env as a commonLabel and gave it the value of staging. We created a new namePrefix with the value of staging-. We also are once again creating an *update_replicas.yaml* that will be used as a patch file to modify the number of replicas when the base deployments YAML files are used in a staging environment. The contents of *update_replicas.yaml* are shown here:

```
apiVersion: apps/v1
kind: Deployment
metadata:
 name: nginx
spec:
 replicas: 5
```

Once again, the *update_replicas.yaml* file contains a patch that modifies the number of replicas. For staging, we have chosen to use five replicas. To run this example, make sure to save the patch in the *staging* folder with the name *update_replicas.yaml*. You can now run Kustomize using the *kustomization.yaml* and *update_replicas.yaml* files by doing the following:

```
$ kubectl kustomize ./staging
```

After you run this command, Kustomize will generate the patched deployment YAML as shown:

```
apiVersion: v1
kind: Service
metadata:
 labels:
  app: webserver
  env: staging
 name: staging-nginx
spec:
 ports:
 - port: 80
   protocol: TCP
 selector:
  app: webserver
  env: staging
---
apiVersion: apps/v1
kind: Deployment
metadata:
 annotations:
  deployment.kubernetes.io/revision: "1"
 labels:
  app: webserver
  env: staging
 name: staging-nginx
spec:
 replicas: 5
 selector:
  matchLabels:
   app: webserver
   env: staging
  strategy:
   rollingUpdate:
    maxSurge: 1
    maxUnavailable: 1
   type: RollingUpdate
  template:
   metadata:
```

```
    labels:
      app: webserver
      env: staging
    spec:
      containers:
      - image: nginx:1.7.9
        name: nginx
        ports:
        - containerPort: 80
```

Once more, we see several changes that resulted from the use of our *kustomization.yaml* and *update_replicas.yaml* files. First, notice that a new `env` label with the value of `staging` now exists in both the service and deployment resources, as well as in the `template` section used to create the container replicas. Also note that all names listed in the deployment YAML have a prefix of `staging-`. Finally, the number of replicas for the development deployment YAML has been modified to denote that five replicas should be created.

For our final example, we will use the same techniques to modify the base deployment YAML files for a production environment. In our production environment, we should have a label of `env` with the value of `production` on all resources, the names of all resources should have a prefix of `prod-`, and the number of replicas that should be used for the production environment is 20. We begin by creating a new folder called *production*. Inside this folder, we create a new *kustomization.yaml* as shown:

```
commonLabels:
  env: production
bases:
- ../base
namePrefix: prod-
patchesStrategicMerge:
- update_replicas.yaml
```

We again create an *update_replicas.yaml* file that will be used as a patch file to modify the number of replicas when the base deployments YAML files are used in the production environment. The contents of *update_replicas.yaml* are as follows:

```
apiVersion: apps/v1
kind: Deployment
metadata:
  name: nginx
spec:
  replicas: 20
```

To run this example, make sure to save the patch in the *production* folder with the name *update_replicas.yaml*. You can now run Kustomize using the *kustomization.yaml* and *update_replicas.yaml* files by doing the following:

```
$ kubectl kustomize ./production
```

After you run this command, Kustomize will generate the patched deployment YAML with the proper labels, prefixes, and replica count value as shown here:

```
apiVersion: v1
kind: Service
metadata:
 labels:
  app: webserver
  env: production
 name: prod-nginx
spec:
 ports:
 - port: 80
   protocol: TCP
 selector:
  app: webserver
  env: production
---
apiVersion: apps/v1
kind: Deployment
metadata:
 annotations:
  deployment.kubernetes.io/revision: "1"
 labels:
  app: webserver
  env: production
 name: prod-nginx
spec:
 replicas: 20
 selector:
  matchLabels:
   app: webserver
   env: production
 strategy:
  rollingUpdate:
   maxSurge: 1
   maxUnavailable: 1
  type: RollingUpdate
 template:
  metadata:
   labels:
    app: webserver
    env: production
  spec:
   containers:
   - image: nginx:1.7.9
     name: nginx
     ports:
     - containerPort: 80
```

As we have demonstrated with this comprehensive example, Kustomize was able to manage deployment YAML files for a development environment, a staging environment, and a production environment, and it reduced the number of deployment YAML files we needed to maintain for all of these environments. We avoided a large amount of copy and paste of files and ended up with a much more manageable solution. In the next section, we show how Kustomize can be used to directly deploy its generated deployment files.

Direct Deploy of Kustomize-Generated Resource Files

In all of the previous Kustomize examples, we generated the modified deployment YAMLs and outputted them to make it clear what Kustomize was generating. Kustomize provides another option in which the generated deployment YAML files can be automatically submitted to Kubernetes for processing. This avoids the step of first generating all the deployment YAML files and instead enables us to use Kustomize to directly deploy what it generates. To use Kustomize to directly deploy to Kubernetes, we use the `kubectl apply -k` option and pass in the desired customization directory. For example, if we wanted to directly deploy the production example we just covered, we would do the following:

```
$ kubectl apply -k ./production/
```

In addition, Kustomize provides commands for viewing and deleting the Kubernetes resources objects that it generates and deploys. More details on these capabilities can be found in the Kustomization documentation (*https://oreil.ly/4kCu4*). In the next section, we introduce the concept of GitOps, which is a popular cloud native methodology for automated continuous delivery that is driven directly from Git repositories.

GitOps

GitOps is the idea of using Git to manage your infrastructure as code. The idea was first popularized by Weaveworks,[2] and with the proliferation of more containerized approaches to software delivery, GitOps has become a popular topic in the industry. The basic GitOps flow is always the same: an update to your source code triggers automation and ultimately validates a potential new change or delivers a new change into a running environment.

Applying GitOps involves the following steps:

1. Containerized applications are represented with declarative infrastructure (easily done with Kubernetes API represented as YAML) and stored in Git.

2. All changes originate from your source control revision system, typically Git-based systems like GitHub, GitLab, Bitbucket, and so on.

---

2 Weaveworks, "Guide to GitOps," *https://oreil.ly/QIQ24*.

3. Code-review techniques like pull requests or merge requests allow you to apply a review process and even automated validation to ensure that changes work correctly before wide rollouts.

4. Kubernetes (or more generally a software agent) is then used to apply and reconcile the desired state whenever changes are merged into the appropriate branch in your repository.

The first half of this flow is really about your team and organizational culture. Is your organization disciplined enough with the appropriate skill set to make all changes indirectly via Git rather than directly manipulating the target infrastructure? Are you at a scale in terms of the number of applications, number of delivery stages, and number of actual clusters that you can manage the proliferation of repositories and branches? As with any cultural change, look for teams in your organization that adapt well to new ideas and can become good representative examples for the broader organization. Focus on a specific application or set of related applications applying this approach from end to end before attempting a broader reorganization of your team's delivery practices.

The second half of the flow is where you have various tools that have evolved to simplify the management of adopting changes out of Git, applying the changes to your running environments, and validating the changes. We will review a few projects that can help you adopt your changes from Git and apply them to your Kubernetes environment in the following sections.

Pull requests/merge requests (PR/MR) allow you to leverage feature branches to complete enhancements and fixes against your code base and validate those changes before integration with the main delivery branches. These PR/MR branches generally apply automated validation to virtually all dimensions of code quality, including security scans, linting or best practices required by your team or organization, automated unit testing, automated functional testing, automated integration testing, and review by other humans on your team to ensure that the change is consistent with the rest of the system's goals and use cases.

GitOps can work well in systems with fewer independent applications and fewer active environments under management (e.g., software as a service, or SaaS). When your delivery output includes software that must be packaged and versioned, GitOps can still add value but likely becomes part of a larger story.

Consider a single application managed with source under management in a Git repository. For each stage of your release process, you will create a distinct Git branch. In the most basic version, you keep a single "main" branch deployed continuously within your end-user accessible production applications. In other cases, your release process may require additional lower environments and thus additional corresponding branches like "main" (for code under active development), "candidate" (for code undergoing user acceptance testing), and "stable" (for code running in production). For example, you might have branches "main" and "stable" where the "main" branch accumulates changes for development and "stable" tracks the version of code and configuration deployed in production. Many organizations likely have additional layers of validation, including quality engineering, user acceptance testing, performance and scale testing, and so on. Each distinct phase that you want control over means potentially another branch in your Git repository.

In the next section, we introduce Razee, which is the first of several production-quality continuous delivery systems for Kubernetes that we survey in this chapter.

Razee

Razee (*https://razee.io*) is an open source continuous deployment system originally developed by IBM to address issues that arise when supporting extreme-scale environments with tens of thousands of Kubernetes clusters that need to be managed. Razee automates the deployment of Kubernetes resources across a large number of clusters and environments and provides several key features to address issues that arise when managing a large number of clusters.

In contrast to other deployment systems, Razee has a pull-based deployment approach that enables Kubernetes clusters to be self-updating. Also, Razee has a dynamic inventory-creation feature that allows it to ascertain what is running in all the Kubernetes clusters that it manages. With this feature, operators can gain insights into what applications and versions run in their clusters. Razee keeps a history of this inventory data and provides alerts to help troubleshoot issues in clusters.

Razee provides a lot of rule-based support for the grouping of clusters that helps to simplify managing large groups of clusters. Razee also uses a rule-based approach to orchestrate its pull-based update deployment model. The combination of all of these features enables Razee to support automated deployment and management of tens of thousands of clusters across multiple availability zones without manual intervention. For more details on Razee's approach to scalability and the key features it provides, see the Razee documentation (*https://oreil.ly/1N0ql*).

Argo CD

Argo CD (*https://oreil.ly/H2UiL*) is a declarative continuous delivery system that will continuously reconcile the contents of a Git repository with a Kubernetes cluster. Argo CD has a number of flexible access control models ranging from a deployment per namespace to per cluster, or you can provide credentials for multiple clusters via Kubernetes secrets to manage multiple clusters.

Argo CD adapts well to Kubernetes applications using Helm charts, Kustomize (*https://oreil.ly/TOE56*), or ksonnet (*https://oreil.ly/9apwT*) for templating changes to your resources for different clusters. Once deployed and configured, Argo CD will respond to postcommit hooks or ongoing polling of changes to the repository and apply those changes to the cluster. In many ways, it resembles a Puppet- or Chef-style convergence model. If changes are made out of band to the cluster, the desired state will eventually be restored.

As of the time of this writing, Argo CD has begun looking at additional API kinds, including ApplicationSet (*https://oreil.ly/5nbsB*), that allow the deployment of resources to more than one cluster. One proposed path would enable Argo CD to leverage the inventory of clusters available from Open Cluster Management to automatically configure GitOps for members of the fleet.

For more information on Argo CD, we recommend the Getting Started (*https://oreil.ly/VJQk5*) materials from the project website.

Tekton

Tekton is a *continuous integration and continuous delivery* (CI/CD) system that runs as a Kubernetes-based cloud native application. Since Tekton runs as a Kubernetes-based application, it is built to run as a scalable cloud native application. This is a significant advantage over more legacy CI/CD systems, which are not cloud native based and thus are more susceptible to failures or performance bottlenecks.

Tekton was originally the build system for the Knative serverless workload platform. Because it provided value as a general-purpose CI/CD platform, it was converted to a standalone project and donated to the Continuous Delivery Foundation in March 2019.[3]

Tekton provides a CLI and a dashboard user interface for managing its CI/CD workloads. It also has event trigger and webhooks support. There are several great tutorials for getting started with Tekton available at the Tekton Pipeline GitHub site (*https://oreil.ly/0yZDx*) and the IBM Developer Tekton Tutorial page (*https://oreil.ly/FSE9g*). In the next few sections, we introduce the fundamental concepts of Tekton: tasks and pipelines.

---

3 "Introducing the Continuous Delivery Foundation, the New Home for Tekton, Jenkins, Jenkins X, and Spinnaker," Google Open Source Blog (March 12, 2019), *https://oreil.ly/FvwF1*.

Tasks

A *task* represents a collection of commands or tools that should be executed in a specific order. Each command or tool is represented as a *step,* which defines the command or tool to be executed and the container image that contains the command or tool. The following example illustrates a simple task with two discrete steps that each run an echo command:

```
apiVersion: tekton.dev/v1beta1
kind: Task
metadata:
 name: simple-task-example
spec:
 steps:
 - name: echo
   image: ubuntu
   command:
   - echo
   args:
   - "This is step one of our first simple task example"
 - name: echo2
   image: ubuntu
   command:
   - echo
   args:
   - "This is step two of our first simple task example"
```

To run this task, first save the previous example in a file called *simpleexample.yaml.* Next, you need to create a TaskRun resource that will be used to run the task in a standalone fashion on a Kubernetes cluster. Here is the YAML for the TaskRun resource that we will use:

```
apiVersion: tekton.dev/v1beta1
kind: TaskRun
metadata:
 name: simple-task-example-run
spec:
 taskRef:
  name: simple-task-example
```

As shown in our sample TaskRun YAML, we create a TaskRun resource and give it a name. Then in the taskRef field, we provide the name of the task that we want to run on a Kubernetes cluster. To deploy the TaskRun resource, save the previous example as *simpleexamplerun.yaml.*

On a Kubernetes cluster that has Tekton installed, run the following commands:

```
$ kubectl apply -f simpleexample.yaml
$ kubectl apply -f simpleexamplerun.yaml
```

After running these commands, you should see output like the following:

```
task.tekton.dev/simple-task-example created
taskrun.tekton.dev/simple-task-example-run created
```

To confirm that the task ran properly, we can use the `tkn taskrun logs --last -f` Tekton command to view the logs from the `simple-task-example` that we just ran:

```
$ tkn taskrun logs --last -f
[echo] This is step one of our first simple task example

[echo2] This is step two of our first simple task example
```

If you need more details on the execution of your task, you can use the `tkn taskrun describe` command to get a much larger list of information:

```
$ tkn taskrun describe simple-task-example-run
Name: simple-task-example-run
Namespace: default
Task Ref: simple-task-example
Timeout: 1h0m0s
Labels:
 app.kubernetes.io/managed-by=tekton-pipelines
 tekton.dev/task=simple-task-example

Status

STARTED       DURATION    STATUS
1 minute ago 16 seconds Succeeded
 Input Resources
No input resources

Output Resources
 No output resources
 Params

 No params

 Steps

 NAME    STATUS
 · echo  Completed
 · echo2 Completed

Sidecars

 No sidecars
```

While not shown in the previous example, Tekton has a large number of built-in capabilities for common integration steps like pulling in content from Git repositories and building container images. In addition, Tekton gives tasks a new feature called *workspaces,* which is a shared persistent volume. The workspace provides an area of shared storage that tasks can use to share files with other tasks that are working with it cooperatively. For more details on workspaces, see the Tekton Workspaces Documentation (*https://oreil.ly/XUZdv*).

In the next section, we describe pipelines, which is Tekton's construct for enabling multiple tasks to work together on common build integration and deployment activities.

Pipelines

Tekton provides the notion of *pipelines* as its mechanism for creating a collection of tasks and ordering the execution of the group of tasks. In some cases, tasks have dependencies on other tasks and must declare that they execute after the tasks they are dependent on. In other cases, tasks may not have dependencies on one another, and those tasks can run concurrently. The pipelines construct manages its collection of tasks and the order in which they execute, as well as the common shared workspaces that each task is entitled to use. To better understand how pipelines work, we need at least two tasks. In the previous section, we defined and deployed the `simple-task-example` task. We will now create a second task called `simple-task-example2`. This task is shown here:

```
apiVersion: tekton.dev/v1beta1
kind: Task
metadata:
 name: simple-task-example2
spec:
 steps:
 - name: echo
 image: ubuntu
 command:
 - echo
 args:
 - "This is step one of our second simple task example"
 - name: echo2
 image: ubuntu
 command:
 - echo
 args:
 - "This is step two of our second simple task example"
```

To deploy this task, save the previous example in a file called *simpleexample2.yaml*. Deploy this task by running the following command:

```
$ kubectl apply -f simpleexample2.yaml
```

You may notice that with our second task example, we did not provide a corresponding `TaskRun` for running it. The reason we don't have a second `TaskRun` is because we are going to group both tasks into a pipeline, and the pipeline will be responsible for creating any `TaskRun` objects it needs to run its tasks.

The pipeline that we are using for this example is named `simple-pipeline`, and it declares that it manages two tasks, which it references as `simple-task-example` and `simple-task-example2` respectively:

```
apiVersion: tekton.dev/v1beta1
kind: Pipeline
metadata:
 name: simple-pipeline
spec:
 tasks:
 - name: simple-task
   taskRef:
     name: simple-task-example
 - name: simple-task2
   taskRef:
     name: simple-task-example2
```

To run this pipeline, first save the previous example in a file called *simplepipeline.yaml*. Deploy this pipeline using the following command:

```
$ kubectl apply -f simplepipeline.yaml
```

Next, we will create a `PipelineRun` object that is responsible for running this pipeline on a Kubernetes cluster:

```
apiVersion: tekton.dev/v1beta1
kind: PipelineRun
metadata:
 generateName: run-simple-tasks
spec:
 pipelineRef:
   name: simple-pipeline
```

Save the previous file as *simplepipelinerun.yaml*. You can then run the `simple-pipeline` example on the cluster by running the following command:

```
$ kubectl create -f simplepipelinerun.yaml
```

To confirm that the pipeline ran properly, use the `tkn pipelinerun logs --last -f` Tekton command and view the logs from the `simple-pipeline` example that you just ran:

```
$ tkn pipelinerun logs --last -f
[simple-task2 : echo] This is step one of our second simple task example
[simple-task : echo] This is step one of our first simple task example

[simple-task2 : echo2] This is step two of our second simple task example


[simple-task : echo2] This is step two of our first simple task example
```

Upon reviewing the log output, we notice that the two tasks ran concurrently. This is consistent with how we defined our tasks. If the two tasks had a dependency and we needed the second task to defer execution until after the first task completed, the Tekton pipeline supports this by adding a `runAfter` declaration to the second task that states it should be run after the first task completes. This is shown in the following example:

```
apiVersion: tekton.dev/v1beta1
kind: Pipeline
metadata:
 name: simple-pipeline
spec:
 tasks:
 - name: simple-task
   taskRef:
    name: simple-task-example
 - name: simple-task2
   runAfter:
   - simple-task
  taskRef:
   name: simple-task-example2
```

Note that the `runAfter` field explicitly references the task named `simple-task` as the task that must be completed before `simple-task2` is permitted to execute.

Tekton has a large number of useful features that are beyond the scope of this book. For more information on Tekton and its capabilities, see the Tekton Pipeline documentation (*https://oreil.ly/nw5yD*). In addition, Tekton pipelines serve as the foundation for OpenShift Pipelines, an offering available from Red Hat.

OpenShift Pipelines

OpenShift Pipelines (*https://oreil.ly/VU8Gr*) is a fully supported software offering from Red Hat based on Tekton. Using the operator paradigm simplifies the configuration of Tekton and helps you get to value from the ecosystem faster.

Let's look at an end-to-end example using OpenShift Pipelines, which is available from the GitHub organization associated with this book (*https://oreil.ly/X749O*). In this example, you'll see the Tekton concepts of tasks and pipelines put to work to build a simple app that lets you play PAC-MAN in your browser.

Configure OpenShift Pipelines by installing the operator from the OperatorHub catalog available within your OpenShift Container Platform web console (4.4 or greater):

1. Navigate to Operators > OperatorHub and search for "OpenShift Pipelines," as shown in Figure 5-1.

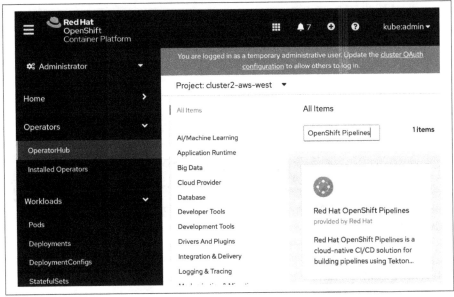

Figure 5-1. OperatorHub catalog filtered by the query "OpenShift Pipelines"

2. Click on the tile to display information about the operator. Scroll to the bottom of the page to download the appropriate command-line version for your platform (see Figure 5-2).

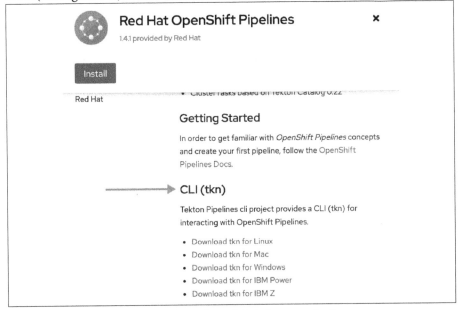

Figure 5-2. Download the CLI for Tekton (tkn) for your platform

3. Click Install.

4. Select the appropriate update channel for your version of OpenShift. For example, if you're running OCP 4.4.x, use ocp-4.4.

5. Click Subscribe.

You can confirm that the installation was successful by navigating to Operators > Installed Operator and filtering the project to "openshift-operators," as shown in Figure 5-3.

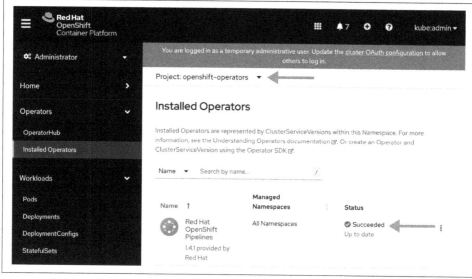

Figure 5-3. Confirm successful installation of the OpenShift Pipelines Operator

When assembling your continuous delivery solution with Tekton Tasks, you have access to a broad community library of existing tasks:

- Tekton task catalog (*https://oreil.ly/INXgA*)
- OpenShift Pipelines task catalog (*https://oreil.ly/z3KwI*)

Let's reuse some of the tasks in the public catalogs to put together our working example. You will also have a set of tasks available after installing the operator:

```
$ tkn clustertasks ls
NAME DESCRIPTION AGE
buildah 25 minutes ago
buildah-v0-11-3 25 minutes ago
git-clone 25 minutes ago
jib-maven 25 minutes ago
kn 25 minutes ago
maven 25 minutes ago
openshift-client 25 minutes ago
```

```
openshift-client-v0-11-3 25 minutes ago
s2i 25 minutes ago
s2i-dotnet-3 25 minutes ago
s2i-dotnet-3-v0-11-3 25 minutes ago
s2i-go 25 minutes ago
s2i-go-v0-11-3 25 minutes ago
s2i-java-11 25 minutes ago
s2i-java-11-v0-11-3 25 minutes ago
s2i-java-8 25 minutes ago
s2i-java-8-v0-11-3 25 minutes ago
s2i-nodejs 25 minutes ago
s2i-nodejs-v0-11-3 25 minutes ago
s2i-perl 25 minutes ago
s2i-perl-v0-11-3 25 minutes ago
s2i-php 25 minutes ago
s2i-php-v0-11-3 25 minutes ago
s2i-python-3 25 minutes ago
s2i-python-3-v0-11-3 25 minutes ago
s2i-ruby 25 minutes ago
s2i-ruby-v0-11-3 25 minutes ago
s2i-v0-11-3 25 minutes ago
tkn 25 minutes ago
```

We will now create a pipeline to build our image and publish to the in-cluster regis-try. First, create a project in your OpenShift cluster to hold the resources we are about to create:

```
$ oc new-project pipelines-tutorial
```

> All of the following examples assume that you are working in this same namespace, pipelines-tutorial. If for some reason your KUBECONFIG is referencing a different namespace, then you can use the oc project command to update your context:
>
> ```
> $ oc project pipelines-tutorial
> ```
>
> Alternatively, you can add the -n pipelines-tutorial flag to the example commands after oc apply, oc create, oc get, and so on. For example:
>
> ```
> $ oc get pipelines -n pipelines-tutorial
> ```

To build and publish an image, the default service account pipeline must have the authorization to push an image into your destination registry. For this example, the Quay.io (*https://quay.io*) registry is used, but any registry will work fine.

To enable the authorization for the pipeline service account, you must create a docker-registry secret and update the pipeline service account. These steps are not related to Tekton specifically but are relevant to our example:

1. Create the Quay.io image repository named `quay.io/<username>/pacman` for your username by following the Quay.io documentation (*https://oreil.ly/N3Ng3*).

2. Download the Kubernetes secret from Quay.io. You can access the secret from the Settings page under "Generate Encrypted Password."

3. Apply the secret (and be sure to update the default name of `<username>-pull-secret` to `quay-registry-secret`) or use the `kubectl` or `oc` command line to create the secret:

```
$ kubectl create secret docker-registry \
  --docker-server="quay.io" \
  --docker-username="YOUR_USERNAME" \
  --docker-password="YOUR_PASSWORD" \
  --docker-email="YOUR_EMAIL" \
  quay-registry-secret
```

4. Patch the `quay-registry-secret` into the `pipeline` service account. The Open-Shift pipelines operator automatically creates the `pipeline` service account in every namespace of your cluster. By updating the service account in the `pipelines-tutorial` namespace, you will allow any Tekton TaskRuns to leverage this authorization for pushing images:

```
$ oc patch sa pipeline -p '{"secrets":[{"name":"quay-registry-secret"}]}'
```

We will start creating a pipeline that will build an image and push it into the image repository that you just defined:

```
pipelines/01-pipeline-build-pacman.yaml

apiVersion: tekton.dev/v1beta1
kind: Pipeline
metadata:
 name: build-pacman
spec:
 workspaces:
 - name: shared-workspace
 resources:
 - name: source-repo
 type: git
 - name: image
 type: image
 params:
 - name: dockerfile-path
 type: string
 description: The path to your Dockerfile
 default: "Dockerfile"
 tasks:
 - name: build-image
 taskRef:
 name: buildah
 kind: ClusterTask
 resources:
```

```
  inputs:
  - name: source
  resource: source-repo
  outputs:
  - name: image
  resource: image
  params:
  - name: TLSVERIFY
  value: "false"
  - name: DOCKERFILE
  value: "$(params.dockerfile-path)"
```

The `build-pacman` Pipeline defines a single task that uses the `buildah ClusterTask`. The input requires a Git repository with the `Dockerfile` and associated source files that are required and the details of the image to build.

We create the pipeline using the oc command-line tool:

```
$ oc apply -f 01-pipeline-build-pacman.yaml
pipeline.tekton.dev/build-and-deploy-pacman created
```

After applying the pipeline definition, we can verify it exists:

```
$ oc get pipelines
NAME                     AGE
build-and-deploy-pacman 8s
```

The `tkn` command-line tool offers a specific set of actions for Tekton resources. In addition to equivalents for commands like `get` or `describe`, there are direct commands to view task logs and other Tekton-specific behaviors:

```
$ tkn pipelines ls
NAME                     AGE            LAST RUN STARTED DURATION STATUS
build-and-deploy-pacman 21 seconds ago ---      ---     ---      ---
```

Tekton pipelines define parameters that drive their behavior. To simplify the management of parameters, Tekton also defines `PipelineResources` that represent different kinds of objects that occur frequently in desired pipeline behavior.

The following are the defined `PipelineResource` types (*https://oreil.ly/KrZlb*):

`git`
> GitHub repository

`storage`
> Storage blob

`image`
> Container image metadata

`cluster`
> Kubernetes cluster description with access credentials

```
pullRequest
```
A GitHub pull request

```
cloudEvent
```
Cloud Event

```
gcs
```
GCSResource backed by a GCS blob/directory

```
build-gcs
```
BuildGCSResources added to be compatible with Knative build

We will create `PipelineResources` that will become inputs to the pipeline and fulfill the required values for the input parameters:

```
pipelines/02-resource-git-repo-pacman.yaml

apiVersion: tekton.dev/v1alpha1
kind: PipelineResource
metadata:
 name: pacman-git
spec:
 type: git
 params:
 - name: revision
 value: master
 - name: url
 value: https://github.com/hybrid-cloud-apps-openshift-k8s-book/k8s-example-apps/
```

```
pipelines/03-resource-pacman-image.yaml

apiVersion: tekton.dev/v1alpha1
kind: PipelineResource
metadata:
 name: pacman-image
spec:
 type: image
 params:
 - name: url
 value: quay.io/mdelder/pacman
```

We will apply these resources and then reference them in our `PipelineRun`:

```
$ oc apply -f 02-resource-git-repo-pacman.yaml \
 -f 03-resource-pacman-image.yaml
```

Now we have a pipeline and we have inputs (our Git repo and our desired image to build). Let's trigger the pipeline by creating a `PipelineRun`:

```
pipelines/04-pipelinerun-build-pacman-01.yaml

apiVersion: tekton.dev/v1beta1
kind: PipelineRun
metadata:
```

```
  generateName: pipelinerun-build-pacman-
spec:
  serviceAccountName: pipeline
  pipelineRef:
  name: build-pacman
  resources:
  - name: source-repo
  resourceRef:
  name: pacman-git
  - name: image
  resourceRef:
  name: pacman-image
  workspaces:
  - name: shared-workspace
  emptyDir: {}
  params:
  - name: dockerfile-path
  value: "pacman-nodejs-app/docker/Dockerfile"
```

The `PipelineRun` will carry out two actions with a single `buildah` task: clone the Git repository, and then build the image and publish it to the Quay.io registry that you previously created.

To run the pipeline, use `oc create`:

```
$ oc create -f pipelines/04-pipelinerun-build-pacman-01.yaml
```

 We are using `oc create` here instead of `oc apply` because the `PipelineRun` uses a generateName instead of a name attribute. The `oc apply` command requires the `name` attribute, whereas `oc create` ate supports additional behavior to generate a suffix for the name automatically.

You can see the running pipelines with the `tkn` command-line tool:

```
$ tkn pipelinerun ls
NAME                             STARTED         DURATION STATUS
pipelinerun-build-pacman-qk5lw 23 seconds ago ---       Running
```

You can follow along with the `PipelineRun` using the `tkn` command line:

```
$ tkn pipelinerun logs -f
```

The output should resemble the following:

```
[build-image : git-source-pacman-git-s2mxf]
{"level":"info","ts":1598817082.1290805,"caller":"git/git.go:105","msg":
"Successfully cloned https://github.com/hybrid-cloud-apps-openshift-k8s-book/
k8s-example-apps/ @ master in path /workspace/source"}
...

[build-image : build] STEP 1: FROM node:boron
[build-image : build] Getting image source signatures
[build-image : build] Copying blob
```

```
sha256:3b7ca19181b24b87e24423c01b490633bc1e47d2fcdc1987bf2e37949d6789b5

...

[build-image : push] Getting image source signatures
[build-image : push] Copying blob
sha256:ec62f19bb3aa1dcfacc9864be06f0af635c18021893d42598da1564beed97448

...

[build-image : push] Writing manifest to image destination
[build-image : push] Copying config
sha256:854daaf20193c74d16a68ba8c1301efa4d02e133d383f04fedc9532ae34e8929
[build-image : push] Writing manifest to image destination
[build-image : push] Storing signatures

...
```

In this example, we built the container image. Let's take it further and apply the change to the cluster. In this step, we will create a pipeline with three distinct stages:

1. Build the application image.

2. Fetch the Git repository that contains our deployment manifests (using Kustomize).

3. Apply Kustomization deployment manifests.

The first step works exactly the same way as before. The additional steps introduce a few new ideas:

- We will create a PersistentVolumeClaim to provide available storage to host the contents of our Git repository. Otherwise, the files retrieved from Git in Step 2 will not be available for use in Step 3.

- We will require additional permissions for our pipeline service account to allow the deployment manifests to be applied to the application namespace on this cluster.

Let's create the PersistentVolumeClaim. The PersistentVolumeClaim should request enough capacity for all persistent file system storage required by all tasks in the pipeline. If the PersistentVolume is reclaimed or recycled in between tasks, you may lose important state and the pipeline run will likely fail. On the other hand, if the same PersistentVolume is reused across many pipeline runs, it may eventually exhaust all available space. If the same PersistentVolume is expected to support multiple pipeline runs in parallel, be sure to set the accessMode to ReadWriteMany:

```
pipelines/00-pvc-shared-workspace.yaml

apiVersion: v1
kind: PersistentVolumeClaim
```

```
metadata:
 name: shared-workspace
spec:
 accessModes:
 - ReadWriteOnce
 resources:
 requests:
 storage: 1Gi
```

```
$ oc apply -f 00-pvc-shared-workspace.yaml
persistentvolumeclaim/shared-workspace created
```

 State management of workspaces could become an issue over time. Tekton 0.12 introduces a `volumeClaimTemplate` that offers to simplify this process. Otherwise, you may always be creating `PersistentVolumeClaims` and `PersistentVolumes` for each `Pipeli neRun`. For any resource that you are creating via automation, be sure to define your reclamation strategy to destroy or allow any unnecessary resources to age out as appropriate.

In our first pipeline, we updated the `system:serviceaccounts:pipelines-tutorial:pipeline` service account to allow the use of an additional secret that authorized our service account to push images into our Quay.io image registry. In our second pipeline, our service account will apply deployment manifests to the same cluster running the pipeline and will require authorization to the application namespace:

```
$ oc adm policy add-role-to-user edit --namespace pacman \
  system:serviceaccount:pipelines-tutorial:pipeline
```

With the `edit` `ClusterRoleBinding` to the `pacman` namespace, the service account will be able to create, modify, and view most of the Kubernetes API objects, including deployments, services, and OpenShift routes. Our chosen example application creates each of these as part of its deployment manifests.

To verify that you have applied the permission correctly, you can use the `can-i` command, which will print a simple "yes" or "no" answer:

```
$ oc auth can-i get deployments \
  --namespace pacman \
  --as system:serviceaccount:pipelines-tutorial:pipeline
```

Now we will create our new pipeline:

```
pipelines/05-pipeline-deploy-pacman.yaml

apiVersion: tekton.dev/v1beta1
kind: Pipeline
metadata:
 name: build-and-deploy-pacman
spec:
```

```
workspaces:
- name: shared-workspace
resources:
- name: source-repo
type: git
- name: image
type: image
params:
- name: kustomization-path
type: string
default: kustomization
- name: kustomization-git-repo-url
type: string
- name: kustomization-git-revision
type: string
default: master
- name: dockerfile-path
type: string
description: The path to your Dockerfile
default: "Dockerfile"
tasks:
- name: build-image
taskRef:
name: buildah
kind: ClusterTask
resources:
inputs:
- name: source
resource: source-repo
outputs:
- name: image
resource: image
params:
- name: TLSVERIFY
value: "false"
- name: DOCKERFILE
value: "$(params.dockerfile-path)"
- name: fetch-repository
taskRef:
name: git-clone
kind: ClusterTask
workspaces:
- name: output
workspace: shared-workspace
params:
- name: url
value: "$(params.kustomization-git-repo-url)"
- name: subdirectory
value: ""
- name: deleteExisting
value: "true"
- name: revision
value: "$(params.kustomization-git-revision)"
runAfter:
- build-image
- name: apply-config
```

```
params:
- name: kustomization-path
value: "$(params.kustomization-path)"
workspaces:
- name: source
workspace: shared-workspace
taskSpec:
params:
- name: kustomization-path
default: "kustomization"
workspaces:
- name: source
steps:
- name: apply-kustomization
image: quay.io/openshift/origin-cli:latest
workingDir: /workspace/source
command: ['/bin/bash', '-c']
args:
- |-
echo "Applying kustomization in DIR \"$(params.kustomization-path)\""
oc apply -k $(params.kustomization-path)
runAfter:
- fetch-repository
```

```
$ oc apply -f 05-pipeline-deploy-pacman.yaml
```

We do not need any additional `PipelineResources` to run this pipeline. In fact, you may notice that the details about the two related Git repositories are managed differently in this pipeline. As you consume different tasks or define your own, you may find slight inconsistencies in how you assemble tasks to accomplish your goals. Specifically, the community `git-clone` task does not use the `git` type `Pipeline Resource` but rather accepts the component parts needed to identify the repository URL and revision.

Just as before, we will create a `PipelineRun` and monitor its progress:

```
$ oc create -f 06-pipelinerun-build-and-deploy-pacman-01.yaml
pipelinerun.tekton.dev/pipelinerun-build-and-deploy-pacman-cjc7b created
```

Again, you can use the `tkn` command-line tool to view all `PipelineRuns`:

```
$ tkn pipelinerun ls
NAME                                         STARTED        DURATION   STATUS
pipelinerun-build-and-deploy-pacman-cjc7b 3 minutes ago  2 minutes  Succeeded
pipelinerun-build-pacman-qk5lw               57 minutes ago 2 minutes  Succeeded
```

You can review or follow the logs as well. Note that if you run this after the `PipelineRun` has completed, the log order will be reversed:

```
$ tkn pipelinerun logs -f pipelinerun-build-and-deploy-pacman-cjc7b
```

Defining and troubleshooting tasks can be a little error prone at first. Use the API reference and don't be afraid to delete or recreate the initial pipelines and pipeline runs to resolve reference issues.

Now we can confirm whether pacman was successfully deployed by opening the route with the web browser (Figure 5-4):

```
$ oc get route pacman --namespace pacman \
  -ojsonpath="{.status.ingress[0].host}"
```

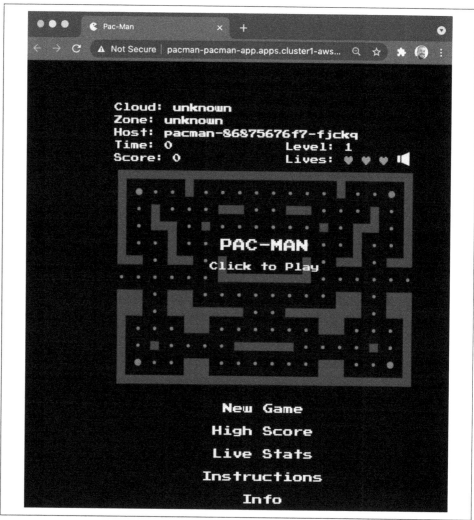

Figure 5-4. Successful deployment of the PAC-MAN application

Open Cluster Management Apps

The Open Cluster Management (*https://oreil.ly/QbBRN*) project is a new approach to managing applications across one or more OpenShift clusters. The approach applies a native GitOps approach to attaching a Kubernetes object to a Git repository. Let's take a simple example based on the open source PAC-MAN app.

The Open Cluster Management project is focused on several aspects of managing Kubernetes clusters, including creating and upgrading clusters, distributed delivery and management of applications, syndicating cluster configuration, and maintaining visibility on the compliance and governance of managed clusters. The *hub* cluster runs the multicluster control plane, and a lightweight agent that runs as a set of pods on the *managed clusters* applies the desired state to all clusters under management and provides a feedback loop for health, search index, and compliance. We will focus only on the application management concepts for the next example.

The Open Cluster Management app model relies on the following concepts:

Application
  A grouping of related resources required to provide a logical service to a consumer.

Channel
  A source of application parts required for deployment. Current supported channels include Git repositories, object store buckets, and Helm repositories.

Subscription
  Connects parts of an application from a channel to one or more clusters. Subscriptions consume a range of versions from a release branch (e.g., "latest," "stable," "production," etc.).

PlacementRule
  Links a subscription to one or more clusters.

Red Hat Advanced Cluster Management (RHACM) (*https://oreil.ly/6x2Ba*) is a fully supported software offering that is based on the Open Cluster Management project. Similar to how OpenShift Pipelines simplifies the setup and life cycle of adopting Tekton and other projects, RHACM for Kubernetes simplifies the adoption of the Open Cluster Management project (Figure 5-5).

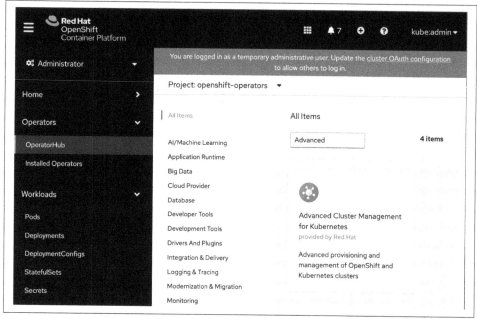

Figure 5-5. Installation of Advanced Cluster Management for Kubernetes in OpenShift

To install RHACM for Kubernetes, follow these steps:

1. Search for the operator by name and click Install.

2. Once the operator is installed, create an instance of the `MultiClusterHub` API:

```
$ oc new-project open-cluster-management

$ oc create -f - <<EOF
apiVersion: operator.open-cluster-management.io/v1
kind: MultiClusterHub
metadata:
 namespace: open-cluster-management
 name: multiclusterhub
spec: {}
EOF
```

3. From the Applications list in the OpenShift Container Platform web console, click the new item to open the RHACM web console, as shown in Figure 5-6. You may need to refresh your web browser for this new link to appear.

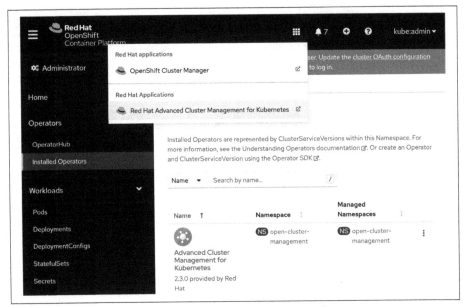

Figure 5-6. Opening the RHACM web console in OpenShift

The example assumes that you have created or imported two clusters in Advanced Cluster Management with the following labels:

```
Cluster 1:
  apps/pacman: deployed
  environment: dev
  region: us-east

Cluster 2:
  apps/pacman: deployed
  environment: dev
  region: europe-west3
```

For reference, we will assume the following two managed clusters: "cluster1-aws-east" and "cluster3-gcp-europe-west3." Notice that one cluster ("cluster1-aws-east") is provisioned on Amazon in North America, while the second ("cluster3-gcp-europe-west3") is provisioned on Google in Europe (see Figure 5-7). So for this example, we're deploying our app to a multicluster and multicloud platform backed by OpenShift!

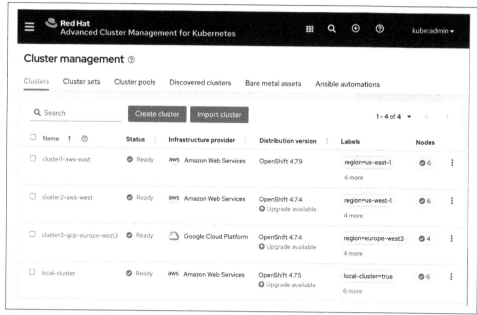

Figure 5-7. Using the RHACM web console to manage both Amazon- and Google-provisioned clusters

We can display these managed clusters from the command line as well:

```
$ oc get managedclusters -o yaml
apiVersion: v1
items:
- apiVersion: cluster.open-cluster-management.io/v1
  kind: ManagedCluster
  metadata:
  labels:
  apps/pacman: deployed
  cloud: Amazon
  clusterID: 7de6ab45-58ac-47f7-897d-b742b7197653
  environment: dev
  name: cluster1-aws-east
  region: us-east
  vendor: OpenShift
  name: cluster1-aws-east
  spec:
  hubAcceptsClient: true
  leaseDurationSeconds: 60
  status:
  ...
  version:
  kubernetes: v1.18.3+b0068a8
- apiVersion: cluster.open-cluster-management.io/v1
  kind: ManagedCluster
  metadata:
  labels:
```

```
apps/pacman: deployed
cloud: Google
clusterID: 9e170dd8-a463-44c7-a59f-39b7459964ec
environment: dev
name: cluster3-gcp-europe-west3
region: europe-west3
vendor: OpenShift
name: cluster3-gcp-europe-west3
spec:
hubAcceptsClient: true
leaseDurationSeconds: 60
status:
...
version:
kubernetes: v1.18.3+b0068a8
kind: List
metadata:
 resourceVersion: ""
 selfLink: ""
```

We start by defining our application and referencing the `Subscription` kind that will make up the application:

```
apiVersion: app.k8s.io/v1beta1
kind: Application
metadata:
 name: pacman-app
 namespace: pacman-app
spec:
 componentKinds:
 - group: apps.open-cluster-management.io
 kind: Subscription
 descriptor: {}
 selector:
 matchExpressions:
 - key: app.kubernetes.io/name
 operator: In
 values:
 - pacman
```

The application provides a way to group a set of related parts into a logical unit for management. As of the current project readiness, the application is used to understand the delivery of parts to different managed clusters. Work is underway to also use the application to aggregate health information and summarize the readiness of the complete application for all supporting clusters where the application or its parts are deployed.

Now let's define the channel and subscription to attach our application to one or more clusters. The channel simply references the Git repository for our application:

```
apiVersion: apps.open-cluster-management.io/v1
kind: Channel
metadata:
 name: pacman-app-latest
```

```
  namespace: pacman-app
  annotations:
  apps.open-cluster-management.io/github-path: kustomization
 spec:
  type: GitHub
  pathname: https://github.com/hybrid-cloud-apps-openshift-k8s-book/
openshift-pipeline-example-pacman.git
  # secretRef:
  # name: github-credentials
```

The subscription then references the channel, includes details about the requested branch for application changes, and isolates the relevant directory structure within the Git repository. Subscriptions can further restrict when deployments are allowed by specifying timeWindows that either explicitly allow or block changes to the cluster that are recognized in the source repository.

Here we see the subscription for the pacman-app with references to the channel defined previously:

```
apiVersion: apps.open-cluster-management.io/v1
kind: Subscription
metadata:
 annotations:
 apps.open-cluster-management.io/git-branch: main
 apps.open-cluster-management.io/github-path: kustomization
 name: pacman-app
 namespace: pacman-app
 labels:
 app.kubernetes.io/name: pacman
spec:
 channel: pacman-app/pacman-app-latest
 placement:
 placementRef:
 kind: PlacementRule
 name: pacman-dev-clusters
 # timewindow:
 # windowtype: blocked
 # location: America/Toronto
 # weekdays: ["Monday","Tuesday","Wednesday","Thursday","Friday"]
 # hours:
 # - start: "06:00AM"
 # end: "05:00PM"
```

The subscription also provides the ability to supply information to the deployment via packageOverrides for Kustomization projects or Helm charts.

The subscription is then matched to a managed cluster by a PlacementRule. The PlacementRule uses match selectors to identify target clusters that are under management that should host the application.

In the following example, a `PlacementRule` defines a selection clause to select at most two clusters that have a region value of us-east, us-west, or europe-west3 and include the labels environment=dev and apps/pacman=deployed:

```
apiVersion: apps.open-cluster-management.io/v1
kind: PlacementRule
metadata:
 name: pacman-dev-clusters
 namespace: pacman-app
spec:
 clusterConditions:
 - status: "True"
 type: ManagedClusterConditionAvailable
 clusterReplicas: 2
 clusterSelector:

 matchExpressions:
 - key: region
 operator: In
 values:
 - us-east
 - us-west
 - europe-west3
 matchLabels:
 environment: dev
 apps/pacman: deployed
```

We can apply all of these API resources from our example project:

```
$ git clone git@github.com:hybrid-cloud-apps-openshift-k8s-book/
openshift-pipeline-example-pacman.git
$ cd openshift-pipeline-example-pacman
$ oc new-project pacman-app
$ oc apply -f deploy/pacman-app.yaml
```

Now let's see what this would look like if we had two clusters under management. Our first cluster is an OpenShift cluster running on Amazon Elastic Compute Cloud (EC2) in the us-east region. Our second cluster is an OpenShift cluster running on Google Compute Platform in the europe-west3 region. We can inspect any managed clusters in RHACM with the following command:

```
$ oc get managedclusters --show-labels
NAME HUB ACCEPTED MANAGED CLUSTER URLS JOINED AVAILABLE AGE LABELS
local-cluster true True True 55m
  cloud=Amazon,clusterID=65333a32-ba14-4711-98db-28c2aa0153d6,
  installer.name=multiclusterhub,installer.
  namespace=open-
cluster-management,local-cluster=true,vendor=OpenShift

cluster1-aws-east true True True 52m
  apps/pacman=deployed,cloud=Amazon,
  clusterID=7de6ab45-58ac-47f7-897d-
b742b7197653,environment=dev,
  name=cluster1-aws-east,region=us-east,vendor=OpenShift
```

```
cluster3-gcp-europe-west3 true True True 52m
  apps/pacman=deployed,cloud=Google,
  clusterID=9e170dd8-a463-44c7-a59f-
39b7459964ec,environment=dev,name=cluster3-gcp-europe-west3,
  region=europe-west3,vendor=OpenShift
```

Our PlacementRule will have identified these two eligible clusters based on the matchLabels and matchExpressions that we defined previously:

```
$ oc get placementrule -n pacman-app pacman-dev-clusters -oyamlapiVersion:
apps.open-cluster-management.io/v1
kind: PlacementRule
metadata:
 name: pacman-dev-clusters
 namespace: pacman-app
 resourceVersion: "3954663"
 selfLink: /apis/apps.open-cluster-management.io/v1/namespaces/pacman-
app/placementrules/pacman-dev-clusters
 uid: 4baae9ee-520c-407e-9cbd-645465e122ea
spec:
 clusterConditions:
 - status: "True"
 type: ManagedClusterConditionAvailable
 clusterSelector:
 clusterReplicas: 2
 matchExpressions:
 - key: region
 operator: In
 values:
 - us-east
 - us-west
 - europe-west3
 matchLabels:
 apps/pacman: deployed
 environment: dev
status:
 decisions:
 - clusterName: cluster1-aws-east
 clusterNamespace: cluster1-aws-east
 - clusterName: cluster3-gcp-europe-west3
 clusterNamespace: cluster3-gcp-europe-west3
```

We can view our application in the Advanced Cluster Management topology view and its relevant parts (described by the subscription) that were deployed to our two managed clusters (identified by the PlacementRule) that originated from our Git repository (identified by the channel). In Figure 5-8, we can see the application has exactly one subscription (it could have multiple) that is placed on two clusters.

We can select elements in the topology to view more information, as shown in Figure 5-9.

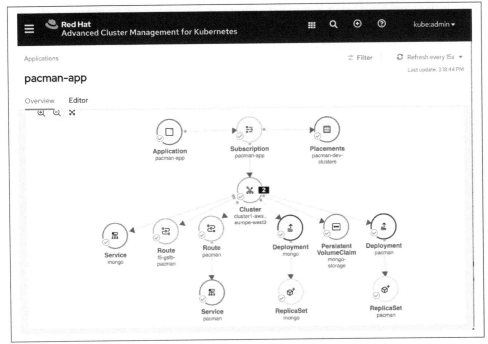

Figure 5-8. Visualization of the application in the RHACM topology view

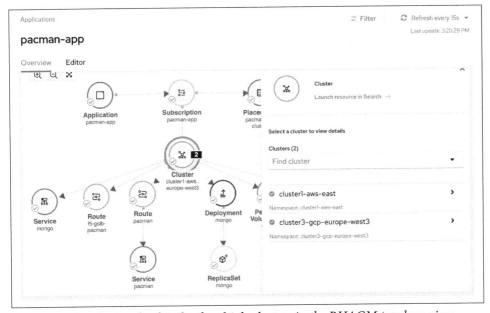

Figure 5-9. Displaying the details of multiple clusters in the RHACM topology view

The cluster icon depicted in Figure 5-10 shows us the clusters that were selected.

Figure 5-10. Displaying the details of a selected cluster in the RHACM topology view

The deployment icons show us how our deployment is doing and whether it was successfully deployed and is currently healthy on our managed clusters.

Clicking "Launch resource in Search" will show us details about the pacman deployment across all managed clusters (see Figure 5-11).

Here we can see our pacman deployment is running on two clusters: cluster3-gcp-europe-west3 and cluster1-aws-east. From here we could further inspect related objects, including the related pods, services, and secrets used by the deployment.

The powerful search capability allows you to understand your application with a holistic view. At a minimum, you are able to validate that parts of the application are deployed as expected. If a problem arises, these views help you isolate what may be the root cause of an observed failure. Making the information available in a more consumable form helps SREs and developers be more effective in dealing with the complexity of a multicluster or multicloud architecture.

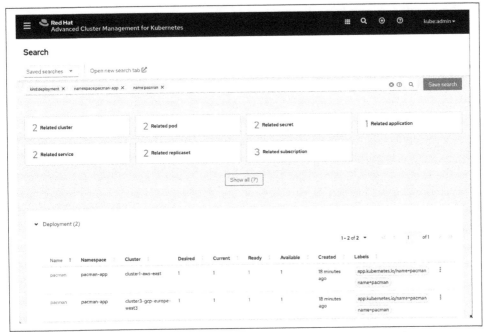

Figure 5-11. Display of the pacman deployment in the RHACM web console

Summary

This chapter provided an overview of several popular tools and methodologies for supporting continuous delivery in production across traditional Kubernetes and OpenShift clusters. We first introduced Helm, which is a popular packaging tool for Kubernetes applications. Next, we described Kustomize, which provides the ability to use your existing Kubernetes YAML files for multiple purposes and configurations while avoiding the use of templates. We then described several popular approaches for supporting continuous delivery pipelines, including GitOps, Razee, Tekton, and Argo CD. Finally, we concluded with an extensive discussion of OpenShift Pipelines and Open Cluster Management tools for deploying and managing OpenShift applications across multiple clusters. With the techniques learned in this chapter, you now have a solid understanding of the most popular and proven continuous delivery options available to you and some hands-on experience managing applications across multiple clusters. In the next chapter, we provide an in-depth examination of the crucial operations of provisioning and upgrading in multicluster environments.

## CHAPTER 6

Multicluster Fleets: Provision and Upgrade Life Cycles

The terms *multicluster* and *multicloud* have become common in today's landscape. For the purposes of this discussion, we will define these terms as follows:

Multicluster
　　Refers to scenarios where more than a single cluster is under management or an application is made up of parts that are hosted on more than one cluster

Multicloud
　　Refers to scenarios where the multiple clusters in use also span infrastructure substrates, which might include a private datacenter and a single public cloud provider or multiple public cloud providers

The differences here are more academic; the reality is that you are more likely than not to have to manage many clusters just as your organization has had to manage multiple VMware ESXi hosts that run VMs.

The differences will matter when your container orchestration platform has variation across infrastructure substrates. We'll talk about some of the places where this currently comes up and may affect some of your management techniques or application architectures.

Why Multicluster?

Let's discuss the use cases that lead to multiple clusters under management.

Use Case: Using Multiple Clusters to Provide Regional Availability for Your Applications

As discussed in Chapter 4, a single cluster can span multiple availability zones. Each availability zone has independent failure characteristics. A failure in the power supply, network provider, and even physical space (e.g., the datacenter building) should be isolated to one availability zone. Typically, the network links across availability zones still provide for significant throughput and low latency, allowing the etcd cluster for the Kubernetes API server to span hosts running in different availability zones. However, your application may need to tolerate an outage that affects more than two availability zones within a region or tolerate an outage of the entire region.

So perhaps one of the most easily understood use cases is to create more than one multiavailability zone cluster in two or more regions. You will commonly find applications that are federated across two "swim lanes," sometimes referred to as a *blue-green architecture* (*https://oreil.ly/82hDU*). The "blue-green" pairing pattern can often be found within the same region, with alternate blue-green pairs in other regions. You may choose to bring that same architecture to OpenShift where you run two separate clusters that host the same set of components for the application, effectively running two complete end-to-end environments, either of which can support most of the load of your users. Additional issues concerning load balancing and data management arise around architectural patterns required to support cross-region deployments and will be covered in Chapter 8.

Use Case: Using Multiple Clusters for Multiple Tenants

The Kubernetes community boundary for tenancy is a single cluster. In general, the API constructs within Kubernetes focus on dividing the compute resources of the cluster into namespaces (also called *projects* in OpenShift). Users are then assigned roles or `ClusterRoles` to access their namespaces. However, cluster-scoped resources like `ClusterRoles`, CRDs, namespaces/projects, webhook configurations, and so on really cannot be managed by independent parties. Each API resource must have a unique name within the collection of the same kind of API resources. If there were true multitenancy within a cluster, then some API concept (like a tenant) would group things like `ClusterRoles`, CRDs, and webhook configurations and prevent collisions (in naming or behavior) across each tenant, much like projects do for applications (e.g., deployments, services, and `PersistentVolumeClaims` can duplicate names or behavior across different namespaces/projects).

So Kubernetes is easiest to consume when you can assign a cluster to a tenant. A tenant might be a line of business or a functional team within your organization (e.g., quality engineering or performance and scale test). Then, a set of cluster-admins or similarly elevated ClusterRoles can be assigned to the owners of the cluster.

Hence, an emerging pattern is that platform teams that manage OpenShift clusters will define a process where a consumer may request a cluster for their purposes. As a result, multiple clusters now require consistent governance and policy management.

Use Case: Supporting Far-Edge Use Cases Where Clusters Do Not Run in Traditional Datacenters or Clouds

There are some great examples of how technology is being applied to a variety of use cases where computing power is coupled with sensor data from cameras, audio sensors, or environmental sensors and machine learning or AI to improve efficiency, provide greater safety, or create novel consumer interactions.[1] These use cases are often referred to generically as *edge computing* because the computing power is outside the datacenter and closer to the "edge" of the consumer experience.

The introduction of high-bandwidth capabilities with 5G also creates scenarios where an edge-computing solution can use a localized 5G network within a space like a manufacturing plant and where edge-computing applications help track product assembly, automate safety controls for employees, or protect sensitive machinery.

Just as containers provide a discrete package for enterprise web-based applications, there are significant benefits of using containers in edge-based applications. Similarly, the automated recovery of services by your container orchestration is also beneficial, even more so when the computing source is not easily accessible within your datacenter.

Architectural Characteristics

Now that we have seen some of the reasons why you may use multiple clusters or clouds to support your needs, let's take a look at some of the architectural benefits and challenges of such an approach.

---

1 Ted Dunning, "Using Data Fabric and Kubernetes in Edge Computing," The Newstack (May 21, 2020), *https://oreil.ly/W3J7f*; "Edge Computing at Chick-fil-A," Chick-fil-A Tech Blog (July 30, 2018), *https://oreil.ly/HcJqZ*.

Region availability versus availability zones

With multiple clusters hosting the application, you can spread instances of the application across multiple cloud regions. Each cluster within a region will still spread compute capacity across multiple availability zones. See Figure 6-1 for a visual representation of this topology.

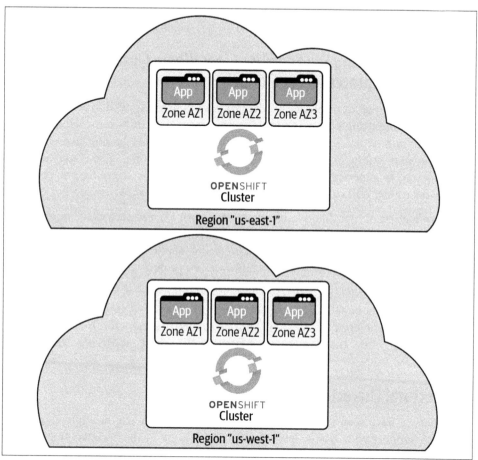

Figure 6-1. Cluster region availability allows multiple clusters to run across independent cloud regions

Under this style of architecture, each cluster can tolerate the total loss of any one availability zone (AZ1, AZ2, or AZ3 could become unavailable but not more than one), and the workload will continue to run and serve requests. As a result of two availability zone failures, the etcd cluster would lose quorum and the control plane would become unavailable.

The reason that a Kubernetes control plane becomes inoperable with more than a single availability zone failure is because of quorum requirements for etcd. Typically, etcd will have three replicas that are maintained in the control plane, each replica supported by exactly one availability zone. If a single availability zone is lost, there are still two out of three replicas present and distributed writes can still be sure that the write transaction is accepted. If two availability zones fail, then write attempts will be rejected. Pods running on worker nodes in the cluster may still be able to serve traffic, but no updates related to the Kubernetes API will be accepted or take place. However, the independent cluster running in one of the other regions could continue to respond to user requests. See Chapter 4 for a deeper analysis of how this process works.

Mitigating latency for users based on geography

If you have users in different locations, using more than one cloud region can also improve response times for your users. When a user attempts to access the web user experience of your application or an API exposed by your workload, their request can be routed to the nearest available instance of your application. Typically, a *Global Server Load Balancer* (GSLB) is used to efficiently route traffic in these scenarios. When the user attempts to access the service, a DNS lookup will be delegated to the nameservers hosted by your GSLB. Then, based on a heuristic of where the request originated, the nameserver will respond with the IP address of the nearest hosted instance of your application. You can see a visual representation of this in Figure 6-2.

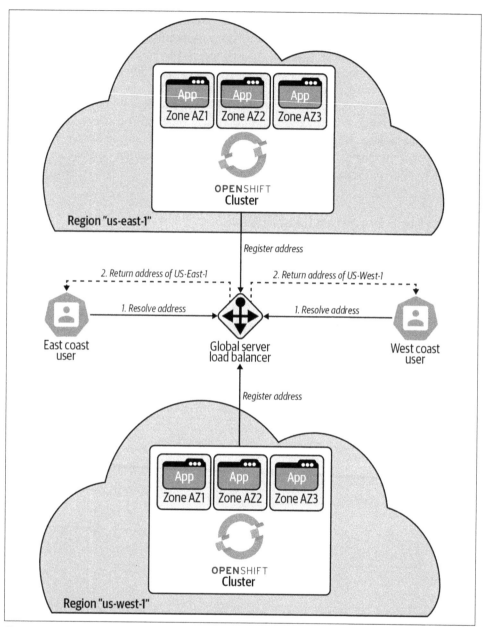

Figure 6-2. Requests to resolve the address of a global service using a GSLB will return the closest instance based on proximity to the request originator

Consistency of your platform (managed Kubernetes versus OpenShift plus cloud identity providers)

One of the major benefits of the OpenShift Container Platform is that it deploys and runs consistently across all cloud providers and substrates like VMware and bare metal. When you consider whether to consume a managed Kubernetes provider or OpenShift, be aware that each distribution of Kubernetes makes various architectural decisions that can require greater awareness of your application to ensure cross-provider portability.

Provisioning Across Clouds

Choosing a Kubernetes strategy affords a great way to simplify how applications consume elastic cloud-based infrastructure. To some extent, the problem of how you consume a cloud's resources shifts from solving the details for every application to one platform—namely, how your organization will adopt and manage Kubernetes across infrastructure substrates.

There are several ways to provision Kubernetes from community-supported projects. For the purposes of this section, we'll focus on how to provision Kubernetes using the Red Hat OpenShift Container Platform. Then we'll discuss how you could alternatively consume managed OpenShift or managed Kubernetes services as part of your provisioning life cycle.

User-Managed OpenShift

When you provision an OpenShift Container Platform 4.x cluster, you have two options for how infrastructure resources are created. *User-provisioned infrastructure* (UPI) allows you more control to spin up VMs, network resources, and storage and then give these details to the install process and allow them to be bootstrapped into a running cluster. Alternatively, you can rely on the more automated approach of *installer-provisioned infrastructure* (IPI). Using IPI, the installer accepts cloud credentials with the appropriate privileges to create the required infrastructure resources. The IPI process will typically define a *virtual private cloud* (VPC). Note that you can specify the VPC as an input parameter if your organization has its own conventions for how these resources are created and managed. Within the VPC, resources, including network load balancers, object store buckets, virtual computing resources, elastic IP addresses, and so forth, are all created and managed by the install process.

Let's take a look at provisioning an OpenShift cluster across three cloud providers: AWS, Microsoft Azure, and Google Cloud Platform. For this discussion, we will review how the install process makes use of declarative configuration (just as Kubernetes does in general) and how this relates to the ClusterVersionOperator (CVO), which manages the life cycle of the OpenShift cluster itself.

First, you will need to download the openshift-installer binary for your appropriate version. Visit Red Hat (*https://cloud.redhat.com*), create an account, and follow the steps to Create Cluster and download the binary for local use. Specific details about the options available for installation are available in the product documentation (*https://oreil.ly/HerIm*).

Let's demonstrate how this approach works by looking at a few example configuration files for the openshift-installer binary. The full breadth of options for installing and configuring OpenShift is beyond the scope of this book. See the OpenShift Container Platform documentation (*https://oreil.ly/wOJ3P*) for a thorough reference of all supported options. The following examples will highlight how the declarative nature of the OpenShift 4.x install methodology simplifies provisioning clusters across multiple substrates. Further, a walk-through example of the MachineSet API will demonstrate how operators continue to manage the life cycle and health of the cluster after provisioning.

Example 6-1 defines a set of options for provisioning an OpenShift cluster on AWS. Example 6-2 defines how to provision an OpenShift cluster on Microsoft Azure, while Example 6-3 defines the equivalent configuration for Google Cloud Platform. Example 6-4—you guessed it!—provides an example configuration for VMware vSphere. With the exception of the VMware vSphere example (which is more sensitive to your own environment), you can use these examples to provision your own clusters with minimal updates. Refer to the OpenShift Container Platform product documentation for a full examination of install methods.

Example 6-1. An example install-config.yaml to provision an OpenShift cluster on AWS

```
apiVersion: v1
metadata:
 name: clusterName
baseDomain: yourcompany.domain.com
controlPlane:
 hyperthreading: Enabled
 name: master
 platform: {}
 replicas: 3
compute:
- hyperthreading: Enabled
 name: worker
 platform:
 aws:
 zones:
 - us-east-1b
 - us-east-1c
 - us-east-1d
 type: m5.xlarge
 rootVolume:
 iops: 4000
 size: 250
```

```
type: io1
replicas: 3
networking:
 clusterNetwork:
 - cidr: 10.128.0.0/14
 hostPrefix: 23
 machineCIDR: 10.0.0.0/16
 networkType: OpenShiftSDN
 serviceNetwork:
 - 172.30.0.0/16
platform:
 aws:
 region: us-east-1
 userTags:
 owner: user@email.domain
publish: External
pullSecret: 'REDACTED'
sshKey: |
 REDACTED
```

Example 6-2. An example install-config.yaml to provision an OpenShift cluster on Microsoft Azure

```
apiVersion: v1
 metadata:
 name: clusterName
baseDomain: yourcompany.domain.com
controlPlane:
 hyperthreading: Enabled
 name: master
 replicas: 3
 platform:
 azure:
 osDisk:
 diskSizeGB: 128
 type: Standard_D4s_v3
compute:
- hyperthreading: Enabled
 name: worker
 replicas: 3
 platform:
 azure:
 type: Standard_D2s_v3
 osDisk:
 diskSizeGB: 128
 zones:
 - "1"
 - "2"
 - "3"
 networking:
 clusterNetwork:
 - cidr: 10.128.0.0/14
 hostPrefix: 23
 machineCIDR: 10.0.0.0/16
 networkType: OpenShiftSDN
```

```
  serviceNetwork:
  - 172.30.0.0/16
 platform:
  azure:
  baseDomainResourceGroupName: resourceGroupName
  region: centralus
 pullSecret: 'REDACTED'
```

Example 6-3. An example install-config.yaml to provision an OpenShift cluster on Google Cloud Platform

```
apiVersion: v1
metadata:
 name: clusterName
baseDomain: yourcompany.domain.com
controlPlane:
 hyperthreading: Enabled
 name: master
 replicas: 3
 platform:
 gcp:
 type: n1-standard-4
compute:
- hyperthreading: Enabled
 name: worker
 replicas: 3
 platform:
 gcp:
 type: n1-standard-4
networking:
 clusterNetwork:
 - cidr: 10.128.0.0/14
 hostPrefix: 23
 machineCIDR: 10.0.0.0/16
 networkType: OpenShiftSDN
 serviceNetwork:
 - 172.30.0.0/16
platform:
 gcp:
 projectID: gcpProjectId
 region: us-east1
 userTags:
 owner: user@email.com
pullSecret: 'REDACTED'
sshKey: |-
 REDACTED
```

Example 6-4. An example install-config.yaml to provision an OpenShift cluster on VMware vSphere

```
apiVersion: v1
metadata:
 name: example
baseDomain: demo.red-chesterfield.com
compute:
- hyperthreading: Enabled
 name: worker
 replicas: 3
platform:
 vsphere:
 vCenter: example.vCenterServer.io
 username: admin
 password: admin
 datacenter: exampleDatacenter
 defaultDatastore: exampleDatastore
 cluster: exampleClusterName
 apiVIP: 10.0.0.200
 ingressVIP: 10.0.0.201
 network: Public Network
pullSecret: 'REDACTED'
sshKey: |-
 REDACTED
```

Any one of these *install-config.yaml* files can be used to provision your cluster using the following command:

```
$ mkdir hubcluster
$ # copy install-config.yaml template from above
$ # or customize your own into the "hubcluster" dir
$ openshift-installer create cluster --dir=hubcluster
```

Note how each example shares some of the same options, notably the clusterName and baseDomain that will be used to derive the default network address of the cluster (applications will be hosted by default at https://*.apps.clusterName.baseDomain and the API endpoint for OpenShift will be available at https://api.cluster Name.baseDomain:6443). When the openshift-installer runs, DNS entries on the cloud provider (e.g., Route 53 in the case of AWS) will be created and linked to the appropriate network load balancers (also created by the install process), that in turn resolve to IP addresses running within the VPC.

Each example defines sections for the controlPlane and compute that correspond to MachineSets that will be created and managed. We'll talk about how these relate to operators within the cluster shortly. More than one MachinePool within the compute section can be specified. Both the controlPlane and compute sections provide con-figurability for the compute hosts and can customize which availability zones are used. Settings including the type (or size) for each host and the options for what kind of storage is attached to the hosts are also available, but reasonable defaults will be chosen if omitted.

Now, if we compare where the *install-config.yaml* properties vary for each substrate, we will find cloud-specific options within the `platform` sections. There is a global `platform` to specify which region the cluster should be created within, as well as `platform` sections under each of the `controlPlane` and `compute` sections to override settings for each provisioned host.

As introduced in Chapter 5, the Open Cluster Management (*https://oreil.ly/D1UvC*) project is a new approach to managing the multicluster challenges that most cluster maintainers encounter. Chapter 5 discussed how applications can be distributed easily across clusters. Now let's look at how the cluster provisioning, upgrade, and decommissioning process can be driven using Open Cluster Management.

In the following example, we will walk through creating a new cluster on a cloud provider. The underlying behavior is leveraging the same openshift-install process that we just discussed. Once provisioned, the Open Cluster Management framework will install an agent that runs as a set of pods on the new cluster. We refer to this agent as a `klusterlet`, mimicking the naming of the `kubelet` process that runs on nodes that are part of a Kubernetes cluster.

> The following assumes the user has already set up the Open Cluster Management project or RHACM for Kubernetes as described in Chapter 5.

From the RHACM for Kubernetes web console, open the Automate Infrastructure > Clusters page and click on the action to "Create cluster" as shown in Figure 6-3.

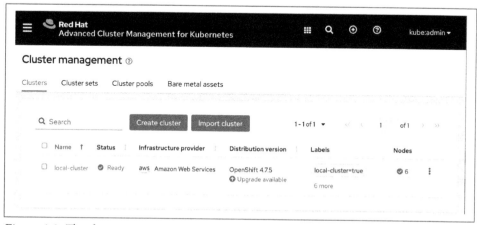

Figure 6-3. The cluster overview page allows you to provision new clusters from the console

The "Create cluster" action shown in Figure 6-4 opens to a form where you provide a name and select one of the available cloud providers.

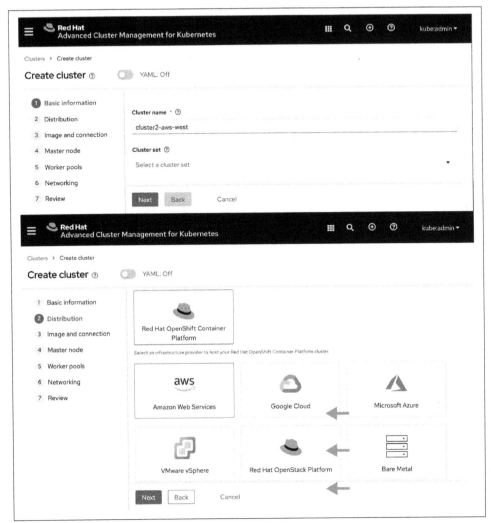

Figure 6-4. Cluster creation form via RHACM for Kubernetes

Next, select a version of OpenShift to provision. The available list maps directly to the ClusterImageSets available on the hub cluster. You can introspect these images with the following command:

```
$ oc get clusterimagesets
NAME            RELEASE
img4.3.40-x86-64 quay.io/openshift-release-dev/ocp-release:4.3.40-x86_64
img4.4.27-x86-64 quay.io/openshift-release-dev/ocp-release:4.4.27-x86_64
img4.5.15-x86-64 quay.io/openshift-release-dev/ocp-release:4.5.15-x86_64
img4.6.1-x86-64  quay.io/openshift-release-dev/ocp-release:4.6.1-x86_64
```

Further down the page, as shown in Figure 6-5, you will also need to specify a provider connection. In the case of AWS, you will need to provide the Access ID and Secret Key to allow API access by the installation process with your AWS account.

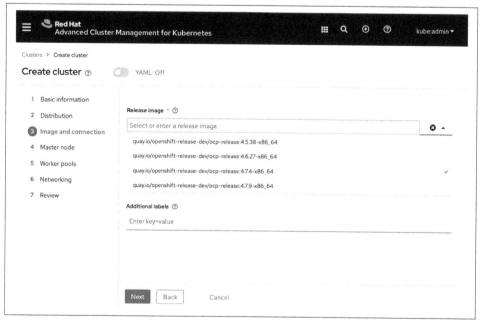

Figure 6-5. Select your release image (the version to provision) and your provider connection

At this point, you can simply click Create and the cluster will be provisioned. However, let's walk through how the `MachinePool` operator allows you to manage `Machine Sets` within the cluster.

Customize the "Worker pool1" `NodePool` for your desired region and availability zones. See Figures 6-6 and 6-7 for an example of what this will look like in the form. You can amend these options after the cluster is provisioned as well.

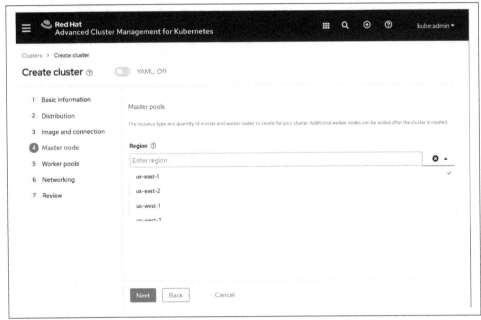

Figure 6-6. Customizing the region and zones for the cluster workers

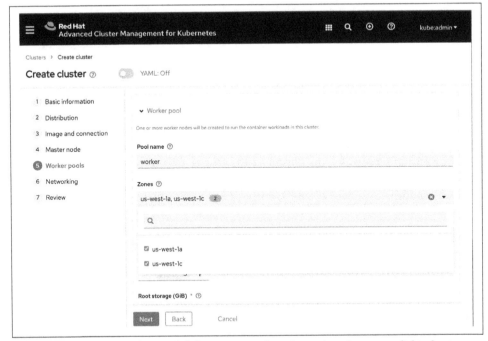

Figure 6-7. Customize the availability zones within the region that are valid to host workers

A final summary of your confirmed choices is presented for review in Figure 6-8.

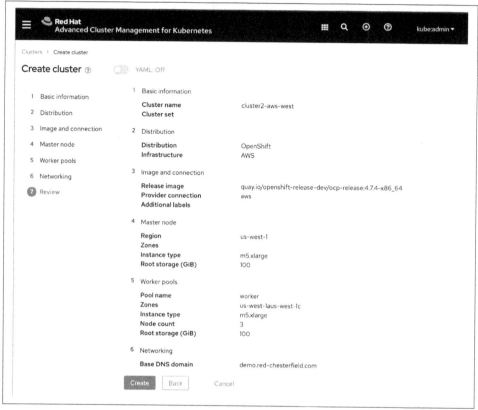

Figure 6-8. Confirmed options selected in the form

Once you have made your final customizations, click Create to begin the provisioning process as shown in Figure 6-9. The web console provides a view that includes links to the provisioning logs for the cluster. If the cluster fails to provision (e.g., due to a quota restriction in your cloud account), the provisioning logs provide clues on what to troubleshoot.

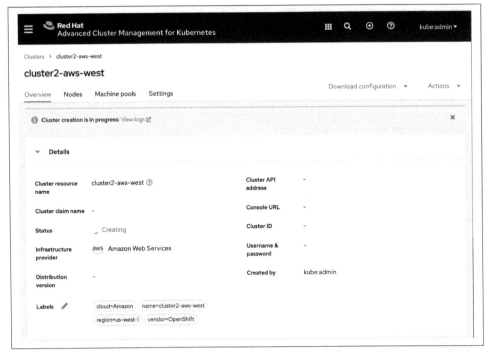

Figure 6-9. RHACM web console view that includes links to the provisioning logs for the cluster

Behind the form editor, a number of Kubernetes API objects are created. A small number of these API objects are cluster scoped (ManagedCluster in particular). The ManagedCluster controller will ensure that a project (namespace) exists that maps to the cluster name. Other controllers, including the controller that begins the provisioning process, will use the cluster project (namespace) to store resources that provide an API control surface for provisioning. Let's take a look at a subset of these that you should become familiar with.

ManagedCluster

ManagedCluster (API group: cluster.open-cluster-management.io/v1; cluster scoped) recognizes that a remote cluster is under the control of the hub cluster. The agent that runs on the remote cluster will attempt to create ManagedCluster if it does not exist on the hub, and it must be accepted by a user identity on the hub with appropriate permissions. You can see the example created in Example 6-5. Note that labels for this object will drive placement decisions later in this chapter.

Example 6-5. Example of the `ManagedCluster` API object

```
apiVersion: cluster.open-cluster-management.io/v1
kind: ManagedCluster
metadata:
  ...
  labels:
  cloud: Amazon
  clusterID: f2c2853e-e003-4a99-a4f7-2e231f9b36d9
  name: mycluster
  region: us-east-1
  vendor: OpenShift
  name: mycluster
 spec:
  hubAcceptsClient: true
  leaseDurationSeconds: 60
 status:
  allocatable:
  cpu: "21"
  memory: 87518Mi
  capacity:
  cpu: "24"
  memory: 94262Mi
  conditions:
  ...
  version:
  kubernetes: v1.18.3+2fbd7c7
```

ClusterDeployment

ClusterDeployment (API group: hive.openshift.io/v1; namespace scoped) controls
the provisioning and decommissioning phases of the cluster. A controller on the hub
takes care of running the openshift-installer on your behalf. If the cluster creation
process fails for any reason (e.g., you encounter a quota limit within your cloud
account), the cloud resources will be destroyed and another attempt will be made
after a waiting period to reattempt successful creation of the cluster. Unlike traditional automation methods that "try once" and require user intervention upon failure,
the Kubernetes reconcile loop for this API kind will continue to attempt to create the
cluster (with appropriate waiting periods in between) as shown in Example 6-6. You
can also create these resources directly through the oc or kubectl like any Kubernetes
native resource.

Example 6-6. Example `ClusterDeployment` created by the form

```
apiVersion: hive.openshift.io/v1
kind: ClusterDeployment
metadata:
  ...
  name: mycluster
  namespace: mycluster
 spec:
```

```
baseDomain: demo.red-chesterfield.com
clusterMetadata:
adminKubeconfigSecretRef:
name: mycluster-0-cqpz4-admin-kubeconfig
adminPasswordSecretRef:
name: mycluster-0-cqpz4-admin-password
clusterID: f2c2853e-e003-4a99-a4f7-2e231f9b36d9
infraID: mycluster-9bn6s
clusterName: mycluster
controlPlaneConfig:
servingCertificates: {}
installed: true
platform:
aws:
credentialsSecretRef:
name: mycluster-aws-creds
region: us-east-1
provisioning:
imageSetRef:
name: img4.5.15-x86-64
installConfigSecretRef:
name: mycluster-install-config
sshPrivateKeySecretRef:
name: mycluster-ssh-private-key
pullSecretRef:
name: mycluster-pull-secret
status:
apiURL: https://api.mycluster.REDACTED:6443
cliImage: quay.io/openshift-release-dev/ocp-v4.0-art-
dev@sha256:8b8e08e498c61ccec5c446d6ab50c96792799c992c78cfce7bbb8481f04a64cb
conditions:
...
installerImage: quay.io/openshift-release-dev/ocp-v4.0-art-
dev@sha256:a3ed2bf438dfa5a114aa94cb923103432cd457cac51d1c4814ae0ef7e6e9853b
provisionRef:
name: mycluster-0-cqpz4
webConsoleURL: https://console-openshift-console.apps.mycluster.REDACTED
```

KlusterletAddonConfig

KlusterletAddonConfig (API group: agent.open-cluster-management.io/v1; namespace scoped) represents the capabilities that should be provided on the remote agent
that manages the cluster. In Example 6-7, the Open Cluster Management project
refers to the remote agent as a klusterlet, mirroring the language of kubelet.

Example 6-7. An example of the KlusterletAddonConfig API object

```
apiVersion: agent.open-cluster-management.io/v1
kind: KlusterletAddonConfig
metadata:
..
name: mycluster
namespace: mycluster
```

```
spec:
 applicationManager:
 enabled: true
 certPolicyController:
 enabled: true
 clusterLabels:
 cloud: Amazon
 vendor: OpenShift
 clusterName: mycluster
 clusterNamespace: mycluster
 iamPolicyController:
 enabled: true
 policyController:
 enabled: true
 searchCollector:
 enabled: true
 version: 2.1.0
```

MachinePool

MachinePool (API group: hive.openshift.io/v1; namespace -scoped) allows you to create a collection of hosts that work together and share characteristics. You might use a MachinePool to group a set of compute capacity that supports a specific team or line of business. As we will see in the next section, MachinePool also allows you to dynamically size your cluster. Finally, the status provides a view into the MachineSets that are available on ManagedCluster. See Example 6-8 for the example MachinePool created earlier, which provides a control surface to scale the number of replicas up or down within the pool and status about the MachineSets under management on the remote cluster.

Example 6-8. The example MachinePool API object

```
apiVersion: hive.openshift.io/v1
kind: MachinePool
metadata:
  ...
 name: mycluster-worker
 namespace: mycluster
spec:
 clusterDeploymentRef:
 name: mycluster
 name: worker
 platform:
 aws:
 rootVolume:
 iops: 100
 size: 100
 type: gp2
 type: m5.xlarge
 replicas: 3
status:
```

```
machineSets:
- maxReplicas: 1
  minReplicas: 1
  name: mycluster-9bn6s-worker-us-east-1a
  replicas: 1
- maxReplicas: 1
  minReplicas: 1
  name: mycluster-9bn6s-worker-us-east-1b
  replicas: 1
- maxReplicas: 1
  minReplicas: 1
  name: mycluster-9bn6s-worker-us-east-1c
  replicas: 1
- maxReplicas: 0
  minReplicas: 0
  name: mycluster-9bn6s-worker-us-east-1d
  replicas: 0
- maxReplicas: 0
  minReplicas: 0
  name: mycluster-9bn6s-worker-us-east-1e
  replicas: 0
- maxReplicas: 0
  minReplicas: 0
  name: mycluster-9bn6s-worker-us-east-1f
  replicas: 0
replicas: 3
```

Once provisioned, the address for the Kubernetes API server and OpenShift web console will be available from the cluster details page. You can use these coordinates to open your web browser and authenticate with the new cluster as the kubeadmin user. You can also access the KUBECONFIG certificates that allow you command-line access to the cluster.

You can download the KUBECONFIG authorization as shown in Figure 6-10 for the new cluster from the RHACM web console under the cluster overview page or access it from the command line. From the web console, click on the cluster name in the list of clusters to view an overview of that cluster. Once the provisioning process has completed, you will be able to download the KUBECONFIG file that will allow you command-line access to the cluster.

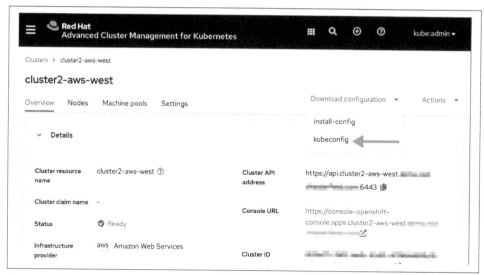

Figure 6-10. Downloading the kubeconfig authorization from the RHACM web console

From the command line, you can retrieve the information stored in a secret under the cluster project (namespace) as in Example 6-9. Save the file contents and configure your `KUBECONFIG` environment variable to point to the location of the file. Then `oc` will be able to run commands against the remote cluster.

Example 6-9. Output of the cluster KUBECONFIG file

```
$ CLUSTER_NAME=mycluster ; oc get secret -n $CLUSTER_NAME \
  -l hive.openshift.io/cluster-deployment-name=$CLUSTER_NAME \
  -l hive.openshift.io/secret-type=kubeconfig \
  -ogo-template="{{range .items}}{{.data.kubeconfig|base64decode}}{{end}}"
```

Now that our cluster is up and running, let's walk through how we can scale the cluster. We will review this concept from the context of the oc CLI.

First, open two terminals and configure the `KUBECONFIG` or context for each of the hub clusters and our newly minted `mycluster`. See Examples 6-10 and 6-11 for examples of what each of the two separate terminals will look like after you run these commands. Note the tip to override your PS1 shell prompt temporarily to avoid confusion when running commands on each cluster.

Example 6-10. An example of what Terminal 1 will look like

```
$ export PS1="hubcluster $ "
hubcluster $ export KUBECONFIG=hubcluster/auth/kubeconfig
hubcluster $ oc cluster-info
Kubernetes master is running at https://api.hubcluster.<baseDomain>:6443
```

```
To further debug and diagnose cluster problems, use 'kubectl cluster-info dump'.
```

Example 6-11. An example of how Terminal 2 will look

```
$ export PS1="mycluster $ "
mycluster $ CLUSTER_NAME=mycluster ; \
  oc get secret -n $CLUSTER_NAME \
  -l hive.openshift.io/cluster-deployment-name=$CLUSTER_NAME \
  -l hive.openshift.io/secret-type=kubeconfig \
  -ogo-template="{{range .items}}{{.data.kubeconfig|base64decode}}{{end}}" \
  > mycluster-kubeconfig
mycluster $ export KUBECONFIG=mycluster-kubeconfig
mycluster $ oc cluster-info
Kubernetes master is running at https://api.mycluster.<baseDomain>:6443

To further debug and diagnose cluster problems, use 'kubectl cluster-info dump'.
```

Now you should have Terminal 1 with a prompt including hubcluster and Terminal 2 with a prompt including mycluster. We will refer to these terminals by the appropriate names through the rest of the example.

In the following walk-through, we will review the MachineSet API, which underpins how an OpenShift cluster understands compute capacity. We will then scale the size of our managed cluster from the hub using the MachinePool API that we saw earlier.

In the mycluster terminal, review the MachineSets for your cluster:

```
mycluster $ oc get machinesets -n openshift-machine-api
NAME                            DESIRED CURRENT READY AVAILABLE AGE
mycluster-9bn6s-worker-us-east-1a 1        1       1     1         1d
mycluster-9bn6s-worker-us-east-1b 1        1       1     1         1d
mycluster-9bn6s-worker-us-east-1c 1        1       1     1         1d
mycluster-9bn6s-worker-us-east-1d 0                      0         1d
mycluster-9bn6s-worker-us-east-1e 0                      0         1d
mycluster-9bn6s-worker-us-east-1f 0                      0         1d
```

Each MachineSet will have a name following the pattern: <clusterName>-<five-character identifier>-<machinePoolName>-<availabilityZone>. In your cluster, you should see counts for the desired number of machines per MachineSet, the current number of machines that are available, and the current number that are considered Ready to be integrated as nodes into the OpenShift cluster. Note that these three counts should generally be equivalent and should only vary when the cluster is in a transition state (adding or removing machines) or when an underlying availability problem in the cluster causes one or more machines to be considered unhealthy. For example, when you edit a MachineSet to increase the desired replicas, you will see the Desired count increment by one for that MachineSet. As the machine is provisioned and proceeds to boot and configure the kubelet, the Current count will increment by one. Finally, as the kubelet registers with the Kubernetes API control plane and marks the node as Ready, the Ready count will increment by one. If at any point the machine becomes unhealthy, the Ready count may decrease. Similarly, if you reduced the Desired count by one, you would see the same staggered reduction in counts as the machine proceeds through various life-cycle states until it is removed.

Next, in the hub terminal, review the worker MachinePool defined for the managed cluster:

```
hubcluster $ oc get machinepool -n mycluster
NAME               POOLNAME CLUSTERDEPLOYMENT REPLICAS
mycluster-worker worker    mycluster          3
```

We will increase the size of the managed cluster mycluster by one node:

```
hubcluster $ oc patch machinepool -n mycluster mycluster-worker \
 -p '{"spec":{"replicas":4}}' --type=merge
machinepool.hive.openshift.io/mycluster-worker patched
```

The size of the worker node will be determined by the values set in the MachinePool mycluster-worker. The availability zone of the new node will be determined by the MachinePool controller, where nodes are distributed across availability zones as evenly as possible.

Immediately after you have patched the MachinePool to increase the number of desired replicas, rerun the command to view the MachineSet on your managed cluster:

```
mycluster $ oc get machinesets -n openshift-machine-api
NAME                              DESIRED CURRENT READY AVAILABLE AGE
mycluster-9bn6s-worker-us-east-1a 1       1       1     1         1d
mycluster-9bn6s-worker-us-east-1b 1       1       1     1         1d
mycluster-9bn6s-worker-us-east-1c 1       1       1     1         1d
mycluster-9bn6s-worker-us-east-1d 1                     1         1d
mycluster-9bn6s-worker-us-east-1e 0                     0         1d
mycluster-9bn6s-worker-us-east-1f 0                     0         1d
```

Over the course of a few minutes, you should see the new node on the managed cluster transition from Desired to Current to Ready, with a final result that looks like the following output:

```
mycluster $ oc get machinesets -n openshift-machine-api
NAME                              DESIRED CURRENT READY AVAILABLE AGE
mycluster-9bn6s-worker-us-east-1a 1       1       1     1         1d
mycluster-9bn6s-worker-us-east-1b 1       1       1     1         1d
mycluster-9bn6s-worker-us-east-1c 1       1       1     1         1d
mycluster-9bn6s-worker-us-east-1d 1       1       1     1         1d
mycluster-9bn6s-worker-us-east-1e 0                     0         1d
mycluster-9bn6s-worker-us-east-1f 0                     0         1d
```

Let's recap what we've just seen. First, we used a declarative method (*install-config.yaml*) to provision our first cluster, called a hub. Next, we used the hub to provision the first managed cluster in our fleet. That managed cluster was created under the covers using the same IPI method but with the aid of Kubernetes API and continuous reconcilers that ensure that the running cluster matches the Desired state. One of the APIs that governs the Desired state is the MachinePool API on the hub cluster. Because our first fleet member, mycluster, was created from the hub cluster, we can use the MachinePool API to govern how mycluster adds or removes nodes. Or indeed, we can create additional MachinePools that add capacity to the cluster.

Throughout the process, the underlying infrastructure substrate was completely managed through operators. The MachineSet operator on the managed cluster was given updated instructions by the MachinePool operator on the hub to grow the number of machines available in one of the MachineSets supporting mycluster.

We will use the term *infrastructure substrate* as a catchall term to refer to the compute, network, and storage resources provided by bare metal virtualization within your datacenter or virtualization offered by a public cloud provider.

Upgrading Your Clusters to the Latest Version of Kubernetes

As we saw with MachinePools and MachineSets, operators provide a powerful way to abstract the differences across infrastructure substrates, allowing an administrator to declaratively specify the desired outcome. An OpenShift cluster is managed by the CVO, which acts as an "operator of operators" pattern to manage operators for each dimension of the cluster's configuration (authentication, networking, machine creation, bootstrapping, and removal, and so on). Every cluster will have a Cluster Version API object named version. You can retrieve the details for this object with the command:

```
$ oc get clusterversion version -o yaml
```

ClusterVersion specifies a "channel" to seek available versions for the cluster and a desired version from that channel. Think of a channel as an ongoing list of available versions (e.g., 4.5.1, 4.5.2, 4.5.7, and so on). There are channels for "fast" adoption of new versions, as well as "stable" versions. The fast channels produce new versions quickly. Coupled with connected telemetry data from a broad source of OpenShift clusters running across infrastructure substrates and industries, fast channels allow the delivery and validation of new releases very quickly (on order of weeks or days). As releases in fast channels have enough supporting evidence that they are broadly acceptable across the global fleet of OpenShift clusters, versions are promoted to stable channels. Hence, the list of versions within a channel is not always consecutive. An example ClusterVersion API object is represented in Example 6-12.

Example 6-12. An example `ClusterVersion` API object that records the version history for the cluster and the desired version—changing the desired version will cause the operator to begin applying updates to achieve the goal

```
apiVersion: config.openshift.io/v1
kind: ClusterVersion
metadata:
 name: version
spec:
 channel: stable-4.5
 clusterID: f2c2853e-e003-4a99-a4f7-2e231f9b36d9
 desiredUpdate:
 force: false
 image: quay.io/openshift-release-dev/ocp-
release@sha256:38d0bcb5443666b93a0c117f41ce5d5d8b3602b411c574f4e164054c43408a01
 version: 4.5.22
 upstream: https://api.openshift.com/api/upgrades_info/v1/graph
status:
 availableUpdates: null
 conditions:
 - lastTransitionTime: "2020-12-02T23:08:32Z"
 message: Done applying 4.5.22
 status: "True"
 type: Available
 - lastTransitionTime: "2020-12-11T17:05:00Z"
 status: "False"
 type: Failing
 - lastTransitionTime: "2020-12-11T17:09:32Z"
 message: Cluster version is 4.5.22
 status: "False"
 type: Progressing
 - lastTransitionTime: "2020-12-02T22:46:39Z"
 status: "True"
 type: RetrievedUpdates
 desired:
 force: false
 image: quay.io/openshift-release-dev/ocp-
release@sha256:38d0bcb5443666b93a0c117f41ce5d5d8b3602b411c574f4e164054c43408a01
 version: 4.5.22
 history:
 - completionTime: "2020-12-11T17:09:32Z"
 image: quay.io/openshift-release-dev/ocp-
release@sha256:38d0bcb5443666b93a0c117f41ce5d5d8b3602b411c574f4e164054c43408a01
 startedTime: "2020-12-11T16:39:05Z"
 state: Completed
 verified: false
 version: 4.5.22
 - completionTime: "2020-12-02T23:08:32Z"
 image: quay.io/openshift-release-dev/ocp-
release@sha256:1df294ebe5b84f0eeceaa85b2162862c390143f5e84cda5acc22cc4529273c4c
 startedTime: "2020-12-02T22:46:39Z"
 state: Completed
 verified: false
 version: 4.5.15
```

```
observedGeneration: 2
versionHash: m0fIO00kMu8=
```

Upgrading a version of Kubernetes along with all other supporting APIs and infrastructure around it can be a daunting task. The operator that controls the life cycle of all of the container images is known informally as "Cincinnati" (*https://oreil.ly/ 6HIZd*) and formally as the *OpenShift Update Service* (OSUS). OSUS (or Cincinnati) maintains a connected graph of versions and tracks which "walks" or "routes" within the graph are known as good upgrade paths. For example, an issue may be detected in early release channels that indicates that the upgrade from 4.4.23 to 4.5.0 to 4.5.18 may be associated with a specific problem. A fix can be released to create a new release 4.4.24 that then allows a successful and predictable upgrade from 4.4.23 to 4.4.24 to 4.5.0 to 4.5.18. The graph records the successive nodes that must be walked to ensure success.

However, the OSUS operator removes the guesswork, allowing the cluster administrator to specify the desired version from the channel. From there, the CVO will carry out the following tasks:[2]

1. Upgrade the Kubernetes and OpenShift control plane pods, including etcd.

2. Upgrade the operating system for the nodes running the control plane pods.

3. Upgrade the cluster operators controlling aspects like authentication, networking, storage, and so on.

4. For nodes managed by the MachineConfigOperator, upgrade the operating system for the nodes running the data plane pods (user workload).

The upgrade takes place in a rolling fashion, avoiding bursting the size of the cluster or taking out too much capacity at the same time. Because the control plane is spread across three machines, as each machine undergoes an operating system update and reboot, the other two nodes maintain the availability of the Kubernetes control plane, including the datastore (etcd), the scheduler, the controller, the Kubernetes API server, and the network ingress controller.

When the data plane is upgraded, the upgrade process will respect PodDisruption Budgets and look for feedback about the health of OpenShift and user workloads running on each node by means of liveness and readiness probes.

---

2 Rob Szumski, "The Ultimate Guide to OpenShift Release and Upgrade Process for Cluster Administrators," Red Hat OpenShift Blog (November 9, 2020), *https://oreil.ly/hKCex*.

Sometimes the group of clusters under management is referred to as *fleet*. Individual clusters under management may be referred to as *fleet members*, primarily to distinguish them from the hub cluster that is responsible for management.

From the RHACM web console, you can manipulate the desired version of a managed cluster for a single fleet member or the entire fleet. From the console, choose the "Upgrade cluster" action for any cluster that shows "Upgrade available." Recall from the discussion around channels that not every channel may have an upgrade currently available. Additionally, the list of versions may not be consecutive. Figures 6-11, 6-12, and 6-13 provide examples of what this actually looks like for a specific cluster or for multiple clusters.

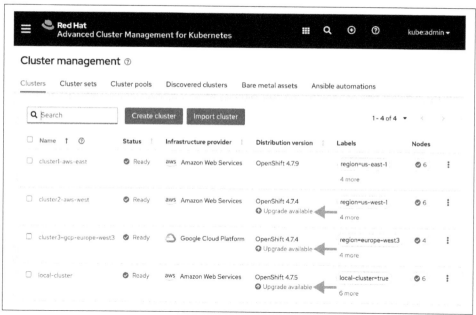

Figure 6-11. Actions permitted on a cluster allow a fleet manager to upgrade the desired version of a cluster

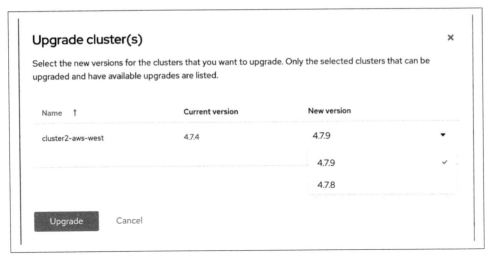

Figure 6-12. The list of available versions is provided for user selection

Upgrade cluster(s)   ✕

Select the new versions for the clusters that you want to upgrade. Only the selected clusters that can be
upgraded and have available upgrades are listed.

Name ↑	Current version	New version	
cluster2-aws-west	4.7.4	4.7.9	▼
		View release notes ☑	
cluster3-gcp-europe-west3	4.7.4	4.7.9	▼
		4.7.9	✓
		4.7.8	

[Upgrade]   Cancel

*Figure 6-13. Multiple clusters may be selected for upgrade, and the versions available
will vary based on the cluster's attached channel configuration in the ClusterVersion
object*

A core topic for this book is how to manage your clusters as a fleet, and for that, we
will rely on policies. The preceding discussion should provide a foundation for you to
understand the moving parts and see that you can explicitly trigger upgrade behavior
across the fleet. In Chapter 7, we will discuss how we can control upgrade behavior
across the fleet by policy.

Summary of Multicloud Cluster Provisioning

Throughout our example, the specific infrastructure substrate showed up in a few declarative APIs, specifically represented by the *install-config.yaml* for the hub cluster and as part of the secrets referenced by the ClusterDeployment API object for the managed cluster. However, the action of provisioning a new cluster and adding or removing nodes for that fleet member was completely driven through Kubernetes API objects.

In addition, the upgrade life cycle managed through the CVO is consistent across supported infrastructure substrates. Hence, regardless if you provision an OpenShift cluster on a public cloud service or in your datacenter, you can still declaratively manage the upgrade process. The powerful realization you should now understand is that managing the infrastructure substrate for OpenShift clusters in multicloud scenarios can be completely abstracted away from many basic cluster-provisioning life-cycle operations.

Beyond controlling the capacity of your fleet from the hub, you can assign policies with Open Cluster Management and drive behavior like fleet upgrades. We will see an example of fleet upgrade by policy in Chapter 7.

OpenShift as a Service

The previous section described how you can abstract the provisioning and life cycle of OpenShift across multiple infrastructure substrates. Under the model we've outlined, you are responsible for the availability of your clusters. For budget or organizational reasons, you may choose to consider a managed service for OpenShift or Kubernetes. Using a vendor-provided "OpenShift as a Service" or "Kubernetes as a Service" can change how you interact with some dimensions, including cluster creation or decommissioning. However, your applications will run consistently regardless of whether the vendor manages the underlying infrastructure or you manage it.

Azure Red Hat OpenShift

Azure Red Hat OpenShift (*https://oreil.ly/0OWW7*) is integrated into the Microsoft Azure ecosystem, including Azure billing. Other aspects, including single sign-on, are automatically configured with Azure Active Directory, simplifying how you expose capabilities to your organization, particularly if you are already consuming other services on Azure. The underlying service is maintained by a partnership between Microsoft and Red Hat.

Red Hat OpenShift on AWS

Red Hat OpenShift on AWS (*https://oreil.ly/fX0a2*) was announced at the end of 2020 with planned availability in 2021. It integrates OpenShift into the Amazon ecosystem, allowing for access and creation through the Amazon cloud console and consistent billing with the rest of your Amazon account. The underlying service is maintained by a partnership between Amazon and Red Hat.

Red Hat OpenShift on IBM Cloud

Red Hat OpenShift on IBM Cloud (*https://oreil.ly/gZBHU*) integrates OpenShift consumption into the IBM Cloud ecosystem, including integration with IBM Cloud single sign-on and billing. In addition, IBM Cloud APIs are provided to manage cluster provisioning, worker nodes, and the upgrade process. These APIs allow separate access controls via IBM Cloud Identity and Access Management for management of the cluster versus the access controls used for managing resources in the cluster. The underlying service is maintained by IBM.

OpenShift Dedicated

OpenShift Dedicated (*https://cloud.redhat.com*) is a managed OpenShift as a Service offering provided by Red Hat. OpenShift clusters can be created across a variety of clouds from this service, in some cases under your own preexisting cloud account. Availability and maintenance of the cluster are handled by the Red Hat SRE team. The underlying service is maintained by Red Hat with options to bring your own cloud accounts on some supported infrastructure providers like AWS.

Kubernetes as a Service

In addition to vendor-managed OpenShift as a Service, many vendors offer managed Kubernetes as a Service distributions. These are typically where the vendor adopts Kubernetes and integrates it into its ecosystem. The following are some examples of these services:

- Amazon Elastic Kubernetes Service
- Azure Kubernetes Service
- Google Kubernetes Engine
- IBM Cloud Kubernetes Service

Because the Kubernetes community leaves some decisions up to vendors or users who assemble their own distributions, each of these managed services can introduce some variations that you should be aware of when adopting them as part of a larger multicloud strategy. In particular, several specific areas in Kubernetes have been evolving quickly:

- Cluster creation
- User identity and access management
- Network routing
- Pod security management
- Role-based access control
- Value-added admission controllers
- Operating system management of the worker nodes
- Different security apparatus to manage compliance

Across each dimension, a vendor providing a managed Kubernetes service must decide how to best integrate that aspect of Kubernetes into the cloud provider's ecosystem. The core API should respond consistently by way of the CNCF Kubernetes Certification process (*https://oreil.ly/sWAXA*). In practice, differences tend to arise where Kubernetes is integrated into a particular cloud ecosystem.

For instance, in some cases a managed Kubernetes service will come with Kubernetes RBAC deployed and configured out of the box. Other vendors may leave it to the cluster creator to configure RBAC for Kubernetes. Across vendors that automatically configure the Kubernetes with RBAC, the set of out-of-the-box `ClusterRoles` and roles can vary.

In other cases, the network ingress for a Kubernetes cluster can vary from cloud-specific extensions to use of the community network ingress controller. Hence, your application may need to provide alternative network ingress behavior based on the cloud providers that you choose to provide Kubernetes. When using Ingress (API group: networking.k8s.io/v1) on a particular cloud vendor–managed Kubernetes, the set of respected annotations can vary across providers, requiring additional validation for apps that must tolerate different managed Kubernetes services. With an OpenShift cluster (managed by a vendor or by you), all applications define the standard Ingress API with a fixed set of annotations or Route (API group: route.openshift.io/v1) API, which will be correctly exposed into the specific infrastructure substrate.

The variation that you must address in your application architectures and multicloud management strategies is not insurmountable. However, be aware of these aspects as you plan your adoption strategy. Whether you adopt an OpenShift as a Service provider or run OpenShift within your own cloud accounts, all of the API-facing applications, including RBAC and networking, will behave the same.

Operating System Currency for Nodes

As your consumption of an OpenShift cluster grows, practical concerns around security and operating system currency must be addressed. With an OpenShift 4.x cluster, the control plane hosts are configured with Red Hat CoreOS as the operating system. When upgrades occur for the cluster, the operating system of the control plane nodes are also upgraded. The CoreOS package manager uses a novel approach to applying updates: updates are packaged into containers and applied transactionally. Either the entire update succeeds or fails. When managing the update of an OpenShift control plane, the result of this approach limits the potential for partially completed or failed installs from the interaction of unknown or untested configurations within the operating system. By default, the operating system provisioned for workers will also use Red Hat CoreOS, allowing the data plane of your cluster the same transactional update benefits.

It is possible to add workers to an OpenShift cluster configured with RHEL. The process to add a RHEL worker node is covered in the product documentation and is beyond the scope of this book.

If you integrate a managed Kubernetes service into your multicluster strategy, pay attention to the division of responsibilities between your vendor and your teams: who owns the currency/compliance status of the worker nodes in the cluster? Virtually all of the managed Kubernetes service providers manage the operating system of the control plane nodes. However, there is variance across the major cloud vendors on who is responsible for the operating system of the worker nodes.

Summary

We have covered quite a bit in this chapter. By now, you should understand how IPI provides a consistent abstraction of many infrastructure substrates. Once provisioned, operators within OpenShift manage the life-cycle operations for key functions of the cluster, including machine management, authentication, networking, and storage. We can also use the API exposed by these operators to request and drive upgrade operations against the control plane of the cluster and the operating system of the supporting nodes.

We also introduced cluster life-cycle management from Open Cluster Management (*https://oreil.ly/3J1SW*) using a supporting offering, Red Hat Advanced Cluster Management. Using RHACM, we saw how to trigger the upgrade behavior for user-managed clusters on any infrastructure substrate.

In the next chapter, we will continue to leverage cluster operators to configure and drive cluster behavior by defining Open Cluster Management policies that we can apply to one or more clusters under management.

## CHAPTER 7

Multicluster Policy Configuration

A key aspect of Kubernetes that we've already seen is how it is a declarative, API-driven system. Initial support for orchestration focused purely on containers and their required support services, such as network services, `PersistentVolumeClaims`, and administrative policies. Now we will look at how we can generalize the underlying pattern that Kubernetes API controllers follow. It turns out, declarative management of applications is also a great way to operate the Kubernetes cluster itself. In this chapter, we will discuss the concept of an operator and how we can use operators to simplify the management of our clusters.

Configuring Your Cluster with Operators

Let's talk a bit about how the Kubernetes system works and how you can extend the system to meet your needs.

Understanding Operators

Each API provider includes a balancing loop (pictured in Figure 7-1): observe actual system state, reconcile with desired system state, apply changes, and report status.

Such a powerful pattern led to more orchestration providers and ultimately was generalized to allow the creation of new CRDs and their responsible controllers in Kubernetes 1.16. Controllers react to the presence of new custom resources (that are instances of CRDs) or updates to existing custom resources. Controllers also interact with objects under management, traditionally containers or pods, but now the vocabulary exposed by CRDs allows for the management of stateful workloads that require additional orchestration behaviors, of VMs, and even of cloud-based services (such as object store, database as a service, etc.). The net is that you can use the Kubernetes API paradigm to program a broad array of infrastructure and application services using a consistent approach and a source-controllable representation of the declarative API.

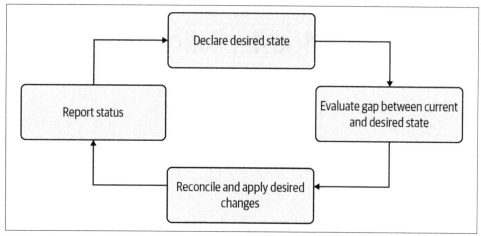

Figure 7-1. A balancing loop reconciles the observed differences between the desired state and current state of the system

Red Hat helped catalyze the community around the operator framework, or a way of applying Kubernetes controllers to manage software life cycles, including deployment, configuration, upgrade, and decommissioning. You can leverage these operators on OperatorHub.io (*https://operatorhub.io*) to more easily manage the containerized software running on your cluster. We will see an example of how to deploy an operator in the next section.

Red Hat OpenShift applies operators to the management of the entire platform, from initiating a cluster and its supporting infrastructure-provisioning life cycle to configuring DNS routes for cluster services to configuring identity providers. In essence, virtually all aspects of cluster state are specified through declarative APIs (via CRDs), and operators implement the intelligent life cycle of reconciliation (e.g., the balancing loop pattern discussed previously).

What distinguishes a controller and an operator? This is largely subjective, and discussion ranges from the intent of the orchestrator (e.g., operators are for the management of software life cycles running in containers) to how you might deploy the orchestrator to your cluster (a simple Kubernetes deployment versus an operator life cycle bundle). Subjective discussion aside, we will talk about operators as custom Kubernetes CRDs and controllers created by the operator-sdk.

In Figure 7-2, we can see the operators available that are built and published by Red Hat alongside the operators that are built and supported by the community.

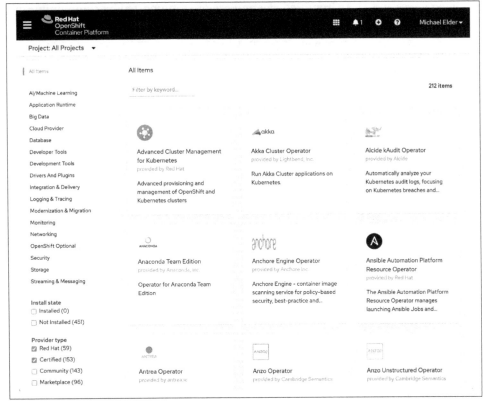

Figure 7-2. The Operator Catalog in Red Hat OpenShift

Example: Container Security Operator

You can consume operators in OpenShift in two steps. First, deploy the operator itself. Second, deploy one or more resources managed by the operator. Let's practice deploying an operator that will help with image security scans in your cluster.

The following example demonstrates how to deploy an example operator, the Container Security operator. You will need an OpenShift Container Platform 4.4+ cluster to follow the demonstration on your own. Follow these steps:

1. **Open the OperatorHub catalog and find the Container Security operator.** From the web console, open the Operators > OperatorHub section and enter "container security" in the filter text box. A tile named "Container Security" should remain in the list.

2. **Open the Container Security operator overview** (as shown in Figure 7-3). Click the tile. If a message about Community operators appears, review the message and click Continue. Community operators do not qualify for official support

guarantees and SLAs from Red Hat and are often supported by community contributors in the upstream.

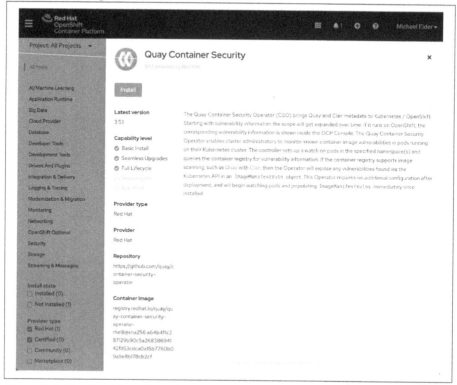

Figure 7-3. The Container Security operator overview page

3. **Review the summary and click Install.** The Summary page describes the operator and other supporting details. Pay attention to the Capability Level and Provider Type attributes, as these are critical to understanding whether you should adopt a particular operator for your needs.

4. **Configure the operator subscription** (as shown in Figure 7-4). Review your desired choices for the Update Channel and Approval Strategy, then click Subscribe.

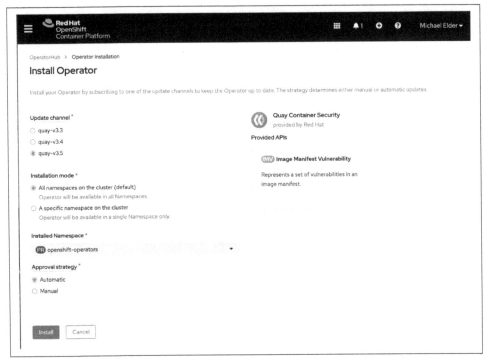

Figure 7-4. Configuring the Operator Lifecycle Manager (OLM) subscription to install the Container Security operator

Subscriptions enable an operator to consume updates as needed, either with manual or automatic approval. For each operator, you must decide what choice to make for the Update Channel and the Approval Strategy.

The *Update Channel* for each operator can be different and reflects how often updates to the operator behavior will be made available and how stable the updates are. Channels might reflect stable, released, supported versions of the operator or early-access developer previews. The channel you pick will depend on the operator and your specific needs and risk tolerance.

The *Approval Strategy* allows you to inject a manual decision prior to upgrades. Operators that follow best practices should be able to apply updates without causing an outage in supported services. The best practice, where possible, is to allow upgrades to proceed automatically, applying the latest security and function fixes that are available.

Now that we have applied an example operator, let's take a look at the new behavior available to our cluster. The act of subscribing to the new operator created two resources on your cluster: `ClusterServiceVersion` and `Subscription`.

The `ClusterServiceVersion` resource provides metadata about the operator, including details like display names and a description, as well as operational metadata about the types of custom resources that the operator can manage and the types of RBAC required to support the operator's behavior on the cluster.

The following example provides a list of the `ClusterServiceVersion` resources defined in the cluster:

```
$ oc get clusterserviceversion
NAME                                  DISPLAY
VERSION    REPLACES    PHASE
advanced-cluster-management.v1.0.0    Advanced Cluster Management for Kubernetes
1.0.0                  Succeeded
container-security-operator.v1.0.5    Container Security
1.0.5                  Succeeded
etcdoperator.v0.9.4                   etcd
0.9.4                  Succeeded
openshift-pipelines-operator.v1.0.1   OpenShift Pipelines Operator
1.0.1                  Succeeded
```

Each of these resources defines metadata about an operator that is installed on the cluster and defines information about what the operator contributes to the cluster, including the CRDs (remember, this is the Kubernetes way of adding new types to the API model).

The `Subscription` resource declares the intent to apply the operator to the cluster. The OLM will apply resources, including roles, `RoleBindings`, a service account, the CRDs acted upon by the operator, and of course the operator's deployment. After all, the operator is just another Kubernetes controller, ever reconciling desired state and actual state.

In the following example, we see which operators are deployed in the cluster based on the subscription API provided by the OLM framework:

```
$ oc get subscriptions.operators.coreos.com -n openshift-operators
NAME                              PACKAGE                       SOURCE
                   CHANNEL
container-security-operator       container-security-operator   community-
operators          alpha
```

The OLM handles the installation, upgrade, and removal of operators on your cluster. For OpenShift Container Platform clusters, the OLM is deployed out of the box. You can optionally deploy OLM against any compliant Kubernetes cluster as well.

Each subscription results in a set of installed CRDs and running pods that act on those custom types.

Using Cluster Operators to Manage OpenShift

As we saw with the provisioning life cycle of OpenShift 4.x clusters, operators play a central role in how the cluster is configured and continuously reconciled. We can introspect the special operators that manage underlying cluster behavior using the following command:

```
$ oc get clusteroperators
NAME                                      VERSION   AVAILABLE   PROGRESSING
DEGRADED    SINCE
authentication                            4.4.3     True        False
False       48d
cloud-credential                          4.4.3     True        False
False       48d
cluster-autoscaler                        4.4.3     True        False
False       48d
console                                   4.4.3     True        False
False       48d
csi-snapshot-controller                   4.4.3     True        False
False       48d
dns                                       4.4.3     True        False
False       48d
etcd                                      4.4.3     True        False
False       28h
image-registry                            4.4.3     True        False
False       48d
ingress                                   4.4.3     True        False
False       48d
insights                                  4.4.3     True        False
False       48d
kube-apiserver                            4.4.3     True        False
False       48d
kube-controller-manager                   4.4.3     True        False
False       48d
kube-scheduler                            4.4.3     True        False
False       48d
kube-storage-version-migrator             4.4.3     True        False
False       48d
machine-api                               4.4.3     True        False
False       48d
machine-config                            4.4.3     True        False
False       48d
marketplace                               4.4.3     True        False
False       48d
monitoring                                4.4.3     True        False
False       41h
network                                   4.4.3     True        False
False       48d
node-tuning                               4.4.3     True        False
False       48d
openshift-apiserver                       4.4.3     True        False
False       38d
openshift-controller-manager              4.4.3     True        False
False       48d
openshift-samples                         4.4.3     True        False
```

```
False      48d
operator-lifecycle-manager              4.4.3    True      False
False      48d
operator-lifecycle-manager-catalog      4.4.3    True      False
False      48d
operator-lifecycle-manager-packageserver 4.4.3   True      False
False      28h
service-ca                              4.4.3    True      False
False      48d
service-catalog-apiserver               4.4.3    True      False
False      48d
service-catalog-controller-manager      4.4.3    True      False
False      48d
storage                                 4.4.3    True      False
False      48d
```

For each of these operators, there will be one or more CRDs that define an API you can configure or query to understand the state of the cluster. What is extremely powerful is that, regardless of the infrastructure substrate supporting the OpenShift 4.x cluster, the API and operators function in a consistent manner.

Example: Configuring the Authentication Operator

Access control is obviously critical for any organization. To support authentication, a Kubernetes provider must establish the identity of a given user or service account. Identity can be established by means of traditional user credentials, *Transport Layer Security* (TLS) certificates, or security tokens, as in the case of service accounts. When no identity information is presented in an API, the user identity is treated as the identity `system:anonymous`.

The Kubernetes API server is configured with options for how to trust information about identity that is provided for each API request. Information about the identity is then asserted for each API request and validated by the Kubernetes API server prior to allowing the request to proceed.

A few special identities beyond typical users to be aware of are listed in Table 7-1.

Table 7-1. Example identities available within a Kubernetes cluster to specify as the subject of a RoleBinding or ClusterRoleBinding

Identity	Description
Anonymous requests without an explicitly provided identity: User: `system:anonymous` Group: `system:unauthenticated`	Provides a default identity for any incoming API requests that have not provided identity information. You can establish what (if any) default API resources are available to anonymous requests by way of Kubernetes RBAC.
All authenticated requests: User: * Group: `system:authenticated`	All authenticated requests will include the group `system:authenticated` to support establishing default permissions across all users.

Identity	Description
Any request using *Mutual Transport Layer Security* (mTLS) authentication by X.509 certificates: User: Common Name specified in the certificate (e.g., CN=username) Group: Organizations specified in the certificate (e.g., O=group1/ O=group2) To create an example X.509 certificate: **$ openssl req -new -key username.pem -out username-csr.pem \\ -subj "/CN=username/O=group1/O=group2"**	Any API request made with mTLS authentication from an X.509 certificate that is signed either by the cluster Certificate Authority (CA) or the `--client-ca-file=SOMEFILE` command option provided to the Kubernetes API server will authenticate as `username` with groups `group1` and `group2`.
Any request made by a service account: User: `system:serviceaccount:<namespace>:<serv iceaccount>` Group: `system:serviceaccounts, system:serviceac counts:<namespace>`	A service account is an identity created by the API server typically for nonhuman actors like bots or long-running jobs. Service accounts establish a token that can be used externally or internally by pods that work with the Kubernetes API server. Service accounts work like any other identity and can be referenced by Kubernetes RBAC to associate permissions.

 Service accounts can be a simple and enticing way to set up automation against your clusters, but take note that service account tokens are long lived and do not automatically rotate or expire. If you have the need for long-running automated access, consider whether to use mTLS certificates (which can have set expiration dates and are resistant to some kinds of security infiltration attacks). Performance of requests using service accounts can also be limited, as for every request made, the kube-apiserver will make a call to itself to retrieve the service account token and validate it. At extremely high API request rates, this can become a bottleneck.

OpenShift simplifies the management of identity by way of *identity providers* (IdPs) that are configured through operators on the platform. When a user or service account authenticates, typically an IdP accepts and validates credential information for the requestor. Through command options to the Kubernetes API server, trust is established between the IdP and the Kubernetes API server for incoming requests and used for authorization in the Kubernetes API server. Later, we'll see how the identity is then authorized using Kubernetes RBAC.

A number of IdPs are available in OpenShift. Here, we will discuss a subset of the most commonly used IdPs. In addition, we will review how managed Kubernetes as a Service providers associate identity in relation to the cloud provider's *identity and access management* (IAM).

The OAuth kind in the API group config.openshift.io with version v1 is a cluster-scoped resource that allows complete control over the available IdPs for OpenShift. The canonical name for this resource is `cluster`:

```
apiVersion: config.openshift.io/v1
kind: OAuth
metadata:
 name: cluster
spec:
 identityProviders: []
 tokenConfig:
   accessTokenMaxAgeSeconds: 86400
```

When configured, the authentication cluster operator will respond to configure the specified IdPs or report the status if there is a problem.

OpenShift htpasswd Identity Provider

The htpasswd IdP is about as simple as it comes. The provider establishes identities and credentials by the standard *.htpasswd* file format, loaded into a secret. If you have a cluster shared by a small group (such as a "department" or "project" scope), consider whether this approach allows you to assign and maintain identities for your needs.

Follow these steps to configure the htpasswd IdP:

1. Create or update an *.htpasswd* file with your users.

2. Create or update the htpasswd secret in openshift-config.

3. Update the cluster OAuth resource to list the htpasswd IdP and reference the htpasswd secret in the openshift-config namespace.

Use htpasswd to generate or update an existing file:

```
$ htpasswd -c -b -B .htpasswd username password
```

Then create or apply updates from this file to the secret maintained in openshift-config:

```
$ oc create secret generic htpass-secret --from-file=htpasswd=.htpasswd -n
openshift-config
```

Finally, update the cluster OAuth API resource as follows:

```
apiVersion: config.openshift.io/v1
kind: OAuth
metadata:
 name: cluster
spec:
 identityProviders:
 - htpasswd:
     fileData:
       name: htpass-secret
   mappingMethod: claim
   name: htpasswdidp
   type: htpasswd
```

```
tokenConfig:
    accessTokenMaxAgeSeconds: 86400
```

Policy and Compliance Across Multiple Clusters

Now let's take a look at how we can declaratively manage the desired configuration after the cluster is provisioned. For this topic, we will introduce additional aspects of the Open Cluster Management project (*https://oreil.ly/3J1SW*) and use RHACM, which provides a supported distribution of this open source project.

First, we need a way to describe policies for our cluster fleet. The Open Cluster Management project introduces the `Policy` (API group: policy.open-cluster-management.io) API to describe the desired configuration, along with rules about whether the expected configuration "must" exist or "must not" exist. Policies can also be configured to audit a cluster and report if the cluster configuration is compliant. Alternatively, policies can be enforced, ensuring that the cluster matches the desired configuration and is considered compliant as a result.

We will express a `Policy` resource that acts as an envelope of one or more (1..*) `ConfigurationPolicies` (API group: policy.open-cluster-management.io). Each `ConfigurationPolicy` is then able to describe one or more (1..*) configurations as a rule set. The policy can be enforced as required, in which case changes are made to ensure compliance, or audit only to report compliance of the fleet (see Figure 7-5). Since we're talking about Kubernetes, each policy is continuously reconciled against fleet members, even when a specific fleet member may lose connectivity to the control plane hub cluster.

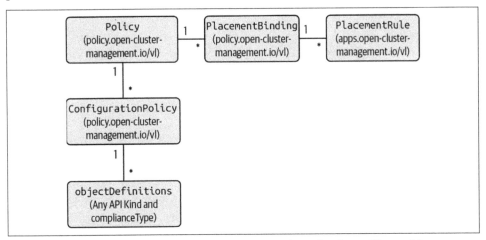

Figure 7-5. Visual representation of the `Policy` API from the Open Cluster Management Project

Policy Example: Federate a Project Across Your Fleet

Let's start with a simple example where we want to federate a specific project across all clusters in the fleet. We have a single `Policy` envelope that contains a single `ConfigurationPolicy` for our desired project, named `frontend-app-prod`, along with a required `LimitRange` configuration to ensure that all pods deployed in our project describe memory requests. This example shows a `Policy` envelope with nested configurations for a project and a `LimitRange` for that project:

```
apiVersion: policy.open-cluster-management.io/v1
kind: Policy
metadata:
 name: policy-project-frontend-app-prod
 namespace: open-cluster-management-policies
 annotations:
   policy.open-cluster-management.io/standards: NIST-CSF
   policy.open-cluster-management.io/categories: PR.IP Information Protection
Processes and Procedures
   policy.open-cluster-management.io/controls: PR.IP-1 Baseline configuration
spec:
 disabled: false
 remediationAction: enforce
 policy-templates:
 - objectDefinition:
     apiVersion: policy.open-cluster-management.io/v1
     kind: ConfigurationPolicy
     metadata:
       name: policy-project-frontend-app-prod
     spec:
       namespaceSelector:
         exclude:
         - kube-*
         include:
         - default
         - frontend-app-prod
       object-templates:
       - complianceType: musthave
         objectDefinition:
           apiVersion: project.openshift.io/v1
           kind: Project
           metadata:
             name: frontend-app-prod
         status:
           Validity: {}
       - complianceType: musthave
         objectDefinition:
           apiVersion: v1
           kind: LimitRange
           metadata:
             name: mem-limit-range
             namespace: frontend-app-prod
           spec:
             limits:
               - default:
```

```
          memory: 512Mi
        defaultRequest:
          memory: 256Mi
        type: Container
---
apiVersion: policy.open-cluster-management.io/v1
kind: PlacementBinding
metadata:
 name: binding-policy-project-frontend-app-prod
 namespace: open-cluster-management-policies
placementRef:
 name: production-clusters
 kind: PlacementRule
 apiGroup: apps.open-cluster-management.io
subjects:
- name: policy-project-frontend-app-prod
 kind: Policy
 apiGroup: policy.open-cluster-management.io
---
apiVersion: apps.open-cluster-management.io/v1
kind: PlacementRule
metadata:
 name: placement-policy-project-frontend-app-prod
 namespace: open-cluster-management-policies
spec:
 clusterConditions:
 - status: "True"
   type: ManagedClusterConditionAvailable
 clusterSelector:
   matchExpressions: []
```

Take note of the following important aspects of the previous example:

- The Policy describes categorization that allows an auditor to quickly understand which technical controls are noncompliant if the given Policy cannot be properly enforced.

- The ConfigurationPolicy specifies namespaces that are governed by the ConfigurationPolicy and can optionally specify an overriding value for remediationAction if the list of ConfigurationPolicies within a single envelope has a mix of enforcement and auditing behavior. Further, the severity of a given ConfigurationPolicy can provide hints to an operator on how to prioritize compliance remediation if violations are detected.

- The object-templates specify a desired template (either an entire API object or a patch) and a complianceType rule of whether the desired configuration should exist, should not exist, or should be unique.

- The PlacementRule describes how to match a Policy against a set of available clusters. We'll talk more about how these work shortly.

- The `PlacementBinding` links the `Policy` to a `PlacementRule`. A given `Policy` can be bound to multiple `PlacementRules`. Each `PlacementRule` can match zero or more clusters.

The annotations applied to the `Policy` allow users to organize violations according to their own technical standards. In the previous example, the annotations link this `Policy` to the National Institute of Standards and Technology Cybersecurity Framework (NIST-CSF) standard under the "Information Protection Processes and Procedures" category as part of the "Baseline configuration" controls:

```
policy.open-cluster-management.io/standards: NIST-CSF
    policy.open-cluster-management.io/categories: PR.IP Information Protection
Processes and Procedures
    policy.open-cluster-management.io/controls: PR.IP-1 Baseline configuration
```

An open library for policies (*https://oreil.ly/hdqzx*) that are categorized according to the NIST-053 is available.

The `complianceType` allows you to define how the `Policy` engine will address a non-compliant rule:

```
object-templates:
        - complianceType: musthave
          objectDefinition:
            apiVersion: project.openshift.io/v1
            kind: Project
            metadata:
              name: frontend-app-prod
            status:
            Validity: {}
```

The enumerated values for `complianceType` include:

musthave
> More than one of the desired configurations may exist, but at least one of the desired configurations must match the given `objectDefinition` as specified. When the `remediationAction` is `enforce`, the relevant `objectDefinitions` will be applied to the cluster. If the `objectDefinitions` cannot be applied, the status of the policy will note the ongoing violation.

mustonlyhave
> Exactly one matching configuration must be present and no more. This is particularly useful when expressing desired configurations for RBAC or security context constraints. If more than one applicable configuration is found, then the status of the policy will note the ongoing violation.

mustnothave

If a matching configuration is found that conforms to the objectDefinition, then a violation has been detected. If a violation is found, then the status of the policy will note the ongoing violation.

PlacementRules to Assign Content to ManagedClusters

PlacementRules (API group: apps.open-cluster-management.io) are a powerful mechanism used by Open Cluster Management to assign content to clusters. Each PlacementRule allows you to specify a clusterSelector and clusterConditions to match available ManagedClusters. Remember that ManagedClusters define labels like any Kubernetes object. The clusterSelector defines a combination of match Expression or matchLabels that is evaluated against available ManagedClusters.

The matchExpressions clause can use binary operators defined by Kubernetes, including In, NotIn, and Exists. For example, if you wanted to match a Managed Cluster with the labels apps/pacman=deployed, region=us-east, env=development, and authenticationProfile=htpasswd, the following combination would work:

```
matchLabels:
    apps/pacman: deployed
  matchExpressions:
    - {key: region, operator: In, values: [us-east, us-west]}
    - {key: env, operator: NotIn, values: [development]}
    - {key: authenticationProfile, operator: Exists}
```

In addition to the clusterSelector, PlacementRules can evaluate the conditions that a ManagedCluster has reported in its status. Three status conditions are available as of the time of this writing that can be used:

HubAcceptedManagedCluster

Indicates that the ManagedCluster was allowed to join by a cluster-manager-admin user

ManagedClusterConditionAvailable

Indicates that the ManagedCluster has updated its lease reservation within the required period of time and is considered available by the hub

ManagedClusterJoined

Indicates that the ManagedCluster has completed the registration protocol and has established a valid connection with the control plane hub cluster

RBAC is important to consider when creating a PlacementRule. When a user creates a PlacementRule, only ManagedClusters that the user has access to are available to be evaluated for set inclusion. Hence, the user or role that is responsible for defining

`PlacementRules` has a lot of control over how broadly content can be applied to the entire fleet.

Policy Example: Managing etcd Encryption Within ManagedClusters

The `APIServer` kind within an OpenShift cluster can be configured to encrypt any sensitive resources, including secrets, `ConfigMaps`, routes, OAuth access tokens, and OAuth authorization tokens. To ensure that all clusters in the fleet use encryption, we can define a policy that will update all cluster `APIServer` kinds to specify what type of encryption should be used. Using `PlacementRules`, we can match this policy against our desired clusters.

In the following example, we see a policy that is ensuring that the `APIServer` CRD, managed by OpenShift, is configured to enforce application-level encryption of sensitive data within etcd:

```
apiVersion: policy.open-cluster-management.io/v1
kind: Policy
metadata:
 name: policy-etcdencryption
 annotations:
   policy.open-cluster-management.io/standards: NIST SP 800-53
   policy.open-cluster-management.io/categories: CM Configuration Management
   policy.open-cluster-management.io/controls: CM-2 Baseline Configuration
spec:
 remediationAction: enforce
 disabled: false
 policy-templates:
   - objectDefinition:
       apiVersion: policy.open-cluster-management.io/v1
       kind: ConfigurationPolicy
       metadata:
         name: enable-etcd-encryption
       spec:
         severity: high
         namespaceSelector:
           exclude:
             - kube-*
           include:
             - default
         object-templates:
           - complianceType: musthave
             objectDefinition:
               apiVersion: config.openshift.io/v1
               kind: APIServer
               metadata:
                 name: cluster
               spec:
                 encryption:
                   type: aescbc
   ---
apiVersion: policy.open-cluster-management.io/v1
```

```
kind: PlacementBinding
metadata:
 name: binding-policy-etcdencryption
placementRef:
 name: placement-policy-etcdencryption
 kind: PlacementRule
 apiGroup: apps.open-cluster-management.io
subjects:
- name: policy-etcdencryption
 kind: Policy
 apiGroup: policy.open-cluster-management.io
---
apiVersion: apps.open-cluster-management.io/v1
kind: PlacementRule
metadata:
 name: placement-policy-etcdencryption
spec:
 clusterConditions:
 - status: "True"
   type: ManagedClusterConditionAvailable
 clusterSelector:
   matchExpressions:
     - {key: environment, operator: In, values: ["dev", "prod"]}
```

After applying this policy, any ManagedCluster with the label environment=dev or environment=prod will be updated to configure the APIServer (API group: config.openshift.io) to use encryption for any sensitive resources. You can connect directly to the managed cluster to review the progress of encrypting the etcd datastore as described in the OpenShift product documentation. In this example, the command is retrieving status conditions from the OpenShiftAPIServer object and printing information about the current progress:

```
$ oc get openshiftapiserver \
  -o=jsonpath='{range.items[0].status.conditions[?(@.type=="Encrypted")]}
  {.reason}{"\n"}{.message}{"\n"}'

EncryptionInProgress
Resource routes.route.openshift.io is not encrypted
…

$ oc get openshiftapiserver \
  -o=jsonpath='{range.items[0].status.conditions[?(@.type=="Encrypted")]}
  {.reason}{"\n"}{.message}{"\n"}'

EncryptionInProgress
Resource routes.route.openshift.io is being encrypted
…
$ oc get openshiftapiserver \
  -o=jsonpath='{range.items[0].status.conditions[?(@.type=="Encrypted")]}
  {.reason}{"\n"}{.message}{"\n"}'

EncryptionCompleted
All resources encrypted: routes.route.openshift.io,
oauthaccesstokens.oauth.openshift.io, oauthauthorizetokens.oauth.openshift.io
```

If you simply wanted to audit for whether sensitive resources managed in the etcd datastore were encrypted, you can change the remediationAction to inform, and the policy will report any ManagedCluster that is not encrypting its API state as noncompliant.

Policy Example: Managing RBAC Within ManagedClusters

One of the benefits of OpenShift's consistency is that you have the same set of ClusterRoles and roles out of the box across all platforms. You may choose to add additional roles to meet your specific organization's needs.

 Of course, modifying the out-of-the-box roles is strongly discouraged because that can be reverted or prevent successful upgrades as you adopt maintenance updates. That said, you can always create new ClusterRoles or roles to meet your organization's standards.

The following example defines two roles: developer-read and developer-write. These are cluster-scoped roles. If you create a ClusterRoleBinding to a user or group, then you are granting cluster-wide access to the resources enumerated in the ClusterRole. If you create a RoleBinding within a specific namespace or project, then the user will have access to the enumerated resources only within that specific project.

In the following code example, a policy with category AC Access Control under the control AC-3 Access Enforcement is defined that will ensure that any matching cluster has the ClusterRoles specified within object-templates defined:

```
apiVersion: policy.open-cluster-management.io/v1
kind: Policy
metadata:
 name: policy-role-developer
 annotations:
   policy.open-cluster-management.io/standards: NIST SP 800-53
   policy.open-cluster-management.io/categories: AC Access Control
   policy.open-cluster-management.io/controls: AC-3 Access Enforcement
spec:
 remediationAction: enforce
 disabled: false
 policy-templates:
   - objectDefinition:
       apiVersion: policy.open-cluster-management.io/v1
       kind: ConfigurationPolicy
       metadata:
         name: policy-role-developer
       spec:
         remediationAction: enforce
          severity: high
         namespaceSelector:
```

```
          exclude: ["kube-*"]
          include: ["default"]
      object-templates:
        - complianceType: mustonlyhave # role definition should exact match
          objectDefinition:
            apiVersion: rbac.authorization.k8s.io/v1
            kind: ClusterRole
            metadata:
              name: developer-read
            rules:
              - apiGroups: ["*"]
                resources: ["deployments", "configmaps", "services", "secrets"]
                verbs: ["get", "list", "watch"]
        - complianceType: mustonlyhave # role definition should exact match
          objectDefinition:
            apiVersion: rbac.authorization.k8s.io/v1
            kind: ClusterRole
            metadata:
              name: developer-write
            rules:
              - apiGroups: ["*"]
                resources: ["deployments", "configmaps", "services", "secrets"]
                verbs: ["create", "delete", "patch", "update"]
---
apiVersion: policy.open-cluster-management.io/v1
kind: PlacementBinding
metadata:
 name: binding-policy-role-developer
placementRef:
 name: placement-policy-role-developer
 kind: PlacementRule
 apiGroup: apps.open-cluster-management.io
subjects:
- name: policy-role-developer
 kind: Policy
 apiGroup: policy.open-cluster-management.io
---
apiVersion: apps.open-cluster-management.io/v1
kind: PlacementRule
metadata:
 name: placement-policy-role-developer
spec:
 clusterConditions:
 - status: "True"
   type: ManagedClusterConditionAvailable
 clusterSelector:
   matchExpressions:
     - {key: environment, operator: In, values: ["dev"]}
```

If you think about how your security protocols provide for separation of duty, you can follow the same pattern to enforce your anticipated permissions for each logical security role provided for your users.

A second policy ensures that any project named pacman-app contains a RoleBinding for a specific group named game-developers. The group would be defined by your

IdP for the cluster (e.g., a Lightweight Directory Access Protocol service). This shows an example to configure the user group game-developers to have a binding to the ClusterRoles developer-read and developer-write:

```
apiVersion: policy.open-cluster-management.io/v1
kind: Policy
metadata:
 name: policy-role-developer-binding
 annotations:
   policy.open-cluster-management.io/standards: NIST SP 800-53
   policy.open-cluster-management.io/categories: AC Access Control
   policy.open-cluster-management.io/controls: AC-3 Access Enforcement
spec:
 remediationAction: enforce
 disabled: false
 policy-templates:
   - objectDefinition:
       apiVersion: policy.open-cluster-management.io/v1
       kind: ConfigurationPolicy
       metadata:
         name: policy-role-developer-binding
       spec:
         remediationAction: enforce
         severity: high
         namespaceSelector:
           exclude: ["kube-*"]
           include: ["default"]
         object-templates:
           - complianceType: mustonlyhave # role definition should exact match
             objectDefinition:
               apiVersion: rbac.authorization.k8s.io/v1
               kind: RoleBinding
               metadata:
                 name: role-developer-read-binding
                 namespace: game-app
               roleRef:
                 apiGroup: rbac.authorization.k8s.io
                 kind: ClusterRole
                 name: developer-read
               subjects:
               - apiGroup: rbac.authorization.k8s.io
                 kind: Group
                 name: "game-developers"
           - complianceType: mustonlyhave # role definition should exact match
             objectDefinition:
               apiVersion: rbac.authorization.k8s.io/v1
               kind: RoleBinding
               metadata:
                 name: role-developer-read-binding
                 namespace: game-app
               roleRef:
                 apiGroup: rbac.authorization.k8s.io
                 kind: ClusterRole
                 name: developer-write
               subjects:
```

```
                - apiGroup: rbac.authorization.k8s.io
                  kind: Group
                  name: "game-developers"
---
apiVersion: policy.open-cluster-management.io/v1
kind: PlacementBinding
metadata:
 name: binding-policy-role-developer-binding
placementRef:
 name: placement-policy-role-developer-binding
 kind: PlacementRule
 apiGroup: apps.open-cluster-management.io
subjects:
- name: policy-role-developer-binding
 kind: Policy
 apiGroup: policy.open-cluster-management.io
---
apiVersion: apps.open-cluster-management.io/v1
kind: PlacementRule
metadata:
 name: placement-policy-role-developer-binding
spec:
 clusterConditions:
 - status: "True"
   type: ManagedClusterConditionAvailable
 clusterSelector:
   matchExpressions:
     - {key: environment, operator: In, values: ["dev"]}
```

If either policy in these two samples were to be in violation, then you would have direct feedback that your access control protocols may be incorrectly configured, either granting certain users too much control or other users not enough control.

Policy Example: Managing IdPs Within ManagedClusters

For every cluster that you provision, you are going to want to define how the cluster recognizes identities. OpenShift has an authentication operator that allows you to define how the cluster validates an identity provided by user credentials. One of the most straightforward IdPs uses an htpasswd-formatted credential file, defined by a secret in a particular namespace (openshift-config). Here we define a policy that configures the OAuth API object on the cluster to respect an IdP of type htpasswd:

```
apiVersion: policy.open-cluster-management.io/v1
kind: Policy
metadata:
 name: policy-htpasswd-auth-provider
 namespace: open-cluster-management-policies
 annotations:
   policy.open-cluster-management.io/standards: NIST-CSF
   policy.open-cluster-management.io/categories: PR.IP Information Protection
Processes and Procedures
   policy.open-cluster-management.io/controls: PR.IP-1 Baseline configuration
 spec:
```

```yaml
        complianceType: mustonlyhave
        remediationAction: enforce
        disabled: false
        policy-templates:
        - objectDefinition:
            apiVersion: policy.open-cluster-management.io/v1
            kind: ConfigurationPolicy
            metadata:
              name: policy-htpasswd-auth-provider
            spec:
              object-templates:
              - complianceType: mustonlyhave
                objectDefinition:
                  apiVersion: config.openshift.io/v1
                  kind: OAuth
                  metadata:
                    name: cluster
                  spec:
                    identityProviders:
                    - htpasswd:
                        fileData:
                          name: htpass-secret
                      mappingMethod: claim
                      name: htpasswdidp
                      type: htpasswd
                    tokenConfig:
                      accessTokenMaxAgeSeconds: 7776000
              - complianceType: mustonlyhave
                objectDefinition:
                  apiVersion: v1
                  data:
                    htpasswd: ""
                  kind: Secret
                  metadata:
                    name: htpass-secret
                    namespace: openshift-config
                  type: Opaque
            # - complianceType: musthave
            #   objectDefinition:
            #     kind: Identity
            #     apiVersion: user.openshift.io/v1
            #     metadata:
            #       name: 'htpassidp:johndoe'
            #     providerName: htpassidp
            #     providerUserName: johndoe
            #     user:
            #       name: johndoe
            #       uid: e4d768dd-a6b5-489c-8900-2c18a160d76f
---
apiVersion: policy.open-cluster-management.io/v1
kind: PlacementBinding
metadata:
 name: binding-policy-htpasswd-auth-provider
 namespace: open-cluster-management-policies
placementRef:
 name: placement-policy-oauth-provider
```

```
  kind: PlacementRule
  apiGroup: apps.open-cluster-management.io
subjects:
- name: policy-htpasswd-auth-provider
  kind: Policy
  apiGroup: policy.open-cluster-management.io
---
apiVersion: apps.open-cluster-management.io/v1
kind: PlacementRule
metadata:
  name: placement-policy-oauth-provider
  namespace: open-cluster-management-policies
spec:
  clusterConditions:
  - status: "True"
    type: ManagedClusterConditionAvailable
  clusterSelector:
    matchExpressions:
    - key: authenticationProfile
      operator: In
      values:
      - htpasswd
    matchLabels: {}
```

In the previous example, we see that the following rules are enforced:

- The OAuth API kind is configured by this policy to use a custom identity provider.
- The htpasswd contents must be updated for this policy to be valid.

To create the contents of the htpasswd secret, use the htpasswd command:

```
$ touch htpasswd.txt
htpasswd -b -B htpasswd.txt username password
```

Then you can create a secret from the generated file to specify as another object Definition in the policy.

Policy Example: Managing Upgrades with Policy Across ManagedClusters

Keeping your cluster fleet up to date will undoubtedly be a core concern for any enterprise that is serious about security and maintenance updates. That's the kind of sentence that just writes itself—of course you want to keep your fleet up to date, and we're going to look at how you can do this with policies across the entire fleet.

As we have already discussed in this chapter, the OpenShift Container Platform encapsulates a substantial amount of in-cluster life-cycle management to upgrade the cluster in the CVO. We've also seen how RHACM can invoke upgrades for one or more clusters from the web console.

How do we accomplish the same thing declaratively? As you've seen, policies are going to play a big role here. To declaratively manage cluster versions, we need to specify the desired state of the `ClusterVersion` API object on a `ManagedCluster`. Here is an example policy that does exactly that:

```
# Upgrade Policy to select known desired version from public connected registry
apiVersion: policy.open-cluster-management.io/v1
kind: Policy
metadata:
 annotations:
   policy.open-cluster-management.io/categories: CM Configuration Management
   policy.open-cluster-management.io/controls: CM-2 Baseline Configuration
   policy.open-cluster-management.io/standards: NIST SP 800-53
 name: upgrade-cluster
 namespace: upgrade-policies
spec:
 disabled: false
 policy-templates:
 - objectDefinition:
     apiVersion: policy.open-cluster-management.io/v1
     kind: ConfigurationPolicy
     metadata:
       name: upgrade-cluster
     spec:
       namespaceSelector:
         exclude:
         - kube-*
         include:
         - '*'
       object-templates:
       - complianceType: musthave
         objectDefinition:
           apiVersion: config.openshift.io/v1
           kind: ClusterVersion
           metadata:
             name: version
           spec:
             desiredUpdate:
               force: false
               image: ""
               version: 4.5.9
       remediationAction: enforce
       severity: high
 remediationAction: enforce
status:
 # Note that the associated PlacementRules are omitted for this example
 placement:
 - placementBinding: binding-upgrade-cluster
   placementRule: placement-upgrade-cluster
 status:
 - clustername: east1
   clusternamespace: east1
   compliant: Compliant
```

The heart of this policy is the specification of the `ClusterVersion`:

```
apiVersion: config.openshift.io/v1
kind: ClusterVersion
metadata:
  name: version
spec:
  desiredUpdate:
    force: false
    image: ""
    version: 4.5.9
```

Here, the desired version (4.5.9) must be available from the associated channel that was configured for the cluster. Additionally, the assumption is that this cluster used the connected install method and remains connected to the public image registries for OpenShift.

What if your cluster cannot be created from the connected install method? OpenShift makes a disconnected install method available. To configure a disconnected image registry, please refer to the product documentation (*https://oreil.ly/rodMz*). The next example assumes that you have already configured a disconnected registry and that all clusters in the fleet are able to consume images from that registry.

For an OpenShift cluster to consume updates from a disconnected registry, the cluster must have a running instance of the OSUS operator deployed and configured. We can define a policy to configure this operator for any cluster in the fleet as follows:

```
# Configure the OpenShift Update Service (OSUS) also known informally as
"Cincinnati".
apiVersion: policy.open-cluster-management.io/v1
kind: Policy
metadata:
 annotations:
   policy.open-cluster-management.io/categories: PR.IP Information Protection
Processes
     and Procedures
   policy.open-cluster-management.io/controls: PR.IP-1 Baseline Configuration
   policy.open-cluster-management.io/standards: NIST-CSF
 name: policy-cincinatti-operator
 namespace: upgrade-policies
spec:
 disabled: false
 policy-templates:
 - objectDefinition:
     apiVersion: policy.open-cluster-management.io/v1
     kind: ConfigurationPolicy
     metadata:
       name: cincinatti-policy-prod
     spec:
       namespaceSelector:
         exclude:
         - kube-*
         include:
         - default
       object-templates:
```

```
        apiVersion: cincinnati.openshift.io/v1beta1
        kind: Cincinnati
        metadata:
          name: example-cincinnati
        spec:
          registry: quay.io
          replicas: 1
          repository: openshift-release-dev/ocp-release
    remediationAction: inform
    severity: low
- objectDefinition:
    apiVersion: policy.open-cluster-management.io/v1
    kind: ConfigurationPolicy
    metadata:
      name: cincinatti-policy-subscription
    spec:
      namespaceSelector:
        exclude:
        - kube-*
        include:
        - default
      object-templates:
      - complianceType: musthave
        objectDefinition:
          apiVersion: operators.coreos.com/v1alpha1
          kind: Subscription
          metadata:
            name: cincinnati-subscription
            namespace: cincinnati-operator
          spec:
            channel: alpha
            installPlanApproval: Automatic
            name: cincinnati-operator
            source: redhat-operators
            sourceNamespace: openshift-marketplace
    remediationAction: inform
    severity: low
- objectDefinition:
    apiVersion: policy.open-cluster-management.io/v1
    kind: ConfigurationPolicy
    metadata:
      name: cincinatti-policy-operatorgroup
    spec:
      namespaceSelector:
        exclude:
        - kube-*
        include:
        - default
      object-templates:
      - complianceType: musthave
        objectDefinition:
          apiVersion: operators.coreos.com/v1
          kind: OperatorGroup
          metadata:
            name: cincinnati-operatorgroup
            namespace: cincinnati-operator
```

```
          spec:
            targetNamespaces:
            - cincinnati-operator
        remediationAction: inform
        severity: low
   remediationAction: enforce
 status:
  placement:
  - placementBinding: binding-policy-cincinatti-operator
    placementRule: placement-policy-cincinatti-operator
 ---
 apiVersion: policy.open-cluster-management.io/v1
 kind: Policy
 metadata:
  annotations:
    policy.open-cluster-management.io/categories:
      PR.IP Information Protection
 Processes
      and Procedures
    policy.open-cluster-management.io/controls: PR.IP-1 Baseline Configuration
    policy.open-cluster-management.io/standards: NIST-CSF
  name: policy-config-imageconfig
  namespace: upgrade-policies
 spec:
  disabled: false
  policy-templates:
  - objectDefinition:
      apiVersion: policy.open-cluster-management.io/v1
      kind: ConfigurationPolicy
      metadata:
        name: policy-config-imageconfig-prod
      spec:
        namespaceSelector:
          exclude:
          - kube-*
          include:
          - default
        object-templates:
        - complianceType: musthave
          objectDefinition:
            apiVersion: config.openshift.io/v1
            kind: Image
            metadata:
              name: cluster
            spec:
              additionalTrustedCA:
                name: trusted-ca
        remediationAction: inform
        severity: low
   remediationAction: enforce
 status:
  placement:
  - placementBinding: binding-policy-config-imageconfig
    placementRule: placement-policy-config-imageconfig
 ---
 apiVersion: policy.open-cluster-management.io/v1
```

```yaml
kind: Policy
metadata:
 annotations:
    policy.open-cluster-management.io/categories: PR.IP Information Protection
Processes
       and Procedures
    policy.open-cluster-management.io/controls: PR.IP-1 Baseline Configuration
    policy.open-cluster-management.io/standards: NIST-CSF
 name: policy-configmap-ca
 namespace: upgrade-policies
spec:
 disabled: false
 policy-templates:
 - objectDefinition:
     apiVersion: policy.open-cluster-management.io/v1
     kind: ConfigurationPolicy
     metadata:
       name: configmapca
     spec:
       namespaceSelector:
         exclude:
         - kube-*
         include:
         - default
       object-templates:
       - complianceType: musthave
         objectDefinition:
           apiVersion: v1
           data:
             cincinnati-registry: |-
               -----BEGIN CERTIFICATE-----
               YOUR_DISCONNECTED_REGISTRY_CERTIFICATE
               -----END CERTIFICATE-----
           kind: ConfigMap
           metadata:
             name: trusted-ca
             namespace: openshift-config
         remediationAction: inform
         severity: low
 remediationAction: enforce
status:
 placement:
 - placementBinding: binding-policy-configmap-ca
   placementRule: placement-policy-configmap-ca
---
apiVersion: policy.open-cluster-management.io/v1
kind: Policy
metadata:
 annotations:
    policy.open-cluster-management.io/categories: PR.IP Information Protection
Processes
       and Procedures
    policy.open-cluster-management.io/controls: PR.IP-1 Baseline Configuration
    policy.open-cluster-management.io/standards: NIST-CSF
 name: policy-namespace-operatorgroup
 namespace: upgrade-policies
```

```
spec:
  disabled: false
  policy-templates:
  - objectDefinition:
      apiVersion: policy.open-cluster-management.io/v1
      kind: ConfigurationPolicy
      metadata:
        name: policy-namespace-operatorgroup-prod
      spec:
        namespaceSelector:
          exclude:
          - kube-*
          include:
          - default
        object-templates:
        - complianceType: musthave
          objectDefinition:
            apiVersion: v1
            kind: Namespace
            metadata:
              name: cincinnati-operator
        remediationAction: inform
        severity: low
    remediationAction: enforce
  status:
    placement:
    - placementBinding: binding-policy-namespace-operatorgroup
      placementRule: placement-policy-namespace-operatorgroup
  # END Policies for cincinnati-operator
```

The previous example policy configures an operator that will support our disconnected installation by providing a valid "update graph" used to calculate how the cluster should proceed from its current version to a new desired version. The following kinds are required for this particular operator to be deployed and configured correctly:

kind: Cincinnati

The configuration of the Cincinnati operator. The OSUS operator defines a CRD that deploys additional pods on the cluster to help calculate the update graphs available to be consumed. A ClusterVersion API object will reference the update graph to know which versions are available to be upgraded. Information about available update graphs is stored within images that are mirrored as part of the disconnected registry that you define for disconnected installs.

kind: Subscription

The OLM subscription to install the OSUS operator on the cluster.

kind: OperatorGroup

The OperatorGroup is a prerequisite for all operators to be installed.

kind: `Image`

The `Image` configuration for a given OpenShift cluster must be told about the CA if you are using a self-signed certificate for your disconnected registry.

kind: `ConfigMap`

The `trusted-ca` referenced from the `Image objectDefinition` is defined here to include the certificate for the registry. If your disconnected registry uses a certificate that is trusted by one of the global CAs, you may not require this part.

kind: `Namespace`

Like all pods in Kubernetes, a namespace must exist on the cluster to run the pods for the OSUS operator.

To consume available updates from your disconnected registry, you would define a policy for your `ClusterVersion` to reference the available update graphs that are made known to the cluster via the OSUS operator:

```
apiVersion: policy.open-cluster-management.io/v1
kind: Policy
metadata:
 annotations:
   policy.open-cluster-management.io/categories: PR.IP Information Protection
Processes
     and Procedures
   policy.open-cluster-management.io/controls: PR.IP-1 Baseline Configuration
   policy.open-cluster-management.io/standards: NIST-CSF
 name: policy-cincinatti-clusterversion
 namespace: upgrade-policies
spec:
 disabled: false
 policy-templates:
 - objectDefinition:
     apiVersion: policy.open-cluster-management.io/v1
     kind: ConfigurationPolicy
     metadata:
       name: policy-cluster-version
     spec:
       namespaceSelector:
         exclude:
         - kube-*
         include:
         - default
       object-templates:
       - apiVersion: config.openshift.io/v1
         complianceType: musthave
         kind: ClusterVersion
         metadata:
           name: version
         objectDefinition:
           spec:
             channel: stable-4.5
             upstream: http://disconnected-cincinnati-policy-engine-route-
```

```
cincinnati-
operator.apps.YOUR_CLUSTER_NAME.YOUR_BASE_DOMAIN/api/upgrades_info/v1/graph
        remediationAction: inform
        severity: low
  remediationAction: inform
status:
  placement:
  - placementBinding: binding-policy-cincinatti-clusterversion
    placementRule: placement-policy-cincinatti-clusterversion
```

The `ClusterVersion` object must reference the update graph made available by the OSUS operator. The upstream field in the preceding `ClusterVersion` spec should reference the route exposed by the OSUS operator.

Summary

In this chapter, we discussed how operators expose additional APIs that provide for the configuration of a Kubernetes or OpenShift cluster. We walked through deploying an example operator that continuously scans running pods for references to container images that have known vulnerabilities.

We then examined how operators support the configuration of all manner of behavior within the cluster and looked at an example of configuring authentication for the Kubernetes API layer by customizing the `OAuth` CRD that is acted upon by the authentication operator within the cluster.

Next we looked at how the rich API surface provided by operators allows you to control all aspects of your cluster and how the Open Cluster Management policy framework allows you to customize policies that define configuration—or indeed even deploy new operators via the OLM framework on all of your clusters. The last policy demonstrates a powerful means for driving the entire upgrade configuration and even triggering active upgrades across the entire collection of managed clusters. You should be able to adapt any one of these working examples to form the foundation of your policies for your multicluster fleet.

In the next chapter, we will look at an example that takes advantage of many of these building blocks to distribute an entire application across multiple clusters that could run across multiple cloud providers.

## CHAPTER 8

Working Example of Multicluster Application Delivery

Let's take a look at a simple working example of a web application with a backing datastore. For our purposes, we will deploy an app that mimics the game PAC-MAN game from Atari. A user will interact with a dynamic frontend that stores information in a backing MongoDB.

We will deploy this application across multiple distinct clusters using the techniques discussed in Chapter 5. Each of the clusters will be provisioned from a hub running Open Cluster Management, as discussed in Chapter 6. Further, we will configure an external load balancer provided by a GSLB service hosted by F5. Incoming user requests will be routed from a global domain into one of the specific clusters. If any one of the clusters or the application experiences a problem, then user requests will no longer be routed to that cluster. We are going to go a little further and demonstrate how to integrate off-cluster resources like an F5 DNS Load Balancer Cloud Service, and we will integrate a ServiceNow change ticket into the example.

In Figure 8-1, we see our PAC-MAN application running on two OpenShift clusters with a load balancer routing traffic to app instances on either cluster. We can see the hub cluster with various resources that are helping to manage the overall system. Through the rest of this chapter, we will explain what these various parts are doing and provide a walk-through that you can do on your own to experiment with all of the moving parts.

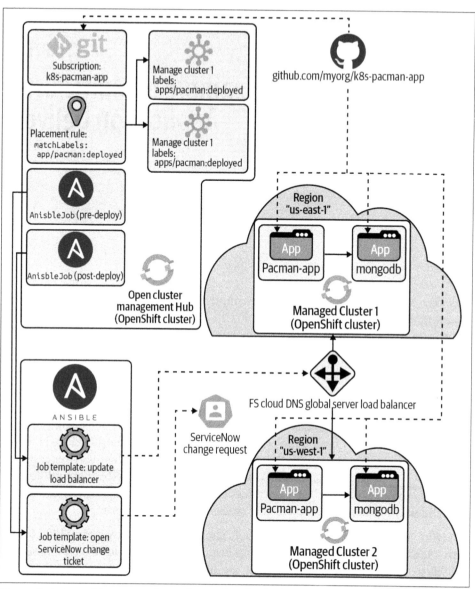

Figure 8-1. A working example made up of multiple clusters and a two-tier web application, managed by an Open Cluster Management hub and integrating off-cluster automation

Failure Is Inevitable

We have seen from many angles how OpenShift recovers from failures of the underlying infrastructure or cloud provider and how you can achieve a responsive and adaptive open hybrid cloud to support your applications. Let's review some of the things we've talked about.

In Chapter 4, we discussed single cluster availability where the control plane of a Kubernetes cluster is able to tolerate the failure of any one availability zone. When an availability zone fails in a single cluster, both the control plane and applications running within the cluster can tolerate loss of supporting compute, network, or storage infrastructure. Your applications must take advantage of Kubernetes concepts like services that act as a load balancer within the cluster, routing user requests to multiple supporting application pods. When an application pod is no longer healthy (as determined by health checks) or the node supporting the pod is no longer healthy, then the Kubernetes scheduler will look for a new home for the failing pod. We design applications for resiliency by having redundant pods that continue to run and service incoming user requests.

Now what happens if the cluster cannot reschedule the failing pod because it has exhausted capacity? What happens if more than a single availability zone fails? Under these scenarios, it may be preferable to deploy additional instances of the application to other clusters in alternative regions or even alternative cloud providers.

As we saw in Chapter 6, we can use OpenShift to provision running clusters across many different cloud providers. The Open Cluster Management (*https://oreil.ly/ 3J1SW*) project allows you to manage those clusters from a central control plane, referred to as the "hub" cluster.

Further, in Chapter 7, we saw how a given cluster was matched to required configurations through a `PlacementRule`. Whenever an Open Cluster Management policy was matched against a cluster because the cluster was selected by a `PlacementRule`, required configuration could be audited or enforced against that cluster. Because OpenShift is very operator-centric both for the control plane and for workloads, using policies to drive declarative configuration is a natural and simple way to ensure that your clusters are ready to support application workloads. An added benefit is that the declarative policies are easily managed in your source control systems if you're adopting a full or semi-GitOps approach.

In Chapter 5, we examined how an appropriate `PlacementRule` can ensure that an application is running across multiple clusters. By running an application across more than one cluster in separate regions, we can now tolerate the failure of an entire cloud region. Alternatively, you can use this when your organization happens to have adopted different cloud providers just due to organizational inertia, because of a merger and acquisition, or because you need to survive the complete outage of a cloud provider. The simplest example of multicluster, though, likely is that you are leveraging your existing datacenter virtualization provider and adopting at least one public cloud provider as well. `PlacementRules` help separate the "what" needs to run from the "where" very easily. `PlacementRules` also enable your application to adjust if the availability or labeling of clusters changes. That is, if either the `PlacementRule` is changed or the set of available clusters changes due to additions or removals, then the application components will be dynamically redeployed across new clusters or taken off of failing clusters.

So, we can create clusters easily (Chapter 6), we can ensure those clusters are configured correctly to support the enterprise configuration and security standards (Chapter 7), and we can deliver applications to those clusters (Chapter 5).

Multicluster Load Balancing

How do we ensure that user requests are routed to healthy application instances? For our example, we will use a cloud-based GSLB service managed by F5.

There are a number of solutions to handle multicluster load balancing. We've chosen to use an cloud-based service from F5 for these reasons:

- It's not supported by an operator at the time of this writing (and yet is still important to automate with our application).
- It's easy to sign up for a lightweight account through the AWS Marketplace.
- We expect most datacenters will need to automate how their applications integrate with an F5 BIG-IP load balancer. Even though the cloud-based service and the F5 BIG-IP appliances use different APIs, we believe the example will give you enough of an understanding that you can adapt the principles that are demonstrated to your own applications. Also, if we used a BIG-IP virtual appliance for the example, it would increase the complexity for users who want to re-create the complete example.
- The F5 service will work for you even if your clusters run across completely different cloud environments or your own datacenters with public routes exposed.

For your own awareness and reference, here are two other options to provide load balancing across clusters:

- The external-dns (*https://oreil.ly/eyHBj*) project extends the typical internal cluster DNS registry for services into a public DNS record. The project is still somewhat young as of the time of this writing but has a number of supported providers.

- The k8gb.io (*https://www.k8gb.io*) project will set up DNS registries within each cluster. An external DNS entry must be configured in some top-level DNS provider that delegates to the cluster-specific DNS registries. The architecture has the benefit that there is no centralized controller that can be a single point of failure. However, features like latency-based routing are not currently supported (as in the F5 or external-dns options).

In our example application, you will establish a top-level DNS record (e.g., `*.www-apps.<clusterName>.<baseDomain>`) that delegates to the F5 DNS Load Balancer to resolve the address (e.g., ns1.f5cloudservices.com and ns2.f5cloudservices.com). Then the general flow of DNS requests to resolve the address will go through the following steps:

1. User resolves `app-name.www-apps.<clusterName>.<baseDomain>` against the top-level DNS provider, which redirects the request to the relevant cloud DNS provider for `*.<baseDomain>`.

2. The `<baseDomain>` is resolved against your cloud provider's DNS (e.g., Amazon Route 53).

3. The cloud DNS provider returns a nameserver record for `*.www-apps.<cluster Name>.<baseDomain>` to route the request to one of ns1.f5cloudservices.com or ns2.f5cloudservices.com.

4. The final resolution request to ns1.f5cloudservices.com or ns2.f5cloudservices.com evaluates the list of managed zones and, based on where the DNS request originated from and current health of backing services, returns the best match to an application route hosted by one of your clusters.

As shown in Figure 8-2, in the F5 DNS Load Balancer Cloud Service, you will have one DNS load balancer zone for each collection of clusters that may host the application. Each of these zones will correspond to a top-level DNS entry in your cloud provider DNS that delegates to F5 to resolve the correct cluster for a requested application route.

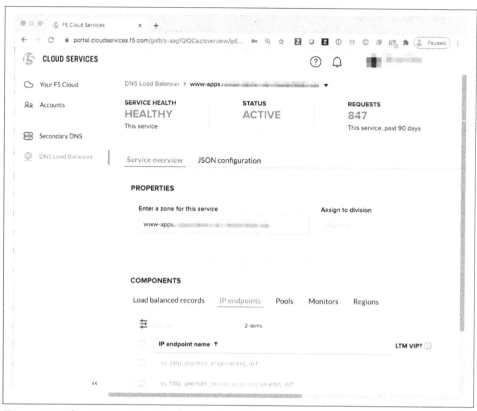

Figure 8-2. The F5 DNS Load Balancer Cloud Service

When logged into the F5 DNS Load Balancer, you will see your various DNS load balancer services (each of these routes to one or more applications provided across multiple clusters) and the IP endpoints that are currently registered. Each IP endpoint resolves to the application router of one of the clusters hosting one of the application instances.

Now each time that your application has an instance that becomes available or is removed from a cluster, we need to update the DNS load balancer zone for that application (identified by `*.www-apps.<clusterName>.<baseDomain>`). How are we going to do this automatically? Here, we're going to introduce how you can automate around your clusters whenever something in your environment is not "native" Kubernetes. To accomplish this, we're going to walk through how Ansible can automate an update to the F5 DNS Load Balancer whenever our application is introduced to a new cluster or removed from an existing cluster.

You will need to carry out the following prerequisites for running our example application:

1. Create an account with the F5 DNS Load Balancer Cloud Service. You can do this at F5 Cloud Services (*https://oreil.ly/tmmSY*) or through the AWS Marketplace (*https://oreil.ly/HF5mw*).

2. Delegate your global domain to the F5 DNS nameservers. Create a nameserver-delegating DNS record with the global domain that you will use with F5. You can do this via Route 53 or your DNS provider. The F5 DNS Load Balancer Cloud Service FAQ (*https://oreil.ly/xK0sK*) answers questions related to this prerequisite.

Automating Without Operators

As we've covered extensively in this book, Kubernetes makes comprehensive use of declarative configuration. While we believe that Kubernetes will underpin most modern applications in the better part of the next decade, we recognize that not all things are Kubernetes native today and may *never* be Kubernetes native.

For those aspects of your application across multiple clusters or even multiple clouds, we introduce Ansible as a method to automate any behavior that you want to occur when the system introduces a change dynamically. As discussed in the previous section, we want to have our OpenShift environment automatically place our application instances across multiple clusters. Whenever our application is deployed on a new cluster or has to be removed because a cluster is unhealthy, we want our global load balancer configuration in front of the system to be updated. Since we are relying heavily on automated recovery from failures, we want this behavior to be automatic as well.

With Ansible, there is a vibrant community that uses automation to simplify the lives of systems administrators managing Linux, containers, clouds, networking devices, security, and so forth. We aren't going to go into a lot of depth to teach you about Ansible. However, we will introduce some basic concepts so that you can see how it works and evaluate whether it is appropriate for your needs.

Note that even if you do not have to automate anything outside of the cluster, all of the details covered around availability, multicluster provisioning, configuration, application delivery, and so on still apply.

For our purposes, you should only need a grasp of the following concepts in Ansible:

Playbook

An Ansible playbook is "a blueprint of automation tasks—which are complex IT actions executed with limited or no human involvement. Ansible playbooks are executed on a set, group, or classification of hosts, which together make up an Ansible inventory."[1]

Project

An Ansible project groups together playbooks along with supporting resources to run those playbooks. Conveniently, projects can be backed by a source control repository that is used to manage the Ansible playbooks and supporting resources.

Ansible Tower

Ansible Tower is a supported version of the open source project Ansible AWX. Ansible Tower provides the capabilities to organize a set of Ansible projects and an automation engine that keeps track of credentials, scheduled jobs, job templates to be invoked as needed, available inventory of systems to run playbooks against, and so on. In essence, think of Tower as a way to organize and track everything you need to automate systems management.

Job template

An Ansible job template defines an available playbook from an Ansible project within Ansible Tower. Job templates can specify exactly which parameters to externalize and which stored credentials to use, and it can associate a list of all invocations of the job template for auditing or diagnostic purposes.

Job

An Ansible job is a running instance of a job template.

As discussed in the previous section, we are going to use Ansible to update the F5 DNS Load Balancer Cloud Service for our application. We are going to use a slightly modified version of an open source tool (*https://oreil.ly/p2AyH*) from F5 that incorporates all of the API calls required to update the service implemented in Ansible. We will load the f5-bd-gslb-tool playbooks into an Ansible project and define a job template that invokes the required playbook, accepting parameters for the clusters that currently host the application. For an example of what the Ansible project within Ansible Tower looks like, see Figure 8-3.

---

1 From "What Is an Ansible Playbook?", Red Hat, *https://oreil.ly/At7XY*.

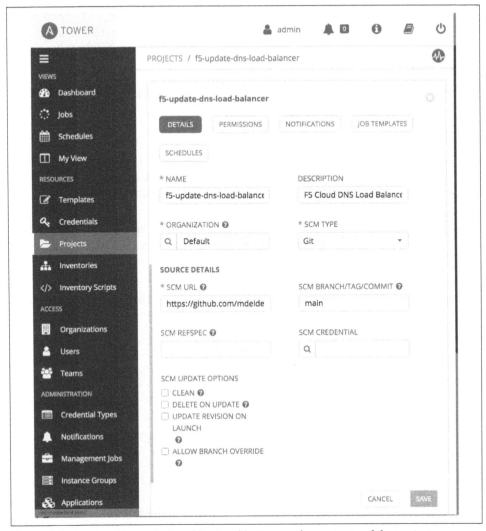

Figure 8-3. An Ansible project within Ansible Tower; the contents of the project are managed under source control (via GitHub)

We will also use Ansible to integrate a simple change management process backed by ServiceNow. Our example is derived from published blogs on the topic.[2] Many IT organizations and operators still make extensive use of ticket-driven change management processes. In our example application, an Ansible job will run before adjusting

---

2 Colin McCarthy, "Ansible + ServiceNow Part 1: Opening and Closing Tickets," Red Hat Ansible Blog (June 6, 2019), *https://oreil.ly/NI9ZX*.

the placement of the app to create a change request in ServiceNow. Our example will make only superficial use of ServiceNow, but you will see one way that you may still use your existing process for record-keeping and auditing purposes even when the system undergoes a dynamic, automatic change.

We have covered several concepts that support application deployment, including the Open Cluster Management Subscription (API Group: apps.open-cluster-management.io/v1) and PlacementRule (API Group: apps.open-cluster-management.io/v1). We now introduce a new API kind that will be part of our example application: AnsibleJob (API Group: tower.ansible.com/v1alpha1). As with other CRDs introduced throughout the book, AnsibleJob is reconciled using an operator known as the Ansible Resource Operator. Let's deploy the Ansible Resource Operator alongside Ansible Tower so that we can link the execution of Ansible jobs whenever the placement of our application instances is updated by the system. The AnsibleJob to create a change request ticket is shown in Example 8-1.

Example 8-1. The AnsibleJob API kind allows us to invoke an Ansible job template configured in Ansible Tower; input parameters are sent via the extra_vars parameter

```
apiVersion: tower.ansible.com/v1alpha1
kind: AnsibleJob
metadata:
 name: snow-create-change-record
 namespace: pacman-app
 labels:
   app.kubernetes.io/name: pacman
spec:
 tower_auth_secret: toweraccess
 job_template_name: snow-create-change-record
 extra_vars:
   app_name: pacman
   change_request:
     severity: 2
     priority: 2
     implementation_plan: "Updated by Red Hat Advanced Cluster Management for
Kubernetes"
     justification: "A new revision was available from the application channel in
GitHub."
     description: "The following resources have been updated: [...]"
     risk_impact_analysis: "Changes are made automatically based on approved
changes in GitHub."
     test_plan: "Run synthetic validation tests post-deployment."
```

In terms of order, the AnsibleJob to create a ServiceNow ticket will run before the new placement decisions are applied (a prehook), and the AnsibleJob to update the F5 load balancer will run last (a posthook).

Deploying the Example Application

We're laying down a lot of capabilities to get to a simple web frontend application—
and the goal is to provide you with a realistic example of some of the concerns that
you will likely encounter as you adopt Kubernetes and OpenShift as part of your
enterprise standards.

We've covered how the application will be replicated across multiple clusters with a
global load balancer in front of those multiple application instances and how whenever the placement decisions change, we will have a simple ticket-based record within
ServiceNow of the change.

We reviewed the PAC-MAN application extensively in Chapter 5, but here is a quick
catchup:

- PAC-MAN is made up of two deployments (the web frontend application and a
  backing MongoDB datastore).
- PAC-MAN exposes two public routes: one for the local cluster and one for the
  global route provided by our F5 DNS Load Balancer.
- The PAC-MAN subscription references a Git repository where our Kubernetes
  manifests are managed. If a change is introduced to those Kubernetes manifests,
  then the update will automatically be rolled out to all active clusters.
- The `PlacementRule` defines a list of conditions that a cluster must match to be
  selected to host the application.

For our purposes (and because we're already dealing with several moving parts), we
are not doing anything to cluster the set of MongoDB replicas that will back the
application across multiple clusters. We could perform additional actions (via Ansible
or operators) to cluster the set of MongoDB replicas and make distributed writes persistent whenever a cluster is lost. Alternatively, we could back the state of the PAC-
MAN application with a cloud-based MongoDB service. You will likely have your
own strong opinions about how persistent the backing datastores of your applications
need to be and what the relevant MTBF and MTTR availability metrics should be for
the application itself.

Now that we've covered the details of how all of the parts fit together, let's dive in and
get our hands on a running example!

To simplify this process, fork the example repository. You will need to make a few
modifications to be able to deliver the application out of your repository fork.

Fork the repository (*https://oreil.ly/8nMgb*) into your own organization and then
clone the repository to your laptop:

```
$ git clone --branch ansible
git@github.com:SPECIFY_YOUR_GITHUB_ORG/k8s-pacman-app.git
```

All of the paths referenced in the following sections refer to files within this repository.

You will need to update the values in the following files according to your specific DNS settings for your OpenShift clusters and Route53:

- *hack/install-config.yaml*
- *deploy/posthook/f5-update-dns-load-balancer.yaml*
- *deploy/pacman-f5-route.yaml*
- *hack/tower-setup/config/inventory*

Table 8-1 shows the required updates.

Table 8-1. Required file updates

Key	Value
SPECIFY_YOUR_CLUSTER_NAME	The name of your hub cluster as defined in the *install-config.yaml*.
SPECIFY_YOUR_BASE_DOMAIN	The value of the base DNS name of your hub cluster as defined in your *install-config.yaml*.
SPECIFY_YOUR_CLUSTER_ADDRESS	The concatenation of *clusterName* and *clusterBaseDomain* separated by a period (e.g., *clusterName.clusterBaseDomain*).
SPECIFY_YOUR_OWN_PASSWORD	Define your own secure password. When in doubt, the output of **uuid** can be a useful password.
SPECIFY_YOUR_EMAIL_ADDRESS	Used to assign a tag for any cloud resources for tracking purposes. You can also just delete the tag if you do not wish to specify your email address.
SPECIFY_YOUR_PULL_SECRET	An image pull secret that you can download from Red Hat (*https://cloud.redhat.com*) after logging into the service.
SPECIFY_YOUR_SSH_RSA_PUBLIC_KEY	An SSH public key that will enable you to connect to hosts that are provisioned as part of your OpenShift cluster.

Configure Your Hub Cluster

Recall that the hub cluster hosts components for Open Cluster Management that allow managed clusters to be managed from a centralized control plane. You can either provision clusters from the hub or import existing OpenShift clusters from a managed provider like Red Hat OpenShift on IBM Cloud or Azure Red Hat OpenShift.

In the following sections, you will create a cluster to act as the hub, install the Open Cluster Management hub, and provision two clusters to host the example application.

Provision an OpenShift Cluster to Host the Open Cluster Management Hub

Provision an OpenShift 4.5 or later cluster following the default instructions. The cluster should have at least three worker nodes with a total of 18 CPU and 80G of memory or m5.xlarge (times three workers) on AWS EC2.

The following example *install-config.yaml* was used to prepare the hub cluster for this example, but so long as your starting cluster has the required capacity, you do not need to provision a cluster exactly like the *install-config.yaml* in Example 8-2.

Example 8-2. An example install-config.yaml to provision a cluster to use as a hub

```
apiVersion: v1
baseDomain: SPECIFY_YOUR_BASE_DOMAIN
controlPlane:
 hyperthreading: Enabled
 name: master
 replicas: 3
 platform:
   aws:
     type: m5.xlarge
     rootVolume:
       iops: 2000
       size: 100
       type: io1
compute:
- hyperthreading: Enabled
 name: worker
 replicas: 4
 platform:
   aws:
     type: m5.xlarge
     rootVolume:
       size: 100
       type: gp2
metadata:
 name: SPECIFY_YOUR_CLUSTER_NAME
networking:
 clusterNetwork:
 - cidr: 10.128.0.0/14
   hostPrefix: 23
 machineCIDR: 10.0.0.0/16
 networkType: OpenShiftSDN
 serviceNetwork:
 - 172.30.0.0/16
platform:
 aws:
   region: us-east-1
   userTags:
     contact: SPECIFY_YOUR_EMAIL_ADDRESS
     purpose: demo
```

```
publish: External
pullSecret: 'SPECIFY_YOUR_PULL_SECRET'
sshKey: |
  ssh-rsa SPECIFY_YOUR_SSH_RSA_PUBLIC_KEY
```

Configure the Open Cluster Management Hub

For our example, we will deploy Open Cluster Management using Red Hat's supported product offering, RHACM. Instructions for configuring RHACM were given in Chapter 5. You can also deploy RHACM directly from the Red Hat Operator Catalog or by using the documented instructions (*https://oreil.ly/a1zlD*).

Provision Two or More Clusters to Host the Application

Once you have configured the hub cluster, you will be able to register your cloud credentials and provision one or more clusters that will be managed automatically by the hub. These clusters can be provisioned across the same cloud provider in different regions or against multiple cloud providers. The example PAC-MAN app is very lightweight, so you will not need a lot of capacity to run the sample application.

Deploy Ansible Tower and the Ansible Resource Operator

In addition to a containerized application, we will configure a DNS Load Balancer provided by F5 and use a ServiceNow developer instance to demonstrate how you might integrate a change management process into the deployment life cycle of your containerized apps. Detailed instructions on setting up the Ansible Tower container-based installation method are available in the Ansible documentation (*https://oreil.ly/Uzm3y*). The following steps capture the specific actions taken to prepare the demo captured in this repository.

To simplify the configuration of this example, we will leverage some pre-defined policies that help prepare the hub cluster to deploy Ansible.

Clone the sample repository and apply the policies under *hack/manifests/policies*:

```
$ cd hack/manifests/policies
$ oc apply -f ansible-tower-policies-subscription.yaml
```

The result of these policies will set up the Ansible Resource Operator, prepare the Ansible Tower project named `tower`, and create a `PersistentVolumeClaim` using the default storage class to support Ansible Tower's database (PostgreSQL).

After a few moments, verify that the resources were correctly applied on your hub cluster. You can see that the `policy-ansible-tower-prep` and `policy-auth-provider` are compliant from your RHACM web console (under "Govern Risk"). You can also verify the resources that were created as follows:

```
$ oc get subs.operators --all-namespaces
NAMESPACE                    NAME                          PACKAGE
           SOURCE                  CHANNEL
open-cluster-management  acm-operator-subscription  advanced-cluster-
management   acm-custom-registry    release-2.2
tower-resource-operator  awx-resource-operator      awx-resource-
operator     redhat-operators       release-0.1

$ oc get pvc -n tower
NAME         STATUS  VOLUME                                      CAPACITY  ACCESS
MODES    STORAGECLASS AGE
postgresql   Bound   pvc-1554a179-0947-4a65-9af0-81c5f2d8b476   5Gi       RWO
         gp2                  3d20h
```

Download the Ansible Tower installer release from the available releases (*https://oreil.ly/utowL*). Extract the archive into a working directory. Configure the inventory for your OpenShift cluster. The inventory file should be placed directly under the folder for the archive (e.g., *ansible-tower-openshift-setup-3.7.2/inventory*).

The inventory in Example 8-3 can be placed under the root directory of the extracted release archive. Be sure to override the following:

SPECIFY_YOUR_OWN_PASSWORD
  Choose a strong password of at least 16 characters.

SPECIFY_YOUR_CLUSTER_ADDRESS
  Provide the correct hostname of the API server for your OpenShift cluster.

SPECIFY_YOUR_OPENSHIFT_CREDENTIALS
  The password for your OpenShift cluster admin user. Be sure to also override kubeadmin if you have defined an alternate administrative user.

Example 8-3. An example inventory file that provides input values for the Ansible Tower installer

```
localhost ansible_connection=local ansible_python_interpreter="/usr/bin/env python"
[all:vars]
# This will create or update a default admin (superuser) account in Tower
admin_user=admin
admin_password='SPECIFY_YOUR_OWN_PASSWORD'
# Tower Secret key
# It's *very* important that this stay the same between upgrades or you will
# lose the ability to decrypt your credentials
secret_key='SPECIFY_YOUR_OWN_PASSWORD'
# Database Settings
# ==================
# Set pg_hostname if you have an external postgres server, otherwise
# a new postgres service will be created
# pg_hostname=postgresql
# If using an external database, provide your existing credentials.
# If you choose to use the provided containerized Postgres depolyment, these
# values will be used when provisioning the database.
```

```
pg_username='admin'
pg_password='SPECIFY_YOUR_OWN_PASSWORD'
pg_database='tower'
pg_port=5432
pg_sslmode='prefer'  # set to 'verify-full' for client-side enforced SSL
# Note: The user running this installer will need cluster-admin privileges.
# Tower's job execution container requires running in privileged mode,
# and a service account must be created for auto peer-discovery to work.
# Deploy into Openshift
# =====================
openshift_host=https://api.SPECIFY_YOUR_CLUSTER_ADDRESS:6443
openshift_skip_tls_verify=true
openshift_project=tower
openshift_user=kubeadmin
openshift_password=SPECIFY_YOUR_OPENSHIFT_CREDENTIALS
# If you don't want to hardcode a password here, just do:
# ./setup_openshift.sh -e openshift_token=$TOKEN
# Skip this section if you BYO database. This is only used when you want the
# installer to deploy a containerized Postgres deployment inside of your
# OpenShift cluster. This is only recommended if you have experience storing and
# managing persistent data in containerized environments.
#
#
# Name of a PVC you've already provisioned for database:
openshift_pg_pvc_name=postgresql
#
# Or... use an emptyDir volume for the OpenShift Postgres pod.
# Useful for demos or testing purposes.
# openshift_pg_emptydir=true
# Deploy into Vanilla Kubernetes
# ==============================
# kubernetes_context=test-cluster
# kubernetes_namespace=ansible-tower
```

Update the default task image that is used to run the defined jobs. Because the jobs use additional modules, we need to ensure that various Python module dependencies are available.

In *group_vars/all*, update the following key:

```
kubernetes_task_image: quay.io/mdelder/ansible-tower-task
```

You can build this image and consume it from your own registry by building the *Dockerfile.taskimage* under *hack/tower-setup/container_task_image*. Optionally, you could build the task image and publish to your own registry. If you're using the existing image as previously defined, you will not need to build your own image. Use the correct Ansible version based on the release you downloaded:

```
$ cd hack/tower-setup/container_task_image
$ docker build -t quay.io/YOUR_USERID/ansible-tower-task:3.7.2 \
-f Dockerfile.taskimage
$ docker push quay.io/YOUR_USERID/ansible-tower-task:3.7.2
```

Once you have made the relevant updates to your inventory file, you can run the Ansible Tower installer. Retrieve an authentication token from the OpenShift web console from the "Copy login command" action under your user name:

```
$ ./setup_openshift.sh -e openshift_token=$TOKEN
```

Launch the Tower web console:

```
$ open https://$(oc get route -n tower ansible-tower-web-svc \
-ojsonpath='{.status.ingress[0].host}')
```

Log in with the user and password that you specified in the inventory file. You must then choose your license for Tower. If you have a Red Hat user identity, you can log in and choose the 60-day evaluation license.

Optionally, you can customize the *hack/manifests/ansible-tower-console-link.yaml* for your own cluster. Then apply the file (note: you must update the URL within the file before this will work in your cluster):

```
$ cd hack/manifests
$ oc apply ansible-tower-console-link.yaml
```

After applying the ConsoleLink, refresh your OpenShift web console and view the shortcut to your Ansible Tower under the Applications drop-down menu in the header.

Configure Projects for ServiceNow and F5 DNS Load Balancer

The example application uses the F5 DNS Load Balancer Cloud Service and Service-Now to demonstrate Ansible automation. This assumes that you have completed the following steps:

1. Create a developer instance of ServiceNow. If you need a developer instance of ServiceNow, follow the directions at ServiceNow Developers (*https://devel oper.servicenow.com*).

2. Create an account with the F5 DNS Load Balancer Cloud Service. If you need to create an account with F5 DNS Load Balancer Cloud Service (*https://oreil.ly/ tmmSY*), you can do this directly or through the AWS Marketplace (*https:// oreil.ly/HF5mw*).

3. Delegate your global domain to the F5 DNS nameservers. Create a nameserver-delegating DNS record with the global domain that you will use with F5. You can do this via Route 53 or your DNS provider. The F5 DNS Load Balancer Cloud Service FAQ (*https://oreil.ly/ObL27*) answers questions related to this prerequisite.

Once you have the credentials for these services, you can configure the Ansible Tower instance that you deployed with the two relevant Ansible projects providing the job templates that will be executed as part of the prehook and posthooks that run when the application is placed or removed on a cluster. For convenience, all of the configuration for Ansible Tower is completely automated (using Ansible playbooks that talk to Ansible Tower to create the projects/job templates/jobs/credentials that are needed for the example).

Create a file named *tower_cli.cfg* under *hack/tower-setup* with the following contents:

```
# hack/tower-setup/tower_cli.cfg
[general]
host = https://ansible-tower-web-svc-tower.apps.cluster.baseDomain
verify_ssl = false
#oauth_token = ALTERNATIVELY_USE_A_TOKEN
username = admin
# password = SPECIFY_YOUR_OWN_PASSWORD
```

If you're unsure of the host address for Tower, you can use oc to find the correct value:

```
$ oc get route -n tower ansible-tower-web-svc \
-ojsonpath='{.status.ingress[0].host}'
```

Create a file named *credentials.yml* under *hack/tower-setup/group_vars* with the following contents:

```
# User and password for the F5 CloudServices account.
f5aas_username: SPECIFY_YOUR_F5_USERNAME
f5aas_password: SPECIFY_YOUR_F5_PASSWORD

# Credentials for ServiceNow
snow_username: admin
snow_password: SPECIFY_YOUR_SERVICENOW_USERNAME
# Specify your ServiceNow developer instance ID.
snow_instance: devXXXXX
```

You may need to install required Python libraries:

```
# Optionally specify the correct version of python required by Ansible
# Of course, you must update the PYTHON var specific to your environment
$ export PYTHON="/usr/local/Cellar/ansible/2.9.13/libexec/bin/python3.8"
$ $PYTHON -m pip install --upgrade ansible-tower-cli
```

Run the playbook that will talk to Ansible Tower and configure our two projects (one for F5 and one for ServiceNow) and the relevant job templates:

```
$ export PYTHON="/usr/local/Cellar/ansible/2.9.13/libexec/bin/python3.8"
$ ansible-playbook -e ansible_python_interpreter="$PYTHON" tower-setup.yml
```

Configure the toweraccess Secret and Create the Ansible Tower Token

From Ansible Tower, create an authorization token. The authorization token will be used in a secret that the application will reference to invoke the Ansible Tower Jobs. Follow these steps:

1. Log in to the Ansible Tower instance:

   ```
   $ open https://$(oc get route -n tower ansible-tower-web-svc \
   -ojsonpath='{.status.ingress[0].host}')
   ```

2. Click on the "admin" user in the header.

3. Click on Tokens.

4. Click on the +.

5. Set the scope to Write.

6. Click Save and be sure to copy and save the value of the token.

7. Create a file *named hack/manifests/toweraccess-secret.yaml* with the following contents:

   ```
   apiVersion: v1
   stringData:
     host: ansible-tower-web-svc-
   tower.apps.SPECIFY_YOUR_CLUSTER_NAME.SPECIFY_YOUR_BASE_DOMAIN
     token: SPECIFY_YOUR_ANSIBLE_TOWER_ADMIN_TOKEN
   kind: Secret
   metadata:
     name: toweraccess
     namespace: pacman-app
   type: Opaque
   ```

Deploy the pacman-app Example to Your Cluster

Now we will deploy the manifests that govern our application placement to the hub. By creating the application, subscription, and `PlacementRule`, you will enable the hub to deploy the application dynamically to one or more of the clusters that you created earlier.

First, create the project for the application and apply the secret:

```
$ oc new-project pacman-app
$ oc apply -f hack/manifests/toweraccess-secret.yaml
```

You can either create the application manifest from the RHACM web console (Managed Applications > Create application) or apply the prebuilt resources from the example Git repository. An example of the final result is provided in Example 8-4.

Example 8-4. The PAC-MAN application manifest and supporting resources to allow the hub cluster to deploy the application to any managed cluster in the fleet

```
---
apiVersion: apps.open-cluster-management.io/v1
kind: Channel
metadata:
  name: pacman-app-latest
  namespace: pacman-app
```

```
    labels:
      app.kubernetes.io/name: pacman
    annotations:

      apps.open-cluster-management.io/github-path: deploy
spec:
  type: GitHub
  pathname: https://github.com/SPECIFY_YOUR_GITHUB_ORG/k8s-pacman-app.git
  # secretRef:
  #   name: github-credentials
---
apiVersion: app.k8s.io/v1beta1
kind: Application
metadata:
  name: pacman-app
  namespace: pacman-app
spec:
  componentKinds:
  - group: apps.open-cluster-management.io
    kind: Subscription
  descriptor: {}
  selector:
    matchExpressions:
    - key: app.kubernetes.io/name
      operator: In
      values:
      - pacman
---
apiVersion: apps.open-cluster-management.io/v1
kind: Subscription
metadata:
  annotations:
    apps.open-cluster-management.io/git-branch: ansible
    apps.open-cluster-management.io/github-path: deploy
  name: pacman-app
  namespace: pacman-app
  labels:
    app.kubernetes.io/name: pacman
spec:
  channel: pacman-app/pacman-app-latest
  hooksecretref:
    name: toweraccess
  placement:
    placementRef:
      kind: PlacementRule
      name: pacman-dev-clusters
---
apiVersion: apps.open-cluster-management.io/v1
kind: PlacementRule
metadata:
 name: pacman-dev-clusters
 namespace: pacman-app
spec:
 clusterConditions:
 - status: "True"
   type: ManagedClusterConditionAvailable
```

```
clusterReplicas: 2
clusterSelector:
  # matchExpressions:
  # - key: region
  #   operator: In
  #   values:
  #    - us-east-1
  #    - us-west-1
  #    - europe-west3
  matchLabels:
    apps/pacman: deployed
```

The channel references the source of Kubernetes manifests in GitHub. Any changes that are made to the supporting GitHub repository will trigger an update across the fleet. The application provides a way to associate a set of subscriptions to a logical unit of deployment and management. The subscription selects a specific branch and directory from within the GitHub repository. You may have a single GitHub repository that feeds multiple subscriptions for one application or multiple applications. Each subscription can be placed independently, so you may have different parts of an application deployed to different clusters. The PlacementRule defines a set of labels and a match expression that must be met for the subscription to be deployed against a managed cluster within the fleet.

Be aware of how you label your clusters and the supporting PlacementRule. You want to ensure that the PlacementRule indicates the selected clusters in their status conditions:

```
$ oc get placementrule -n pacman-app -oyaml
apiVersion: apps.open-cluster-management.io/v1
kind: PlacementRule
metadata:
name: pacman-app-placement-0
namespace: pacman-app
spec:
clusterSelector:
    matchLabels:
    apps/pacman: deployed
status:
decisions:
- clusterName: foxtrot-ap-northeast-1
    clusterNamespace: foxtrot-ap-northeast-1
- clusterName: foxtrot-gcp-europe
    clusterNamespace: foxtrot-gcp-europe
```

Now that you have deployed all of the supporting pieces, you can experiment by adding or removing matching clusters or changing the desired labels specified in the PlacementRule. The application instances will be added or removed to supporting clusters while keeping the F5 DNS Load Balancer Cloud Service up to date automatically.

From the topology view, your application deployment should resemble Figure 8-4.

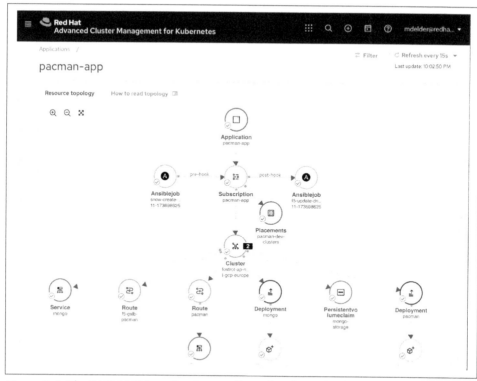

Figure 8-4. The PAC-MAN application configured with pre-hooks and post-hooks with Ansible Tower Jobs

Summary

In this chapter, we focused on providing a practical example that demonstrates how to deliver an application across multiple clusters, how to manage any parts of your system that are still not natively programmable from Kubernetes operators, and how to integrate a set of clusters behind a global load balancer service. Many specific examples from earlier in the book were used to pull all of this together, including the PAC-MAN application that used a Tekton pipeline to build its supporting images in Chapter 5. We used policies to configure an operator on our cluster (the Ansible Resource Operator on the hub) and used the Open Cluster Management hub to provision clusters that were used to support the running application. We also introduced one way that you can adapt your existing change management process using Ansible to create change request tickets whenever the system dynamically reacts to a change.

Hopefully, by now you have a firm grasp of what is possible with Kubernetes and OpenShift and how you can use some of these capabilities to streamline your adoption of these technologies for your organization.

## CHAPTER 9

The Future of Kubernetes and OpenShift

Spend some time at a KubeCon + CloudNativeCon conference these days and you will quickly conclude that the future of Kubernetes is very bright. Attendance at KubeCon + CloudNativeCon conferences is experiencing an explosive level of growth. In addition, the Kubernetes open source community of contributors continues to expand and strengthen. The number of industries that are adopting Kubernetes is astounding.[1] Similarly, OpenShift has seen its customer base grow from 1,000 to 1,700 in the past year and has also seen strong adoption among Fortune 2000 companies.[2] In this chapter, we make some predictions about what the future holds for both traditional Kubernetes and OpenShift. We discuss our expectations for how these technologies will grow and increase their impact across numerous facets of cloud native computing, including legacy application migration, high performance computing, machine learning and deep learning applications, open source marketplaces, and multicloud environments. We then conclude this chapter with a discussion of recommended resources for further study.

Increased Migration of Legacy Enterprise Applications to Cloud Native Applications

Over the years, both traditional Kubernetes and OpenShift have made dramatic improvements that will result in accelerating the migration of legacy enterprise applications to cloud native applications. With the introduction of the operator framework, these platforms are now much more capable of supporting stateful applications,

---

1 The Cloud Native Computing Foundation website (*https://www.cncf.io*) provides more information.

2 Jeffrey Burt, "OpenShift, Kubernetes, and the Hybrid Cloud," The Next Platform (April 28, 2020), *https://oreil.ly/aNyAD*.

as well as managing the complete software management life cycle for these applications. Additionally, as mentioned earlier in this book, the OpenShift platform continues to innovate in areas of tooling that reduce the complexity of moving from source code to having a fully functional containerized cloud native application. At the same time, Kubernetes and OpenShift are greatly increasing the types of applications they can support by leveraging new projects like Knative to support serverless and function-based programming models. The convergence of all these innovations makes traditional Kubernetes and OpenShift in particular well-suited to support an even greater domain of enterprise applications. Thus, we anticipate that in the near future there will be a dramatic acceleration in the migration of legacy enterprise applications to cloud native applications that run on traditional Kubernetes and OpenShift. Furthermore, we anticipate even greater interoperability and integration will occur between traditional mainframe applications and cloud native applications. In fact, there is already some early experimental work demonstrating that COBOL applications can be containerized and run on both Kubernetes and OpenShift.[3]

Increased Adoption of Kubernetes for High Performance Computing

There is a long, rich history of using server clusters for supporting high performance computing initiatives. Pioneering work in this space began in the late 1980s with platforms like the Parallel Virtual Machine.[4] Over the years, the high performance computing community has embraced new technologies that improve efficiency and scalability. Kubernetes and its container-based approach provide several benefits that make the environment well-suited for high performance computing applications. Because Kubernetes is container based, the platform experiences less overhead to start up new tasks, and the tasks can be of a finer grain operation than those supported by VM-based cloud computing environments. The reduction of latency associated with the creation and destruction of computational tasks that occur when using containers instead of VMs improves the scalability of a high performance computing environment. Furthermore, the increased efficiency that is possible by packing a larger number of containers onto a physical server in contrast to the limited number of VMs that can be placed on a physical server is another critical advantage for high performance applications.

---

3 JJ Asghar, "Run a COBOL Program on Kubernetes," IBM Developer (May 14, 2019), *https://oreil.ly/qhqwg*; IBM Developer Staff, "Getting COBOL Working on Red Hat OpenShift and Kubernetes," IBM Developer (April 20, 2020), *https://oreil.ly/FcFJ8*.

4 VS Sunderam, "PVM: A Framework for Parallel Distributed Computing," *Concurrency: Practice and Experience* 2:4 (1990): 315–339.

In addition to reduced latency, Kubernetes environments support a parallel work queue model. An excellent overview of the Kubernetes work queue model can be found in *Kubernetes Up and Running* (O'Reilly). The work queue model described in this book is essentially the "bag of tasks" parallel computing model. Research has shown that this parallel computing model is a superior approach for the execution of high performance parallel applications in a cluster environment.[5]

Even though the Kubernetes project has matured substantially since its inception, it continues to innovate in ways that improve its ability to efficiently run workloads. Most recently, Kubernetes made significant advances to its workload-scheduling algorithms that enable it to achieve better cluster utilization and high availability for its workloads.[6] The efforts the Kubernetes SIG Scheduler team has made over the years has culminated in Kubernetes being a platform that is incredibly flexible and efficient in how it schedules workloads for a variety of custom application needs.[7]

Because of all these factors, as well as the large number of cloud computing environments that offer Kubernetes-based environments, we expect huge growth in adoption of Kubernetes by the high performance computing community.

Kubernetes and OpenShift Will Become the De Facto Platforms for Machine Learning and Deep Learning

Machine learning and deep learning applications typically require highly scalable environments. Data scientists with expertise in these domains want easy-to-use platforms that enable their applications to run in production at scale. Similar to our justification provided for adopting Kubernetes for high performance computing, we anticipate that machine learning and deep learning environments will greatly benefit from adopting Kubernetes-based environments as their primary platforms. In fact, initiatives like Kubeflow (*https://oreil.ly/NjZxV*), which are focused on providing an open source Kubernetes-based platform for machine learning applications, are already attracting a significant number of contributors to their open source projects.

---

5 BK Schmidt and VS Sunderam, "Empirical Analysis of Overheads in Cluster Environments," *Concurrency Practice & Experience* 6 (1994): 1–32.

6 Wei Huang and Aldo CulquiCondor, "Introducing PodTopologySpread," Kubernetes Blog (May 5, 2020), *https://oreil.ly/iKzaV*.

7 See Kubernetes Scheduler (*https://oreil.ly/exRO9*) in the documentation for more information.

Open Cloud Marketplaces Will Accelerate Adoption of Cloud Native Applications

An increasing number of enterprises are beginning to use both multiple public clouds and private datacenters hosting their on-premises clouds. These enterprises are quickly realizing that they need an easy way to purchase, deploy, and manage cloud native application software that runs across all these environments. To address this situation, open cloud marketplaces are emerging. In these marketplaces, cloud native applications are packaged up using the Kubernetes operator packaging model. This approach enables the open cloud marketplace to automatically install, deploy, update, scale, and back up cloud native applications.

A recent example of an open cloud marketplace is the Red Hat Marketplace (*https://oreil.ly/oE1vW*), which enables customers to purchase cloud native application software that works across all major cloud environments as well as on-premises clouds. The Red Hat Marketplace provides certification, vulnerability scans, and support for the cloud native application software no matter which cloud you choose to deploy it on. Figure 9-1 is a snapshot of the home page for the Red Hat Marketplace.

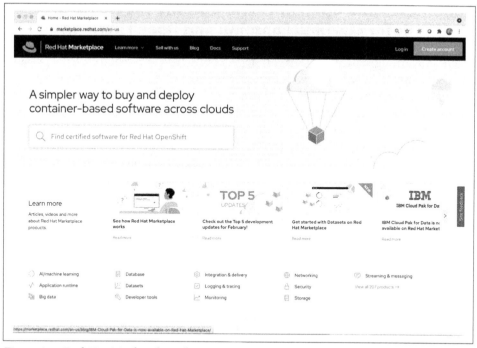

Figure 9-1. Red Hat Marketplace (https://oreil.ly/oE1vW)

Because the software on Red Hat Marketplace is vetted and certified, it provides developers with a curated view of the best tools and software stacks for building enterprise solutions to run on Red Hat OpenShift. This allows developers to focus on the capabilities the software provides, not on whether it's suitable for the environment in which they'll run it.

Because developers may begin a new development project only a few times a year, they have few opportunities to select an application stack and associated tooling. An open cloud marketplace like Red Hat Marketplace enables developers to try their desired software for free and progress seamlessly to a commercially supported version when they are ready. In addition, Red Hat Marketplace can provide visibility to development managers into how much consumption of deploying applications to each cloud is occurring. This lets them see how utilization is occurring across each platform and enables them to better manage development costs.

OpenShift Will Be the Platform for Enterprise Multicloud

After reading this book, this last prediction should come as no surprise to you. Open-Shift has proven that it provides superior interoperability and workload portability and is available from all major cloud providers, including IBM Cloud, Google Cloud, Amazon Cloud, Azure, and many others. In addition, OpenShift leverages the Istio Service Mesh, and this critical networking technology reduces the complexity of connecting applications that reside in different clouds. It also has built-in tools specifically tailored for managing multicloud clusters. For all these reasons we fully expect OpenShift to be the preferred platform for enterprise multicloud activities. In fact, many enterprise customers that use OpenShift have already embraced the use of multiple clusters, and these clusters are deployed across multiple clouds or in multiple datacenters. This behavior can result from several factors. First, an enterprise might inherit applications that run on a different cloud due to an acquisition. Second, different clouds may offer different services, and the enterprise may require a best-of-breed solution that encompasses the use of a multicloud solution. Third, data locality constraints can serve as an anchor for critical applications on certain clouds or perhaps on a premises cloud. For all these reasons, OpenShift is well positioned to be the ideal platform for enterprise multicloud applications.

Recommended Resources

This book has covered many concepts related to running both traditional Kubernetes and OpenShift in production. In this section, we provide a list of recommended resources that are excellent sources for expanding your skills and understanding of Kubernetes, OpenShift, and cloud native applications.

IBM Developer Website

The IBM Developer Website (*https://developer.ibm.com*) provides a large number of developer-training resources for learning Kubernetes, OpenShift, and over one hundred other open source technologies. The website contains lots of reusable code patterns that are complete solutions to problems developers face every day. In addition the website has tutorials, training videos, articles, and a list of both online and in-person workshops for learning open source technologies. A large part of the IBM Developer Website is focused on Kubernetes, OpenShift, and adjacent technologies like Istio, Knative, and containers. The OpenShift portion of the IBM Developer Website is shown in Figure 9-2.

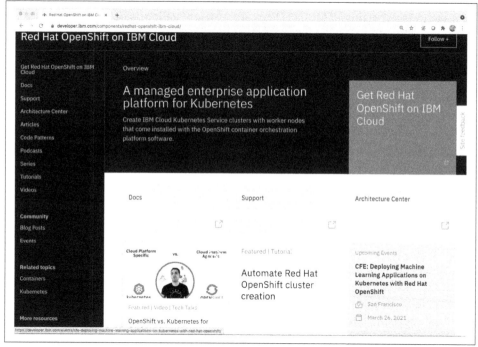

Figure 9-2. IBM Developer Website OpenShift content (https://oreil.ly/FllKH)

Learn OpenShift

Another option for online learning about OpenShift is the Learn OpenShift Interactive Learning Portal (*https://learn.openshift.com*). This interactive learning website provides free, preconfigured OpenShift environments that allow you to do hands-on learning about numerous OpenShift-related topics, such as continuous delivery, building operators, adding persistence to OpenShift, and developing OpenShift applications. Figure 9-3 provides a snapshot of the hands-on courses available from Learn OpenShift.

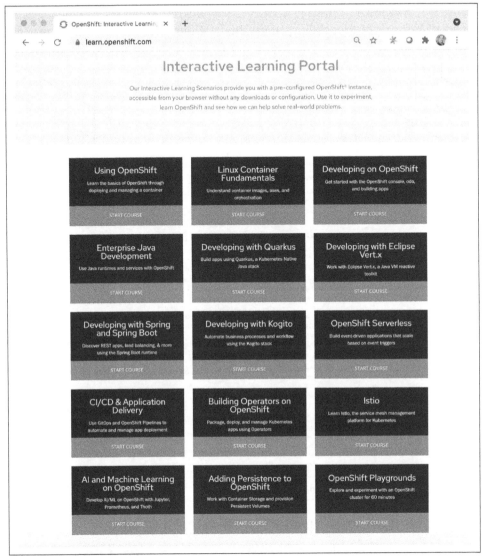

Figure 9-3. Learn OpenShift interactive learning portal course offerings

Kubernetes Website

The primary Kubernetes website (*https://kubernetes.io*) is an excellent place to start for information on Kubernetes. This website has links to more information on topics like documentation, community, blogs, and case studies. In the community (*https://oreil.ly/wCjyS*) section of the Kubernetes GitHub repository, you will find more information on how to join the large number of Kubernetes special interest groups. A snapshot of the Kubernetes Special Interest Group information page is shown in

Figure 9-4. As shown in the figure, each special interest group focuses on a specific aspect of Kubernetes. Hopefully, you can find a group that excites you and matches your interests.

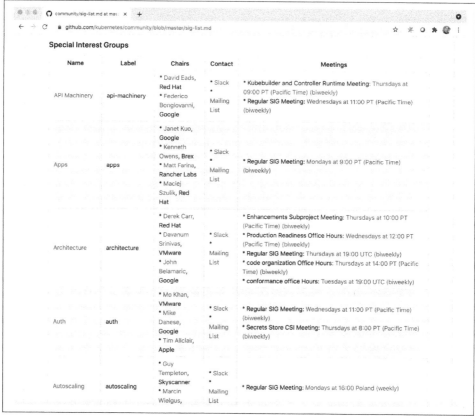

Figure 9-4. List of Kubernetes special interest groups

Kubernetes IBM Cloud Provider Special Interest Group

If you are interested in following the evolution of the IBM Cloud Kubernetes Service and its adjacent technologies, this is the group for you. Many developers and leaders from IBM Cloud work openly in this group to determine the future of IBM contributions and involvement in the Kubernetes community. You can also interact with the team that builds and operates IBM Cloud. More information on the group and their meetings can be found at the Cloud Provider Special Interest Group website (*https://oreil.ly/Ie44a*).

Kubernetes Contributor Experience Special Interest Group

The Kubernetes community takes the happiness of its contributors very seriously. In fact they have an entire special interest group, the Contributor Experience SIG, dedicated to improving the contributor experience. The Contributor Experience SIG is an amazing group of folks who want to know more about you and understand the issues you may be encountering as you become a Kubernetes contributor. Visit the Contributor Experience SIG website (*https://oreil.ly/TrYlt*) for more information on how to contact the group and learn about the contributor topics they focus on.

Summary

In this book, we have covered a broad array of topics to help you successfully run both Kubernetes and OpenShift in production. We provided a historical overview of traditional Kubernetes and OpenShift and discussed the key benefits of both platforms that have driven the huge growth in their popularity. We described the architecture for both environments and important Kubernetes and OpenShift concepts. We then began a journey into foundational production-related topics, such as advanced resource management, single cluster high availability, and continuous delivery. Next, we explored the more advanced topic of multicluster utilization with a focus on multicluster provisioning, upgrading, and policy support. We then looked at a working example of multicluster application delivery. Finally, we ended with a short discussion on what the future holds for Kubernetes and OpenShift, and we presented several recommended resources for further study. We hope you have found this book helpful and that it has given you the in-depth skills and confidence to develop and deploy cloud native applications on the most sophisticated and advanced Kubernetes and OpenShift production-level environments you could possibly encounter.

Index

About the Authors

Michael Elder is the senior Distinguished Engineer for Red Hat Advanced Cluster Management for Kubernetes. His technical focus is enabling enterprises to deploy a common application programming model and operational model based on Kubernetes in hybrid architectures deployed across a multicloud infrastructure. Prior to joining Red Hat, Michael led the launch of IBM Cloud Private and helped launch IBM Multicloud Manager, which both focused on enabling an open, hybrid platform based on Kubernetes. Prior to his work on container orchestration platforms, he led DevOps solutions, including IBM UrbanCode and IBM Cloud Continuous Delivery.

Michael has delivered talks at KubeCon, Red Hat Summit, IBM Think, O'Reilly Software Architecture, VMworld, IBM Interconnect, OpenStack Summit, SaltConf, ChefConf, and EclipseCon on topics ranging from his open source contributions to the Eclipse project to hybrid cloud deployment strategies and proof points. He has numerous awarded patents and has been honored with an IBM Corporate Award for technical achievement and three IBM Outstanding Technical Achievement awards. He is a coauthor of *Kubernetes in the Enterprise* (O'Reilly).

Jake Kitchener is senior technical staff member at IBM, responsible for the architecture, implementation, and delivery of the IBM Cloud Kubernetes Service, Red Hat OpenShift on IBM Cloud, and IBM Cloud Satellite. Jake is a habitual open source cloud adopter, starting with OpenStack and then migrating to containers and Kubernetes. He has been developing and delivering IBM Cloud container platforms for more than six years. Jake also has a passion for all things DevOps. He dreams of team organization, pipeline, and operations, with the hope of one day realizing product delivery nirvana. He is a coauthor of *Kubernetes in the Enterprise*. He has received the IBM Corporate Award for technical achievement and three IBM Outstanding Technical Achievement awards. Jake has delivered conference talks on Kubernetes and OpenShift at KubeCon, All Things Open, and IBM Think.

Dr. Brad Topol is an IBM Distinguished Engineer leading efforts focused on open technologies and developer advocacy. In his current role, Brad leads a development team with responsibility for contributing to and improving Kubernetes and several other cloud native open source projects. Brad is a Kubernetes contributor, serves as a member of the Kubernetes Conformance Workgroup, and is a Kubernetes documentation maintainer. He also serves as chair of the Kubernetes SIG Docs Localization Subgroup. He is a coauthor of *Kubernetes in the Enterprise*. In addition, he is a coauthor of *Identity, Authentication, and Access Management in OpenStack* (O'Reilly). He received a PhD in computer science from the Georgia Institute of Technology in 1998.

Colophon

The animal on the cover of *Hybrid Cloud Apps with OpenShift and Kubernetes* is a bean goose (*Anser fabalis*). This goose was named for its habit of grazing on bean fields in the winter. There are five subspecies of bean geese throughout Europe and Asia, but they are usually categorized by their breeding habitat. *Taiga* bean geese inhabit the forests of subarctic Scandinavia, Russia, and Siberia, while *tundra* bean geese are mostly found in Northern Russia and Siberia.

Bean geese are medium-sized birds with dark brown plumage, black and orange bills, and orange legs. They are typically between two and three feet long, with wingspans of over five feet. There is some variation in body size and pattern among the different subspecies, but they can often be distinguished by the size of their bills. Taiga bean geese have longer and slimmer bills with a larger portion of yellow-orange coloring than their counterparts in the tundra. They eat many different kinds of vegetation, including grass, seeds, corn, rice, potatoes, soybeans, and wheat and other grain crops. In the winter, bean geese migrate south to the British Isles, Belgium, Germany, and the Mediterranean, as well as parts of China, Mongolia, Korea, and Japan.

Bean geese are monogamous and mate for life. Courtship rituals begin when they reach maturity around two or three years old, and they perform a special "Triumph Ceremony" once a mate is chosen. This ceremony is sometimes repeated throughout their lifetime, and the young often participate, too! Bean geese lay four to six eggs at a time, and they incubate for about a month. Both parents raise the young together. Bean geese are not considered an endangered species, but their populations have been declining due to hunting, climate change, and loss of habitat. Many of the animals on O'Reilly covers are endangered; all of them are important to the world.

The cover illustration is by Karen Montgomery, based on a black and white engraving from *British Birds*. The cover fonts are Gilroy Semibold and Guardian Sans. The text font is Adobe Minion Pro; the heading font is Adobe Myriad Condensed; and the code font is Dalton Maag's Ubuntu Mono.

O'REILLY®

There's much more where this came from.

Experience books, videos, live online training courses, and more from O'Reilly and our 200+ partners—all in one place.

Learn more at oreilly.com/online-learning

Lightning Source UK Ltd.
Milton Keynes UK
UKHW031116261022
411122UK00002B/10